Intellectual Disability and Stigma

Katrina Scior • Shirli Werner
Editors

Intellectual Disability and Stigma

Stepping Out from the Margins

Editors
Katrina Scior
Department of Psychology
University College London
London, United Kingdom

Shirli Werner
Paul Baerwald School of Social Work
and Social Welfare
Hebrew University of Jerusalem
Jerusalem, Israel

ISBN 978-1-137-52498-0   ISBN 978-1-137-52499-7   (eBook)
DOI 10.1057/978-1-137-52499-7

Library of Congress Control Number: 2016950063

Printed on acid-free paper

This Palgrave Macmillan imprint is published by Springer Nature
The registered company is Macmillan Publishers Ltd. London

Foreword

The stigma of intellectual disabilities is as troubling for people with these disabilities as the impairments that accompany them. Disabilities are socially constructed, representing the interface between dysfunctions that result from disease and obstacles in the community that combined prevent people from attaining personally meaningful life goals. Consider the irony: people who learn to master challenges and are ready for work or independent living only to have their community say "no" to their aspirations. Stigma, particularly public beliefs that people with intellectual disabilities can't…, is among the greatest of obstacles to self-determination. Stigma teaches that people with intellectual disabilities can't work competitive jobs, so why should employers hire them. They can't develop mature and intimate relationships so should not be allowed to date, marry, or have children. The benefits of rehabilitation and independent living programs grind to a halt when confronted by community prejudice promoting can'ts. Just as advocates and experts in rehabilitation have developed innovative ways for people to overcome their dysfunctions to meet personal goals, so they need to develop effective strategies to tear down community barriers to these goals.

Scior and Werner have assembled a masterful team of scientists and advocates to summarize the state of research on the stigma of intellectual disabilities. Parts I and II begin by focusing on what I call the basics, understanding conceptual foundations of stigma and its egregious impact. They ground their discussion in research methods to make sure prescriptions are based on evidence. Part III segues into the practical. What are effective strategies for erasing the stigma? Focusing on the practical reflects the advocates' imperative in stigma research. The ultimate value of investigations on stigma is their utility in tearing down stigma and replacing it with affirming attitudes (such as hope and self-determination) and affirming behaviors (reasonable accommodations and community supports).

What role does research have in stigma change? After all, neither Mahatma Gandhi in India nor Martin Luther King Jr in the USA had social scientists at their right hand when envisioning and actualizing their journey towards social justice. The social inequities wrought by stigma stir the progressive emotions of many. As a result, advocates plunge headlong into efforts to change stigma. Plunging evokes purpose and energy which is needed to sustain the righteous goals of these efforts. But plunging also reminds us of risk, of what happens when someone dives into the deep end to find it is only three feet deep. Research humbly has the role of guide to the optimism of progressives.

The interaction between impairments and disabling environments people with intellectual disabilities face significantly hamper their ability to participate in anti-stigma efforts, especially when compared to the articulate leadership of people pressing for civil rights around the globe. As a result, one might ask, "How can a person with an intellectual disability, who may have trouble understanding or communicating about stigma, have an effective role in stigma change?" This question is NOT meant to promote research that identifies who can and who cannot participate in this kind of effort. Such research in itself is stigmatizing, presupposing that some people lack what's necessary to pursue social justice for them and their group. Rather, this question reflects the advocate's imperative. What reasonable accommodations are necessary so the person with an intellectual disability can fully participate in anti-stigma efforts?

Who therefore drives that anti-stigma agenda? There are many stakeholders: people with disabilities, their family members, service providers, and other progressive members of one's community. A theme of the chapters in Scior and Werner suggests who should be leading this charge: people with disabilities themselves. As a white male living in the USA,

I absolutely endorse African American rights agendas. However, I need to take the back seat in these efforts. Only African Americans themselves fully know the injustice and must be empowered to correct it. Hence, research on the stigma of intellectual disabilities must be community-based and participatory (CBP). According to principles of CBP research, the most impactful research relies on partnership between the community affected by the phenomenon of concern and experts in methods and analyses. CBP research is especially important for disenfranchised groups—people of color, those with low income, and individuals with intellectual disabilities—who are traditionally left out of the kind of research-based, social decision-making that leads to education, health, and social policy. CBP research changes the scope of research relationships. People with lived experience participating in CBP research are full partners in the research enterprise and not relegated to being subjects of study. The same should be the case for research in the intellectual disability field.

Patrick W. Corrigan

Contents

About the Editors

Katrina Scior is a senior lecturer in Clinical Psychology at University College London, UK, and a chartered clinical psychologist. She has published widely on lay people's attitudes and stigma concerning intellectual disability and is concerned with identifying effective interventions to tackle such stigma in diverse cultural and economic contexts. In the past she has worked with young people and adults with intellectual disabilities in community services and the UK National Health Service, where she witnessed first-hand the negative effects ostracism and discrimination can have on people with intellectual disabilities, their families, and paid carers.

Shirli Werner is a senior lecturer at the Paul Baerwald School of Social Work and Social Welfare, Hebrew University of Jerusalem, Israel. Previous to her academic career, Shirli worked as a social worker in the field of intellectual disability. Her field experience has provided her with contact and knowledge of this population and the difficulties which they encounter in various aspects of everyday life. Shirli has published widely on intellectual disability stigma, focusing on theoretical considerations and measurement issues related to the conceptualization of stigma in this field. Further, her research has focused on issues of public stigma, stigma held by service providers, and the impact of stigma on family members.

Notes on Contributors

Afia Ali is a senior clinical lecturer at University College London, UK, and honorary consultant psychiatrist working with adults with intellectual disabilities in North London. Her research interests include the experience of stigma and health inequalities in people with intellectual disabilities.

Sian Anderson is a research fellow in the Living with Disability Research Centre and sessional lecturer in the discipline of Social Work at LaTrobe University in Melbourne, Australia. She recently completed a PhD at LaTrobe which examined the impact of engagement in self-advocacy groups on the social identity of adults with intellectual disabilities.

Dorit Barak is the academic coordinator of the network of self-advocacy groups in Israel led by the organizations Beit Issie Shapiro and Elwyn. Her current research interests include empowerment and self-advocacy of people with disabilities and grassroots organizations for social change. She is active in the establishment, planning, design, and capacity building of a social movement of people with disabilities in Israel.

Christine Bigby is Professor of Social Work and Director of the Living with Disability Research Centre at La Trobe University, Melbourne, Australia. Her research has focused on the effectiveness of social programs and policies that aim to support the social inclusion of people with intellectual disabilities in adulthood and later life. She has published extensively in peer-reviewed journals and is the founding editor of the *Journal of Policy and Practice in Intellectual and Developmental Disabilities*.

Elizabeth E. Biggs is a doctoral candidate in the Department of Special Education at Vanderbilt University, USA. Her interests include promoting meaningful inclusion for students with severe disabilities in school and community settings. She is particularly interested in social and communication interventions for students with limited or no verbal speech.

Carly L. Blustein is a doctoral candidate in the Department of Special Education at Vanderbilt University, USA. She is interested in understanding how young people with severe disabilities navigate the school-to-work transition and prepare for postsecondary outcomes.

Erik W. Carter is a professor in the Department of Special Education at Vanderbilt University, USA, and a Vanderbilt Kennedy Center Investigator. His research focuses on evidence-based strategies for supporting inclusion and valued roles in school, work, and community settings for children and adults with severe disabilities.

Patrick W. Corrigan is Distinguished Professor of Psychology at the Illinois Institute of Technology, USA, and principal investigator of the US National Consortium on Stigma and Empowerment. His work focuses on understanding ways to replace the stigma of mental illness with affirming attitudes and behaviors.

Jason W. Crabtree is lead clinical psychologist in a community team for adults with intellectual disabilities in inner London, UK. His work and research interests include interventions for individuals with complex and challenging behavior, diagnosis and interventions for individuals with autism spectrum conditions, and stigma, self-identity, and self-evaluation in individuals with intellectual disabilities.

Nicole Ditchman is an assistant professor in the Department of Psychology at Illinois Institute of Technology, USA. She is a certified rehabilitation counselor and licensed clinical professional counselor. Her professional and research work have aimed to advance our understanding of quality of life and successful outcomes for young adults with disabilities. Her research focuses on factors affecting community integration, sense of community, and social reciprocity for people with disabilities.

János Fiala-Butora is a doctor of juridical science candidate at Harvard Law School, USA, and director of the Central European Program of the Harvard Law School Project on Disability. He has represented several persons with disabilities in strategic litigation before international tribunals and has been involved in law reform activities on behalf of persons with disabilities in several Central European countries.

Nev Jones is a postdoctoral fellow and a mental health services researcher at Stanford University, USA. Her work focuses on the sociocultural determinants of psychiatric disability and recovery, the subjective experience of psychosis, and the relationship between mental health challenges and identity development.

Callista Kahonde is a doctoral candidate in disability studies at the University of Cape Town, South Africa. Her research focuses on the responses of families to young adults with intellectual disabilities' sexuality. She grew up and trained as a physiotherapist in Zimbabwe. Since 2008 she has been working and studying in South Africa. She is a passionate disability activist and researcher, with special interests in family support, advocacy, and development programs for persons with intellectual disabilities.

Kristin Kosyluk is an assistant professor at the University of Texas at El Paso, USA. She is a certified rehabilitation counselor and rehabilitation counseling educator. Her research focuses on addressing environmental barriers, such as stigma, to the full inclusion of individuals with disabilities in their communities. Prior to entering academia, she spent eight years providing services to individuals with disabilities.

Eun-Jeong Lee is an associate professor in the Department of Psychology at Illinois Institute of Technology, USA. She is a certified rehabilitation counselor. Her work aims to enhance the educational and career advancement opportunities of people with disabilities from ethnic minority backgrounds. Her research focuses on the cognitive vulnerability model of depression for people with disabilities, positive psychology and wellness, cultural and psychosocial aspects of disability, and caregivers' adjustment.

William Mandy is a senior lecturer in Clinical Psychology at University College London, UK. His research focuses on improving ways to identify and help people who have social communication difficulties, including autism spectrum conditions.

Roy McConkey is Emeritus Professor of Developmental Disabilities at the University of Ulster, Northern Ireland, and visiting professor at Trinity College Dublin and the University of Cape Town, South Africa. His research interests include family support, early childhood intervention, community-based services, and social inclusion. He has acted as consultant to various UN and international NGOs. He is coeditor of *Disability and Human Rights: A Global Perspective* published by Palgrave in 2015.

Judith McKenzie is a postdoctoral research fellow in the disability studies programme, University of Cape Town, South Africa. She has conducted research into the education and living arrangements of people with intellectual disabilities in South Africa. She has an ongoing interest in inclusive education as a vehicle for social inclusion and participation. Her current research focuses on how to enable families to support the learning, participation, and rights of their family members with disabilities.

Hannah L. Mustard is a clinical psychologist in an HIV and sexual health service in London, UK. Her research interests include the experience of individuals who belong to stigmatized groups and how to reduce the negative impact stigma can have on self-esteem.

Anna Neller is a graduate assistant at the University of Toledo, USA. She is cochair of the Student Forum Advisory Board of the American Sociological Association. Her research focuses on the social construction of identities regarding people with restricted growth, disability and social barriers, the connections between maternal blame and disability, how impairment affects people with restricted growth, and bioethics.

Heli (Rachel) Peretz is a program evaluator in the Research and Evaluation Department of Beit Issie Shapiro, Israel. She has over 15 years of experience in research and evaluation of social services, especially services focusing on the improvement of the quality of life of people with disabilities and their families.

Rebecca Renwick is a professor in the Department of Occupational Science and Occupational Therapy, University of Toronto, Canada. She trained in occupational therapy and physical therapy at the University of Toronto before earning a PhD in psychology from the University of Lancaster, UK. Her research focuses on people with disability in society: social relationships, media representations, civic engagement, and quality of life.

James G. Rice is an assistant professor of Anthropology at the University of Iceland and has been a member of the Centre for Disability Studies at the University of Iceland since 2008. His research focuses on disability and power. He recently contributed to the volume *Disability Research Today* (2015) edited by Tom Shakespeare.

Dana Roth is the founder and director of the Research and Evaluation Department at Beit Issie Shapiro, Israel's leading organization furthering rights, opportunities, and services for people with disabilities. She has a particular interest in developing and applying inclusive participatory and collaborative approaches in all research and evaluation procedures in the disability field. Her current research focuses on technology, self-advocacy, attitudes, and stigma towards individuals with disability.

Hanna Björg Sigurjónsdóttir is an associate professor and Chair of Disability Studies at the University of Iceland. Much of her research has focused on families headed by parents with intellectual disabilities and their children. One of her major themes of interest over the years has been the representations of disability in art, literature, and popular culture.

Rory Sheehan is an academic clinical fellow in the Division of Psychiatry at University College London, UK. His research work spans a range of contemporary issues in intellectual disability. He is also a clinician working with people with intellectual disabilities and mental health problems in north London.

Mark Sherry is Professor of Sociology at the University of Toledo, USA. His book *Disability Hate Crime: Does Anyone Really Hate Disabled People?* was published in 2010. He is editor of the Ashgate Interdisciplinary Disability Studies Series and is currently the chair of the Disability Section of the American Sociological Association. His current work is on disability hate crimes, human trafficking of people with disabilities, and developing a social model of impairment.

Michael Ashley Stein is Cofounder and Executive Director of the Harvard Law School Project on Disability, a visiting professor at Harvard, and extraordinary professor at the University of Pretoria Faculty of Law. An internationally acclaimed expert on disability law and policy, he participated in the drafting of the UN Convention on the Rights of Persons with Disabilities, works with disabled persons organizations around the world, consults with governments on their disability laws and policies, advises UN bodies, and has brought landmark litigation and written extensively on disability rights.

List of Figures and Tables

Figures

Tables

Part I

Theory and Concepts

1

Toward Understanding Intellectual Disability Stigma: Introduction

Katrina Scior

The recent *World Report on Disability* (World Health Organization and World Bank 2011) concluded that 15 %, more than a billion people, around the world experience some form of disability. Eighty percent of these live in developing countries. Wherever they live, people with disabilities generally have poorer health, lower educational attainment, fewer economic opportunities, and higher rates of poverty than people without disabilities. A very prominent but often invisible form of disability is intellectual disability, which affects around 2 % of the population. Intellectual disability, like disability in general, is more common in developing countries due to poorer health and maternity care, and increased risk of exposure to diseases, toxins, and severe malnutrition. Persons with intellectual disabilities experience the same sources of disadvantage and inequities as people with other types of disabilities, but often face the

K. Scior (✉)
Division of Psychology & Language Sciences,
University College, London, UK
e-mail: k.scior@ucl.ac.uk

3

K. Scior, S. Werner (eds.), *Intellectual Disability and Stigma*,
DOI 10.1057/978-1-137-52499-7_1

additional disadvantage of having their needs inadequately understood and met and having limited recourse to assert their rights.

Historically, the category of 'intellectual disability' as a discrete entity was created and defined through a medical model that used labels such as 'feebleminded', 'mental defective', 'subnormal', and 'retarded'. Such terms became generic insults, as well as insults specifically aimed at this population. The characterization of people with intellectual disabilities as less worthy, subhuman, found its most extreme advocates in the Eugenics movement, resulting in the forceful sterilization of tens of thousands of persons with intellectual disabilities and later under the Nazi regime experimentation on them and their extermination (Grenon and Merrick 2014; Wolfensberger 1981). While we may think such sentiments belong to some other 'dark' era, of note the American Association on Intellectual and Developmental Disabilities, one of the world's foremost scientific organizations focused on intellectual disability, only abandoned use of the term 'mental retardation' as recently as 2006, having referred to itself until this time as the American Association on Mental Retardation. The word 'retard' and other highly pejorative terms are still commonly used in many parts of the world (Scior et al. 2015).

The very concept of intellectual disability presumes that it is possible to draw a clear demarcating line between intellectual ability and disability. This notion is rooted in Western classificatory systems but is of little relevance in many other parts of the world, not least as such a label would result in few if any additional resources being provided outside of the family. Having noted this qualification, in this book we have adopted the most prominent current definition of intellectual disability as (1) significant impairment of intellectual (cognitive) functioning, indicated by a full-scale IQ below 70; (2) alongside significant impairment of adaptive (social) functioning that affects how a person copes with everyday tasks; (3) both of which must have their onset during childhood (before age 18) (American Psychiatric Association 2013; World Health Organization 1994). Rather than concern ourselves with impairment (a problem in body function or structure), though, in this book we very much focus on intellectual *disability* (the interaction between features of a person's body and features of the society in which they live), as it is at the point of interaction between individual and society that the oppressive consequences of disability stigma are experienced. Importantly though, as several of the authors in Part II of this book note, a frequent failure to recognize impairment and make adjustments to accommodate the needs of persons with intellectual disabilities is in itself disabling and closely related to stigma.

What Is Intellectual Disability Stigma?

Intellectual disability elicits mixed reactions. While many respond to visible disability with compassion, sympathy, and a desire to help, intellectual disability also elicits many negative responses including pity, anxiety, avoidance, hostility, and even hatred and disgust. Such negative responses arise from stigma, a term that originates in ancient Greek and was reintroduced into common parlance by Goffman (1963), who defined stigma as the process by which the reaction of others spoils normal identity. A prominent current conceptualization defines stigma as the co-occurrence of labeling, stereotyping (negative evaluation of a label), and prejudice (endorsement of negative stereotypes), which lead to status loss and discrimination for the stigmatized individual or group (Link and Phelan 2001). Widely endorsed negative stereotypes about people with intellectual disabilities are that they are invariably severely academically and socially impaired (McCaughey and Strohmer 2005), lack the potential to change (Jahoda and Markova 2004), and are childlike (Gilmore et al. 2003).

Importantly, for stigmatization to occur, power must be exercised; that is, members of the stigmatized group are disempowered by having their access to rights, resources, and opportunities determined by those invested with more power in the social hierarchy—a condition that is clearly met for this population. The attention paid to power in social processes that continue the subjugation of people with intellectual disabilities is one of the key reasons why we have adopted the term 'stigma', in preference over the term 'attitude', which dominates research and discussion in the intellectual disability field. Furthermore, contemporary psychological theorizing on attitudes draws attention to three aspects of attitudes: a cognitive component (how we *think* about X), an emotional component (how we *feel* about X), and a behavioral component (how we *act* toward X). However, in common parlance the term 'attitude' continues to be mostly used to refer to the cognitive component alone and less so to emotions and actions or behaviors, which after all are most likely to negatively affect people with intellectual disabilities. In contrast, stigma more clearly draws our attention to negative outcomes such as devaluation and discrimination.

Why Is Intellectual Disability Stigmatized?

While in many parts of the world attitudes to people with intellectual disabilities have undoubtedly improved over time, evidence suggests that their position near the bottom of the social hierarchy remains largely unchanged. Studies consistently find that the general public rate social interactions with people with intellectual disabilities as much less desirable than contact with people with physical or sensory disabilities (but contact with individuals with severe mental health problems is viewed as at least equally undesirable). To answer the question why intellectual disability is stigmatized we need to look to social psychology. Although generally thought of in negative terms, social psychologists stress that stigma meets some important human needs. It allows people to reduce potentially overwhelming complexity and to feel better about themselves or their groups—functions that have evolved from a need for humans to live in effective groups to assure their survival (Major and O'Brien 2005; Neuberg et al. 2000). As a flipside, it also allows them to justify their preferential status in society. Stigma has been theorized both as a social construction, as in the labeling theories referred to above, and in evolutionary terms. The fact that intellectual disability appears to be stigmatized across cultures yet stereotype contents and the extent of discrimination associated with intellectual disability vary across historical, social, and cultural contexts suggests that both types of theories should be borne in mind to advance our understanding of intellectual disability stigma.

Evolutionary theorists have proposed that disability has been stigmatized as it prevents individuals from contributing (equally) to the group's effective functioning, efforts, and resources (Neuberg et al. 2000). As societies evolve and the most valued tasks shift from physical to cognitive, people with physical disabilities are able to contribute in alternative, valued ways;

consequently, physical disability becomes less stigmatized. However, as long as intellectual disability is viewed as impeding someone's contribution to society, it will continue to be stigmatized. While Neuberg et al. (2000) view non-reciprocity as central to disability stigma and to avoidance, the most common response to people with disabilities, another evolutionary psychological perspective views disease avoidance as central to disability stigma (Park et al. 2003). The latter should be particularly relevant in situations where misconceptions exist that disability is infectious, or in cultures where consanguineous marriage and parenthood are prominent, carrying with them a markedly increased risk of disability resulting from genetic abnormalities. Other selected conceptual explanations for negative reactions to disability advanced by social psychologists are detailed in Box 1.1 (for a review see Heatherton et al. 2000). To date researchers have tested few of these theories in relation to intellectual disability stigma.

Box 1.1 Social-Psychological Theories of Stigma

Attributional Approaches: *Blaming the Victim* (Ryan 1971); *Belief in a just world* (Lerner 1980; Furnham and Procter, 1989); *Attributions of Control and Responsibility* (Weiner 1985)

Demand Evaluations: *Interactional uncertainty; Required Effort; Resource Evaluations* (Blascovich et al. 2000)

Attitudinal ambivalence (Conner and Armitage 2008; Thompson et al. 1995)

The Impact of Intellectual Disability Stigma

Stigma exerts its potential profound negative effects on persons with intellectual disabilities and those close to them in several ways. It can lead to their exclusion from community life, being denied opportunities and equal rights, and being avoided in social situations (Jahoda and Markova 2004). Stigma has also been linked to psychological distress (Dagnan and Waring 2004), decreased self-esteem (Paterson et al. 2012), and increased vulnerability to mental health problems (Mak et al. 2007). These and other consequences of stigma are considered in detail in Part II of this book.

Stigma not only affects the person but may extend to include his or her whole family as well. Families may be affected in three ways: (1) through negative attitudes others may hold about the families of someone with intellectual disability, what has been termed 'courtesy stigma' (Ali et al. 2012; Birenbaum 1992); (2) through their fear that others view them negatively as parents or family members of someone with an intellectual disability, referred to as 'anticipated stigma' (Weiss 2008); and (3) by internalizing others' negative attitudes toward them, referred to as 'affiliate stigma' (Mak and Cheung 2008). To date, only limited research has been conducted on these three aspects and the relationships between them.

Stigma and Identity

One question which crops up repeatedly in discussions of stigma, particularly its potential internalization and the need to organize in self-advocacy groups to take collective action against stigma, is whether the individuals concerned in fact view themselves as having an intellectual disability. Some have proposed that in order to develop a positive sense of self, coming to accept one's intellectual disability and learning to manage the stigmatized identity are crucial (Szivos and Griffiths 1990). Others, in contrast, have argued that the label of intellectual disability is so toxic that individuals given this label have very good reason to reject it (Gillman et al. 2000). Yet others have questioned the whole notion of accepting or rejecting this label and have pointed to the fluid, context-dependent nature of identity (Rapley 2004). A young woman, for example, who is of short stature and has Down syndrome, when surrounded by tall people may view her stature as a prominent and possibly defining feature. When on a girls' night out though, being short or tall is likely to be of much less relevance than being female, someone who shares others' interest in Karaoke, or perhaps a wearer of trainers of a certain popular brand. Even in relation to the label of intellectual disability, answers to the question whether or not someone ascribes this label to themselves are much less clear cut than often suggested. To illustrate, the young woman may identify with the label of intellectual disability in some regards, such as annoyance at everyone taking a much closer interest in her relationship with her boyfriend than they do for her younger sister, while she may reject the label when invited to attend segregated activities. Perhaps then an even fleeting alignment with others similarly labeled, without necessarily assuming an 'intellectual disabled identity', is all that is called for as basis for collective action.

While touching on identity politics, we accept that in drawing attention to intellectual disability stigma in this book, we inevitably imply the existence of an essential entity—a group unified by its distinctive features, rather than focusing on the myriad distinctions between the millions of children and adults around the world labeled as having intellectual disabilities. As such, we recognize that we are guilty of what Gergen (1999) termed an essentialist presumption implicit in much identity politics.

This Book

Our aim in producing this edited text is to generate debate around a topic that has received limited attention but has a major impact on people with intellectual disabilities, their families, and society at large. We have arranged the book in three parts that we hope make sense to the reader. Consideration of broader theoretical issues in Part I is followed with in-depth analysis of the consequences of intellectual disability stigma in Part II. In Part III, perhaps the most important part, how to tackle intellectual disability stigma is addressed.

Looking to the future, in relation to long-term illness it has been suggested that we are perhaps witnessing the end of stigma (Green 2009). Recent testimonies we gathered from around the globe suggest, sadly, that this is far from the reality where intellectual disability is concerned (Scior et al. 2015). While huge progress has been made toward the inclusion and protection of the fundamental rights of persons with intellectual disabilities, they are still mostly far from being accepted as equal citizens.

In highly industrialized Western countries we are witnessing an interesting paradox—in the midst of frantic activity and the idolization of autonomy and independence, more and more people are embracing the slow movement. Where for a long time one's value in the (Western) world has been measured in part by one's capacity for autonomy, and to perform under pressure and at maximum speed, increasingly this notion is being questioned and a desire to address time poverty and to create more connections appears to sweep across industrialized nations. As increasing numbers of people are seeking a greater sense of connectedness with their communities and downshifting, or dreaming of doing so, is the time perhaps right to question not only whether prejudice and discrimination directed at people with intellectual disabilities are morally and legally wrong but also whether a section of society that requires us to slow down and to pay closer attention to one another's humanness can perhaps teach us all some valuable lessons and skills. This is not to say for a moment that they cannot contribute to society in many other ways that are at present frequently closed to them, but that in addition perhaps they can help us relearn some human values and skills that are at risk of being lost.

Key Learning Points

- Terminology and policy relating to intellectual disability may have improved, but interactions between the public and people with intellectual disabilities are still rare and viewed as undesirable by many.
- The concept of stigma, with its emphasis on power in the process of devaluing people with intellectual disabilities has advantages over the concept of attitudes which dominates the intellectual disability literature.
- Social psychologists have advanced numerous theories that can explain why intellectual disability is stigmatized but these have not been tested in relation to intellectual disability.
- Stigma results in many negative outcomes for people with intellectual disabilities and their families and carers.

Accessible Summary

- People with intellectual disabilities around the world often face bad attitudes and actions.
- This often makes life more difficult for them and their families.

- Researchers have produced different ideas why attitudes to disability are negative.
- These ideas can help us understand stigma and how to challenge it.

References

Ali, A., Hassiotis, A., Strydom, A., & King, M. (2012). Self stigma in people with intellectual disabilities and courtesy stigma in family carers: A systematic review. *Research in Developmental Disabilities, 33*, 2122–2140. doi:10.1016/j.ridd.2012.06.013.

American Psychiatric Association (2013). *Diagnostic and statistical manual of mental disorders* (5th ed.) (DSM-5).Washington, DC: American Psychiatric Association.

Birenbaum, A. (1992). Courtesy stigma revisited. *Mental Retardation, 30*, 265–268.

Blascovich, J., Mendes, W. B., Hunter, S. B., & Lickel, B. (2000). Stigma, threat and social interactions. In T. F. Heatherton, R. E. Kleck, M. R. Hebl, & J. G. Hull (Eds.), *The social psychology of stigma* (pp. 307–331). New York, NY: Guilford Press.

Conner, M., & Armitage, C. J. (2008). Attitudinal ambivalence. In W. D. Crano & R. Prislin (Eds.), *Attitudes and attitude change* (pp. 261–286). New York, NY: Psychology Press.

Dagnan, D., & Waring, M. (2004). Linking stigma to psychological distress: Testing a social cognitive model of the experience of people with intellectual disabilities. *Clinical Psychology and Psychotherapy, 11*, 247–254. doi:10.1002/cpp.413.

Furnham, A., & Procter, E. (1989). Belief in a just world: Review and critique of the individual difference literature. *British Journal of Social Psychology, 28*, 365–384. doi:10.1111/j.2044-8309.1989.tb00880.

Gergen, K. (1999). *Social construction and the transformation of identity politics.* Retrieved from https://www.swarthmore.edu/sites/default/files/assets/documents/kenneth-gergen/Social%20Construction_and_the_Transformation.pdf

Gillman, M., Heyman, B., & Swain, J. (2000). What's in a name? The implications of diagnosis for people with learning difficulties and their family carers. *Disability and Society, 15*, 389–409. doi:10.1080/713661959.

Gilmore, L. A., Campbell, J., & Cuskelly, M. (2003). Developmental expectations, personality stereotypes, and attitudes towards inclusive education:

Community and teacher views of Down syndrome. *International Journal of Disability, Development and Education, 50*, 65–76. doi:10.1080/103491203 2000053340.

Goffman, E. (1963). *Stigma: Notes on the management of spoiled identity.* London: Prentice-Hall.

Green, G. (2009). *The end of stigma? Changes in the social experience of long-term illness.* London: Routledge.

Grenon, I., & Merrick, J. (2014). Intellectual and developmental disabilities: Eugenics. *Frontiers of Public Health, 2*, 201. doi:10.3389/fpubh.2014.00201.

Heatherton, T. F., Kleck, R. E., Hebl, M. R., & Hull, J. G. (2000). *The social psychology of stigma.* New York, NY: Guilford Press.

Jahoda, A., & Markova, I. (2004). Coping with social stigma: People with intellectual disabilities moving from institutions and family home. *Journal of Intellectual Disability Research, 48*, 719–729. doi:10.1111/j.1365-2788.2003.00561.x.

Lerner, M. (1980). *The belief in a just world: A fundamental delusion.* New York, NY: Plenum Press.

Link, B. G., & Phelan, J. C. (2001). Conceptualizing stigma. *Annual Review of Sociology, 27*, 363–385. doi:10.1146/annurev.soc.27.1.363.

Major, B., & O'Brien, L. T. (2005). The social psychology of stigma. *Annual Review of Psychology, 56*, 393–421. doi:10.1146/annurev.psych.56.091103.070137.

Mak, W. W., Poon, C. Y., Pun, L. Y., & Cheung, S. F. (2007). Meta-analysis of stigma and mental health. *Social Science and Medicine, 65*, 245–261. doi:10.1016/j.socscimed.2007.03.015.

Mak, W. W., & Cheung, R. Y. (2008). Affiliate stigma among caregivers of people with intellectual disability or mental illness. *Journal of Applied Research in Intellectual Disabilities, 21*, 532–545. doi:10.1111/j.1468-3148.2008.00426.x.

McCaughey, T. J., & Strohmer, D. C. (2005). Prototypes as an indirect measure of attitudes toward disability groups. *Rehabilitation Counseling Bulletin, 48*, 89–99. doi:10.1177/00343552050480020301.

Neuberg, S. L., Smith, S. M., & Asher, T. (2000). Why people stigmatize: Toward a biocultural framework. In T. F. Heatherton, R. E. Kleck, M. R. Hebl, & J. G. Hull (Eds.), *The social psychology of stigma* (pp. 31–61). New York, NY: Guilford Press.

Park, J. H., Faulkner, J., & Schaller, M. (2003). Evolved disease-avoidance processes and contemporary anti-social behavior: Prejudicial attitudes and avoidance of people with physical disabilities. *Journal of Nonverbal Behavior, 27*, 65–87.

Paterson, L., McKenzie, K., & Lindsay, B. (2012). Stigma, social comparison and self-esteem in adults with an intellectual disability. *Journal of Applied Research in Intellectual Disabilities, 25*, 166–176. doi:10.1111/j.1468-3148.2011.00651.x.

Rapley, M. (2004). *The social construction of intellectual disability*. Cambridge: Cambridge University Press.

Ryan, W. (1971). *Blaming the victim*. New York, NY: Pantheon Books.

Scior, K., Hamid, A., Hastings, R., Werner, S., Belton, C., Laniyan, A., et al. (2015). *Intellectual disabilities: Raising awareness and combating stigma—A global review*. London: University College London.

Szivos, S. E., & Griffiths, E. (1990). Group processes involved in coming to terms with a mentally retarded identity. *Mental Retardation, 6*, 333–341.

Thompson, M. M., Zanna, M. P., & Griffin, D. W. (1995). Let's not be indifferent about (attitudinal) ambivalence. In R. E. Petty & J. A. Krosnick (Eds.), *Attitude strength: Antecedents and consequences* (pp. 361–386). Mahwah, NJ: Erlbaum.

Weiner, B. (1985). An attributional theory of achievement motivation and emotion. *Psychological Review, 92*, 548–573. doi:10.1007/978-1-4612-4948-1_6.

Weiss, M. G. (2008). Stigma and the social burden of neglected tropical diseases. *PLoS Neglected Tropical Diseases, 2*(5), e237. doi:10.1371/journal.pntd.0000237.

Wolfensberger, W. (1981). The extermination of handicapped people in World War II Germany. *Mental Retardation, 19*, 1–7.

World Health Organization (1994). *International classification of diseases* (10th ed., ICD-10). Geneva: WHO.

World Health Organization & World Bank (2011). *World report on disability*. Geneva: WHO.

2

Measurement Methods to Assess Intellectual Disability Stigma

Shirli Werner

Adequate measurement tools are needed to allow researchers to examine the extent and severity of stigma. Specific tools for intellectual disability stigma are needed because stigma may differ across disabilities. However, measurement of stigma in the intellectual disability field has not received the same level of attention and rigorous investigation as in other areas. First, the theoretical and methodological challenges facing this field are discussed, followed by a brief summary of several leading instruments. This chapter focuses on both stigma and attitude scales that aim to measure the perceptions held by adults and children regarding individuals with intellectual disabilities.

S. Werner (✉)
Paul Baerwald School of Social Work and Social Welfare,
Hebrew University of Jerusalem, Jerusalem, Israel
e-mail: shirli.werner@mail.huji.ac.il

© The Editor(s) (if applicable) and The Author(s) 2016   **15**
K. Scior, S. Werner (eds.), *Intellectual Disability and Stigma*,
DOI 10.1057/978-1-137-52499-7_2

Theoretical and Methodological Challenges of Existing Scales

Measurement of the intellectual disability stigma construct is based on its theoretical conceptualization. Although attitudes and stigma are frequently used interchangeably, attitudes (consisting of cognitive, affective, and behavioral components) do not capture the entirety of the stigma construct (the chain from stereotypes through prejudice to discrimination). While up-to-date measures should focus on the stigma construct, most available scales in this field have various theoretical limitations because they focus on examining attitudes rather than stigma. These scales do not include the components of stereotypes, prejudice, and discrimination. Furthermore, most studies fail to measure multidimensional theoretical underpinnings because they do not examine all three dimensions of stigma or attitudes, or study them only as separate dimensions lacking the conceptual interrelationships that a theory underlying the process of stigma provides.

Several methodological limitations should be noted in relation to existing scales. Only a few report conducting wide literature reviews as a basis for their development, whereas others are based on previously existing scales. Thus, it remains unclear how their items were derived. Several scales are outdated; thus, some of the items have limited relevance. Most scales' psychometric properties have not been evaluated and they have been developed and used primarily in Western countries. Some scales have only been used by the research group that developed them. Finally, most scales measure explicit attitudes (those that are consciously accessible and controllable) via self-report questionnaires based on direct questioning methods. These methods are subject to the effects of social desirability, where the human inclination to present oneself in the best possible light can distort the information provided (Fisher 1993). A full review of these issues is provided in Werner et al. (2012).

Summary of Leading Scales

The scales presented below include those that are more widely used and more recently developed.

The Mental Retardation Attitude Inventory—Revised (MRAI). This scale was developed by Antonak and Harth (1994) by adapting a scale of attitudes toward racial minority groups (Woodmansee and Cook 1967). The scale includes 29 items scored on a 4-point Likert scale which relate to different contexts in which stigma might occur (school, employment, and living arrangements).

The MRAI consists of four subscales with confirmed construct validity: (1) *Social distance* assesses the willingness to live near or be 'asocial' to people with intellectual disabilities; (2) *Integration-segregation* evaluates views toward including those with intellectual disabilities in the classroom; (3) *Private rights* measures the belief in having rights to express one's views on intellectual disability inclusion; and (4) *Subtle derogatory beliefs* assesses perceptions of individuals with intellectual disabilities. Intercorrelations between the scale scores provide evidence for the specificity of the four scales. Further, internal reliability was found to be adequate ($\alpha = 0.91$ for the overall scale and $\alpha = 0.76$ to $\alpha = 0.86$ for the subscales) (Antonak and Harth 1994).

Recently, a question has been raised regarding the items' content, suggesting further examination of their face validity (Sam et al. 2016). Specifically, several items seem overly hypothetical. For example, to answer 'I would allow my child to accept an invitation to a birthday party given for a child with an intellectual disability', participants who do not have children first need to imagine what it might be like to have a child and how they would feel in the described situation. Further, the item 'School officials should not place children with intellectual disabilities and children without intellectual disabilities in the same classes' could be outdated in many countries in which integration within schools is a mandatory policy.

Nevertheless, the MRAI has been one of the most widely employed attitude measures in the intellectual disability field to date. The scale has been utilized with many different populations including students, volunteers, and clinicians and has been employed worldwide, including studies conducted in Australia, Canada, China, Japan, Kuwait, and the USA.

Community Living Attitudes Scale (CLAS-ID). This scale was developed by Henry et al. (1996) to assess attitudes toward the social inclusion of people with intellectual disabilities. Since social inclusion is closely linked to attitudes and stigma, this scale has been frequently utilized to measure attitudes. Items were developed in consultation with self-advocates and users of intellectual disability services.

The CLAS-ID includes 40 items (17 in the short version) scored for degree of agreement on a 6-point Likert scale. It consists of four subscales: (1) *Empowerment*—the view that persons with intellectual disabilities should be able to make their opinions known in decisions and policies that affect their lives; (2) *Exclusion*—the desire to segregate persons with intellectual disabilities from community life; (3) *Sheltering*—the extent to which one believes that individuals with intellectual disabilities need to have others supervise them in their daily lives or protect them from the dangers of community life; and (4) *Similarity*—the extent to which one perceives persons with intellectual disabilities to be basically like themselves and others regarding life goals and basic human rights. All subscales show acceptable internal consistency ($\alpha = 0.75$ to $\alpha = 0.86$) and acceptable test-retest reliability ($\alpha = 0.70$ to $\alpha = 0.75$), indicating that they measure relatively stable attitudes (Henry et al. 1996).

The CLAS-ID has been widely used across populations, including professionals working with individuals with intellectual disabilities, college, university, and medical students, and the general public. It has been used in Australia, Canada, Hong Kong, Israel, Japan, the Netherlands, the UK, and the USA.

Attitudes toward Intellectual Disability Questionnaire (ATTID). This scale, developed by Morin et al. (2013), adopts a multidimensional perspective by measuring the cognitive, affective, and behavioral dimensions of attitudes. The scale was developed based on previously validated instruments, items inspired by the Montreal Declaration on Intellectual Disability (Pan-American Health Organization and World Health Organization 2004), and literature in the field. This scale takes into consideration that attitudes may differ according to level of intellectual disability by using two vignettes that illustrate different levels of intellectual disability.

The ATTID consists of 67 items rated for their degree of agreement on a 5-point Likert scale. It consists of five subscales: two cognitive, two affective, and one behavioral. Specifically, *Knowledge of the capacity and rights* of persons with intellectual disabilities and *Knowledge of the causes* of intellectual disability. *Discomfort* refers to situations that can create discomfort or fear. *Sensitivity and compassion* refer to the affect of sadness and pity and *Interaction* refers to everyday interactions and social distance from an individual with an intellectual disability. The overall Cronbach reliability of the scale was $\alpha = 0.92$ and subscale reliabilities ranged between $\alpha = 0.59$ and $\alpha = 0.89$.

The ATTID and its norms were developed using a large representative random sample of Quebec's general adult population (Morin et al. 2015). It was also used with elementary school teachers in Canada. To the best of my knowledge, no other studies have been published using this scale. However, the ATTID scale is new and several studies utilizing this scale are underway.

The ID Stigma Scale. This scale was developed by Werner (2015a) based on the theoretical conceptualizations of social psychology models of mental illness stigma and on the previously validated Multidimensional Attitudes Scale (Findler et al. 2007). The scale includes 35 items measuring cognitive, affective, and behavioral reactions when meeting a man with an intellectual disability described in a vignette.

The scale consists of three dimensions: stereotypes, prejudice, and behavioral aspects, each comprising several factors. Stereotypes include positive cognitions of *Acceptance* and negative cognitions of *Low ability* and *Dangerousness*. Prejudice consists of both *Negative affect* and *Calm affect*. Finally, behavioral aspects include discrimination (*Withdrawal* and *Social distance*), as well as positive behaviors of *Helping*. Internal reliabilities of subscales were found to range from acceptable to good ($\alpha = 0.60$ to $\alpha = 0.89$).

To overcome the effects of social desirability, researchers have advocated the use of indirect questioning, by asking respondents to report what they believe other people think about sensitive issues (Snijders and Matzat 2007), thus projecting their own attitudes using the façade of 'another person'. Accordingly, the ID Stigma Scale has been adapted to an indirect version (Werner 2015b) using the same vignette and items described above. However, participants are asked to report on the reactions that they believe another person would have in the same situation. Subscale reliabilities of the indirect version range from $\alpha = 0.66$ to $\alpha = 0.91$.

The ID Stigma Scale has only been used, thus far, by the original author. However, the scale is new and many studies worldwide have used the Multidimensional Attitudes Scale (Findler et al. 2007) on which it is based.

Single-Target Implicit Association Test (ST-IAT). An additional method to overcome the limitations of explicit attitude measures is to use measures that assess implicit attitudes. Implicit attitudes are automatically activated without effort or intention (Prestwich et al. 2008), providing a more accurate reflection of attitudes (Wilson and Scior 2015). The Implicit Association Test (IAT, Greenwald et al. 1998) is a computer-based task that measures the relative strength of the association between pairs of concepts/images and words. Participants are asked to categorize the presented image/word into two groups, each related to a target concept (e.g., White vs. Asian) and to an attribute concept (e.g., pleasant vs. unpleasant) (Lane et al. 2007). The IAT has been found to be a valid and reliable measure of implicit attitudes and is fairly robust against social desirability (Cunningham et al. 2001).

In contrast to the traditional IAT, the ST-IAT (Karpinski and Steinman 2006) allows measurement of attitudes toward only one attitude object. A ST-IAT version designed to measure implicit attitudes toward individuals with intellectual disabilities has recently been developed by Wilson and Scior (2015). In the ST-IAT, participants categorize two sets of attribute category words (five 'pleasant' words: happiness, laughter, joyful, rainbow, and sunshine and five 'unpleasant' words: sickness, hatred, disease, terrible, and poison) and five words representing the target category of 'intellectual disability' (dependent, mental handicap, slow learner, impaired, and special needs) using two keyboard keys. In the different blocks, the attribute category words are paired with either pleasant or negative attribute words.

Participants' implicit attitudes are reflected in the difference in response time to the different pairings. If participants are quicker in categorizing words when 'intellectual disability' and 'pleasant' are paired, this indicates positive implicit attitudes. Conversely, if they are quicker to categorize words when 'intellectual disability' and 'unpleasant' are paired, this indicates negative implicit attitudes. The authors found no significant associations between implicit and explicit attitudes (Wilson and Scior 2015).

It is important to note that debates have arisen regarding the psycho-metric properties of the ST-IAT versus the traditional IAT (Greenwald et al. 1998). Whereas some argue that the traditional IAT is more psy-chometrically sound than the ST-IAT (Greenwald, personal communication), others argue that the choice of a counter category against which the target object of interest is contrasted may sometimes be highly subjective (Karpinski 2004). In these instances, the ST-IAT has the advantage of reliably and efficiently capturing the evaluation of a single target category without a nonrelative evaluation (Bluemke and Friese 2008).

Social Distance Scales. Social distance relates to the willingness of an individual to have social contact with a member of another group in situations having varying degrees of intimacy (Bogardus 1959). Many researchers have used some form of social distance scale to measure external stigma, although these scales are not specific to intellectual disability.

For example, Scior and Furnham (2011), as part of their Intellectual Disability Literacy Scale, adapted four statements representing varying degrees of intimacy taken from a previously validated scale (Link et al. 1999). Participants rate their level of agreement with each statement on a scale from 1 to 7. Lately, the scale has been used with the addition of a fifth item referring to social distance toward a potential work colleague with an intellectual disability (Connolly et al. 2013). Another frequently used social distance measure is the social distance subscale of the MRAI (Harth 1974), which contains eight items that have been used in isolation in some studies.

Scales for Children. Studying children's stigmatic attitudes toward individuals with intellectual disabilities is highly important because these frequently influence the acceptance and inclusion of children with disabilities within the classroom and in society. Most scales used among children have similar limitations to those described within the first section of this chapter. Most scales do not focus on all three attitude components and most research conducted with children has focused on disability groups other than intellectual disability. Furthermore, most studies have been based on attitude scales developed to measure attitudes toward disability in general.

Notwithstanding these limitations, two scales are considered the most comprehensive in this field, measuring all three attitude components (see Vignes et al. 2008 for a comprehensive review). First, the Acceptance Scale (Voeltz 1980) was developed for a 9- to 12-year-old target population. This scale consists of 21 items scored on a 3-point rating scale. It has high internal consistency (α = 0.77) and test-retest reliability (coefficient = 0.68). Nevertheless, it is important to note that the three factorial structure model of this scale was not repeated in other research (Bossaert and Petry 2013).

Second, the Chedoke-McMaster Attitudes toward Children with Handicaps Scale (CATCH, Rosenbaum et al. 1986) was developed for use with a 9- to 13-year-old target population, although it has been used with youths up to age 16. This scale consists of 36 items rated on a 5-point scale, with 12 items for each of the cognitive, affective, and behavioral attitude components. The scale has high internal consistency (α = 0.89) and good test-retest reliability (coefficient = 0.70).

Although the CATCH has been recommended as one of the more complete scales and has been used in research in many countries, some questions have arisen regarding its suitability. First, the factorial validity of the scale remains unclear: some researchers have found a two-dimensional structure (Rosenbaum et al. 1986) and others a unidimensional structure (Bossaert and Petry 2013). Recently, Bossaert and Petry (2013) suggested a better fit by using a shortened unidimensional scale that includes 7 items (5 affective and 2 behavioral). Within this version, none of the cognitive items were found to be sufficiently related to the overall attitude measure. Second, when used to learn about attitudes toward individuals with intellectual disabilities, it is presumed that children completing the scale know what an intellectual disability is. This may well not be the case, more so for younger children. Third, careful consideration is needed for items that may be at risk of actually promoting prejudice; for example, 'I would try to stay away from a handicapped child.'

Conclusions and Recommendations

The field of intellectual disability stigma measurement is still in its infancy. Most available scales have some shortcomings and limitations, both in terms of theory and methodology. Nevertheless, the few leading scales presented can serve as a beginning point for continued development of scales in this field.

Several recommendations can be made for future development of scales in this field. First, I encourage additional qualitative research with various intellectual disability stakeholder groups, including the lay public, professionals, and policy makers, as well as individuals with intellectual disabilities and their families. Each of these groups most likely holds differing perspectives; therefore, including all would help elicit all stereotypes specific to intellectual disability. Second, there is a clear gap between the theoretical level of attitudes and stigma and its measurement. Hence, scales should be improved in order to measure stigma multidimensionally, thus allowing for a more holistic and comprehensive picture of stigma in this field. Third, all scales must undergo a strict examination of their psychometric characteristics among random samples in both Western and non-Western countries. Fourth, all items on scales for both children and adults should be closely examined to determine whether they are up to date, that none is at risk of perpetuating stigma, and that all are appropriate for the population for which they are intended, not least in relation to age and culture. Fifth, researchers should examine the option of integrating the use of quantitative scales along with observing behavior to obtain a more complete picture. Finally, more research is needed in non-Western countries in order to examine how existing scales are used in other cultural contexts.

Key Learning Points

- Adequate measurement tools to measure stigma toward individuals with intellectual disabilities are a mandatory first step in order to be able to examine the extent and severity of stigma and to offer appropriate stigma change interventions.
- Available scales to measure stigma and attitudes toward individuals with intellectual disabilities have many inherent theoretical and methodological limitations.
- Several of the leading scales presented in this chapter can be used as a starting point from which to continue scale development in this area.

- Scale development should focus on bridging the gap between the theoretical and the methodological levels by developing multidimensional scales intended to measure the stigma construct, rather than by simply measuring attitudes.

Accessible Summary

- It is important to accurately measure stigma before the professional staff can offer a program to change it.
- The available measurement tools have some problems and limitations.
- In this chapter, I describe some measurement scales that have fewer problems.
- New scales need to measure stigma by examining all of its various aspects.

References

Antonak, R. F., & Harth, R. (1994). Psychometric analysis and revision of the mental retardation attitude inventory. *Mental Retardation, 32*, 272–280.

Bluemke, M., & Friese, M. (2008). Reliability and validity of the Single-Target IAT (ST-IAT): Assessing automatic affect towards multiple attitude objects. *European Journal of Social Psychology, 38*, 977–997. doi:10.1002/ejsp.487.

Bogardus, E. S. (1959). *Social distance.* Los Angeles: University of Southern California Press.

Bossaert, G., & Petry, K. (2013). Factorial validity of the Chedoke-McMaster Attitudes towards Children with Handicaps Scale (CATCH). *Research in Developmental Disabilities, 34*, 1336–1345. doi:10.1016/j.ridd.2013.01.007.

Connolly, T., Williams, J., & Scior, K. (2013). The effects of symptom recognition and diagnostic labels on public beliefs, emotional reactions and stigma associated with intellectual disability. *American Journal on Intellectual and Developmental Disabilities, 13*, 211–223. doi:10.1352/1944-7558-118.3.211.

Cunningham, W. A., Preacher, K. J., & Banaji, M. R. (2001). Implicit attitude measure: Consistency, stability and convergent validity. *Psychological Science, 12*, 163–170. doi:10.1111/1467-9280.00328.

Findler, L., Vilchinsky, N., & Werner, S. (2007). The Multidimensional Attitudes Scale toward persons with disabilities (MAS): Construction and validation. *Rehabilitation Counseling Bulletin, 50*, 166–176. doi:10.1177/00 343552070500030401.

Fisher, R. J. (1993). Social desirability bias and the validity of indirect questioning. *Journal of Consumer Research, 20*, 303–315. doi:10.1086/209351.

Greenwald, A. G., McGhee, D. E., & Schwartz, J. L. K. (1998). Measuring individual differences in implicit cognition: The implicit association test. *Journal of Personality and Social Psychology, 74*, 1646–1480. doi:10.1037/0022-3514.74.6.1464.

Harth, R. (1974). Attitudes toward minority groups as a construct in assessing attitudes toward the mentally retarded. *Education and Training of the Mentally Retarded, 6*, 142–147.

Henry, D. B., Keys, C. B., Jopp, D., & Balcazar, F. (1996). The community living attitudes scales, mental retardation form: Development and psychometric properties. *Mental Retardation, 34*, 149–158.

Karpinski, A. (2004). Measuring self-esteem using the implicit association test: The role of the other. *Personality and Social Psychology Bulletin, 30*, 22–34. doi:10.1177/0146167203258835.

Karpinski, A., & Steinman, R. B. (2006). The single category implicit association test as a measure of implicit social cognition. *Journal of Personality and Social Psychology, 9*, 16–32. doi:10.1037/0022-3514.91.1.16.

Lane, K. A., Banaji, M. R., Nosek, B. A., & Greenwald, A. G. (2007). Understanding and using the implicit association test: IV. What we know (so far). In B. Wittenbrink & N. S. Schwarz (Eds.), *Implicit measures of attitudes: Procedures and controversies* (pp. 59–102). New York, NY: Guilford Press.

Link, B. G., Phelan, J. C., Bresnahan, M., Stueve, A., & Pescosolido, B. A. (1999). Public conceptions of mental illness: Labels, causes, dangerousness and social distance. *American Journal of Public Health, 89*, 1328–1333. doi:10.2105/AJPH.89.9.1328.

Morin, D., Crocker, A. G., Beaulieu-Bergeron, R., & Caron, J. (2013). Validation of the attitudes toward intellectual disability: ATTID questionnaire. *Journal of Intellectual Disability Research, 57*, 268–278. doi:10.1111/j.1365-2788.2012.01559.x.

Morin, D., Rivard, M., Boursier, C. P., Crocker, A. G., & Caron, J. (2015). Norms of the attitudes toward intellectual disability questionnaire. *Journal of Intellectual Disability Research, 59*, 462–467. doi:10.1111/jir.12146.

Pan-American Health Organization & World Health Organization (2004). *Montreal Declaration on Intellectual Disability.* Retrieved from www.jaid.org. jm/membersdocs/declaration_eng.pdf

Prestwich, A., Kenworthy, J., Wilson, M., & Kwan-tat, N. (2008). Differential relations between two types of contact and implicit and explicit racial attitudes. *British Journal of Social Psychology, 47,* 575–588. doi:10.1348/014466 607X267470.

Rosenbaum, P., Armstrong, R., & King, S. (1986). Children's attitudes toward disabled peers: A self-report measure. *Journal of Pediatric Psychology, 11,* 517–530. doi:10.1093/jpepsy/11.4.517.

Sam, K. L., Li, C., & Lo, S. K. (2016). Validation of the Mental Retardation Attitude Inventory-Revised (MRAI-R): A multidimensional rasch analysis. *International Journal of Social Science and Humanity, 6,* 519–524. doi:10.7763/IJSSH.2016.V6.703.

Scior, K., & Furnham, A. (2011). Development and validation of the intellectual disability literacy scale for assessment of knowledge, beliefs and attitudes to intellectual disability. *Research in Developmental Disabilities, 32,* 1530–1541. doi:10.1016/j.ridd.2011.01.044.

Snijders, C. C. P., & Matzat, U. (2007). Reducing social desirability bias through indirect questioning in scenarios: When does it work in online surveys? *Proceedings of the General Online Research, GOR07, March 26–28, 2007,* Leipzig.

Vignes, C., Coley, N., Grandjean, H., Godeau, E., & Arnaud, C. (2008). Measuring children's attitudes towards peers with disabilities: A review of instruments. *Developmental Medicine and Child Neurology, 50,* 182–189. doi:10.1111/j.1469-8749.2008.02032.x.

Voeltz, L. (1980). Children's attitudes toward handicapped peers. *American Journal of Mental Deficiency, 84,* 455–464.

Werner, S. (2015a). Stigma in the area of intellectual disabilities: Examining a conceptual model of public stigma. *American Journal of Intellectual and Developmental Disabilities, 120,* 460–475. doi:10.1352/1944-7558-120.5.460.

Werner, S. (2015b). Public stigma in intellectual disability: Do direct versus indirect questioning make a difference? *Journal of Intellectual Disability Research, 59,* 958–969. doi:10.1111/jir.12207.

Werner, S., Corrigan, P., Ditchman, N., & Sokol, K. (2012). Stigma and intellectual disability: A review of measures and future directions. *Research in Developmental Disabilities, 33,* 748–765. doi:10.1016/j.ridd.2011.10.009.

Wilson, M. C., & Scior, K. (2015). *Implicit attitudes towards individuals with intellectual disabilities: Their relationship with explicit attitudes, social distance, emotions and contact* (pp. 1–19). *September: Plos One.* doi:10.1371/journal.pone.013790.

Woodmansee, J. J., & Cook, S. W. (1967). Dimensions of verbal racial attitudes: Their identification and measurement. *Journal of Personality and Social Psychology, 39,* 848–860. doi:10.1037/h0025078.

Part II

The Consequences of Intellectual Disability Stigma

3

How Stigma Affects the Lives of People with Intellectual Disabilities: An Overview

Nicole Ditchman, Kristin Kosyluk, Eun-Jeong Lee, and Nev Jones

Worldwide, children and adults with intellectual disabilities face social exclusion, marginalization, and abuse as a result of stigma. The societal treatment of people with intellectual disabilities reflects a tension between fear and concern for their protection. Fear, evident in its most extreme form in eugenic practices, and paternalism have resulted in limited choices and restricted rights for people with intellectual disabilities. Acknowledgment of the rights and concerns of people with intellectual disabilities has led to laws and policies protecting their right to community inclusion. Also, the change in terminology from 'mental retardation' and other pejorative terms to 'intellectual disability' in many countries highlights a growing awareness of intellectual disability stigma. However, stigmatizing attitudes among the general public persist throughout the world.

N. Ditchman (✉) • K. Kosyluk • E.-J. Lee
Department of Psychology, Illinois Institute of Technology, Chicago, IL, USA
e-mail: nditchma@iit.edu

N. Jones
Felton Institute, San Francisco, CA, USA

© The Editor(s) (if applicable) and The Author(s) 2016
K. Scior, S. Werner (eds.), *Intellectual Disability and Stigma*,
DOI 10.1057/978-1-137-52499-7_3

This chapter provides an overview of the effects of stigma in perpetuating social inequalities and violating the basic rights of people with intellectual disabilities in the following areas: poverty, safety, education, employment, community integration and participation, health, intimate relationships and reproductive rights, and self-determination. We do not consider self-stigma here among stigma's effects as this is covered in Chap. 7 of this book. The chapter closes with considerations for future research in this area.

Poverty

Of an estimated 150 to 200 million people with intellectual disabilities worldwide, 26 million live on less than $1 a day (Inclusion International 2006). The cycle of poverty and disability is caused and maintained in part by stigma, denial of opportunities for economic and social development, and reduced political engagement. Exclusion of people with intellectual disabilities from the workforce, and the financial and social impact of parents caring for children with intellectual disabilities in social systems that do not provide adequate, and oftentimes *any*, support perpetuate poverty (Emerson 2007). In developing countries, the stigma associated with the birth of a child with a disability can lead fathers to abandon the family, leaving mothers with the sole responsibility for care. Thus, the largest unreimbursed cost associated with intellectual disabilities is that of caregiving by family members (Inclusion International 2006).

Safety

Poverty and isolation in and of themselves increase risks to safety, and people with disabilities are at greater risk of harassment, violence, and abuse compared to individuals without disabilities. Individuals with intellectual disabilities often experience abuse, ranging from physical injury, sexual assault, emotional trauma, financial abuse, medication mismanagement, and/or refusal to provide necessary personal assistance by others in the community. Although some countries have created or expanded existing hate crime laws to include crimes motivated by an actual or perceived disability, harassment, bullying, and violence are still regular experiences for many people with intellectual disabilities (Disability Rights Commission 2004).

Research suggests that children and adults with intellectual disabilities are far more likely to be sexually abused compared to those without disabilities (Johnson and Sigler 2000). When people with intellectual disabilities are dehumanized and thought to be unable to understand what is happening to them, service providers may not see anything wrong with behaviors or treatments they would see as impermissible with other groups. Historically, individuals with intellectual disabilities have not been considered reliable reporters of abuse, and most strategies to address these issues have been aimed at training service providers to recognize abuse and intervene to protect victims, as opposed to assisting people with intellectual disabilities to develop and utilize their own capacities to self-advocate and call attention to violence and abuse (Powers and Oschwald 2004). This situation is starting to change in some places as people with intellectual disabilities are directly involved in raising awareness about stigma and hate crimes. For example, the state of Maryland, USA, has initiatives in place that include people with intellectual disabilities directly in the training of police officers. (*Note.* The discussion on disability hate crime is expanded in Chap. 8.)

Finally, people with intellectual disabilities are also more likely to be designated as criminal suspects or offenders. This overrepresentation may be related to communication barriers, limited training of police officers, the potential suggestibility of individuals with intellectual disabilities, and/or inappropriate interrogation procedures. In addition, suspects or defendants may hide or deemphasize their own disabilities due to stigma. In the USA, persons with intellectual disabilities were regularly executed until the Supreme Court in 2002 declared such executions to be in violations of the US Constitution (Appelbaum 2009). Over the past decade, a series of reinvestigations of death row convictions of prisoners with intellectual disabilities have concluded that those convicted were wrongfully imprisoned and not guilty of the crimes for which they were convicted, leading to their exoneration (Mai-Duc 2014).

Education

Stigma and structural discrimination have led children to be routinely excluded from education or educated in segregated, and often lower-quality, facilities. Globally, many children and youth with intellectual disabilities are not in school due to barriers such as stigma, limited access to transportation, and prohibitive school fees (Inclusion International 2006; UNESCO 2015). Over 98 % of children with disabilities in developing countries do not receive any formal education (United Nations 2007). Further, negative attitudes and lowered expectations by community members, teachers, and peers can lead parents to remove children from school (Inclusion International 2006). Even in countries where policies and laws mandate inclusive education, implementation is often lacking. This is particularly concerning given that studies show that children with intellectual disabilities who are included in regular education are more likely to finish school, work, and become active community members (Bach and Burke 2002).

Findings from the US National Longitudinal Transition Survey-2 (NLTS2), a large-scale study examining postsecondary outcomes for young adults 1 month to 8 years post school, reveal that less than one-third of young adults with intellectual disabilities were engaged in any kind of postsecondary education post high school—the lowest among all the disability groups studied (Newman et al. 2011). These trends persist in spite of students and families wanting access to higher education (Mock and Love 2012). Moreover, attempts to fully participate in postsecondary education have been met with resistance. For example, in the case of *Fialka-Feldman v. Oakland University Board of Trustees* (2009), a student with an intellectual disability attending a special program at Oakland University requested to live in campus housing. After his request was denied by the university, he sued and the university was ordered to allow him to move into on-campus housing.

Employment

Stigma has also resulted in the denial of work for people with intellectual disabilities who continue to face very high rates of unemployment and underemployment, despite the desire of many for employment in an open, competitive labor market. In the USA, estimates suggest that only around 15 % of people with intellectual disabilities are working in paid, community-based jobs (Anderson et al. 2011). In England, an even lower proportion, 7 % of people with intellectual disabilities of working age are in any form of employment (Hatton et al. 2014). Societal beliefs that the majority of adults with intellectual disabilities are unemployable (Shaw et al. 2004) or should only work in special workshops (Siperstein et al. 2003) foster this continued segregation. This is concerning given that research findings suggest that sheltered work is associated with poorer job satisfaction and well-being compared to competitive and supported employment for people with intellectual disabilities (Anderson et al. 2011; Jahoda et al. 2008).

Furthermore, recent class action lawsuits in the USA (e.g., *Lane v. Brown*) have challenged sheltered workshops that pay subminimum wages and operate as segregated environments as a civil rights violation. On the other hand, there is also some evidence of more positive public views toward the inclusion of people with intellectual disabilities in employment (Burge et al. 2007). The authors suggested that structural stigma in the form of inadequate employment training programs for people with intellectual disabilities represents a greater barrier than public attitudes. Meanwhile, in the competitive workplace, research demonstrates that employers appear to prefer people with physical or sensory disabilities over individuals with intellectual disabilities (Kersh 2011). Discrimination in the workplace occurs as well, with over one-fourth of the claims filed with the US Equal Employment Opportunity Commission (EEOC) alleging discrimination at least in part on the basis of disability—although it is unclear how many of these cases involve individuals with intellectual disabilities (EEOC 2014).

Community Integration and Participation

Individuals with intellectual disabilities have lower levels of community participation, fewer social relationships, and less engagement in leisure activities than those without disabilities (Verdonschot et al. 2009). Although community living alone does not solve the problem of inclusion, some research has shown that those who physically live in the community, particularly in smaller and more integrated group homes, experience increased levels of community integration, especially when compared to those living in large institutions (Kozma et al. 2009). However, moving persons with intellectual disabilities from institutional settings into the community without addressing underlying societal and structural barriers cannot ensure meaningful inclusion; it often results in physical presence alone while potentially exposing those concerned to negative community attitudes (Cummins and Lau 2003). Findings from a nationally representative study in the USA of transition outcomes (NLTS2) indicate that almost half of all young adults with intellectual disabilities report no participation in organized community activities in the previous year, and over one-third were not registered to vote, which was statistically lower than voter registration rates for most other disability groups (Newman et al. 2011).

Failure to adequately address barriers to full participation in community and civic life should be recognized as a reflection of multiple intersecting areas of structural stigma. For example, transportation is a major barrier to community involvement and participation in leisure activities, as it is often unavailable or residential facilities are located far from convenient public transportation hubs (Buttimer and Tierney 2005). Furthermore, it is rare to find public information presented in a cognitively accessible format, which poses a significant barrier to full inclusion in social and civic life (Yalon-Chamovitz 2009). In addition, nowadays a major digital divide separates many people with intellectual disabilities from the rest of the population (McCarron et al. 2011). Inaccessible websites, apps, and software, coupled with financial barriers affecting access to Internet and technology, likely play a large role in limiting participation in social media and networking opportunities.

Health

Individuals with intellectual disabilities die at a younger age and experience poorer health than people without disabilities, mostly for reasons that are avoidable and unjust (Emerson and Hatton 2014). A recent study examined matched US data to compare health status, health risks, and preventative health care for over 20,000 people with intellectual disabilities (Havercamp and Scott 2015). The findings suggest that people with intellectual disabilities are more likely to experience health risks compared to people without disabilities in a number of areas, including obesity and physical inactivity.

While some of these health disparities are related to biological aspects of disability (e.g., Down syndrome is associated with higher risk for a number of health conditions), oftentimes negative provider attitudes and failure of institutional policies to adequately address health prevention and health concerns of people with intellectual disabilities are to blame. People with intellectual disabilities are less likely to receive routine screenings and are over four times more likely to have poor overall health than the general population (Havercamp and Scott 2015). A review of UK and international literature paints a similar picture of inequalities in both access to and outcomes of health care and cites social determinants of health, such as discrimination, as contributors (Emerson and Baines 2010). In developing countries, there remains a paucity of information regarding the health status and needs of people with intellectual disabilities, even though inequalities are likely to be even more pronounced than those in developed countries (Evenhuis et al. 2000).

While many factors, including environmental conditions, health promotion, and medical care, contribute to these health inequalities, stigma clearly plays a major role. One of the better documented components of such stigma concerns the negative attitudes often held by health care providers toward people with intellectual disabilities (Lewis and Stenfert Kroese 2010; Ryan and Scior 2014). At the level of public stigma on the part of health care providers, disparities in patterns of utilization of preventative health services, such as prostate, cervical, and breast cancer screening, may be attributed to physicians' attitudes toward sexuality among individuals with intellectual disabilities and beliefs about life expectancy and quality of life (Burge et al. 2008). Overall, the literature suggests more negative attitudes than would be expected from 'caring' professionals, and training related to this patient group is often lacking or perpetuating negative attitudes (Lewis and Stenfert Kroese 2010; Ryan and Scior 2014). The need to provide better mental health care for those with intellectual disabilities and the negative attitudes that characterize such care are also well established (Rose et al. 2012; Werner and Stawski 2012).

At a more structural level, negative attitudes affect health care by reducing the number of medical professionals willing and/or able to provide high-quality care to this patient group. Among other things, improved training can help prevent diagnostic overshadowing, that is, the attribution of health concerns or unusual behavior to the intellectual disability diagnosis. Other barriers that at least in part reflect structural stigma include scarcity of services, physical barriers to access, and failure to accommodate the needs of individuals with intellectual disabilities with regard to literacy and communication (Emerson and Baines 2010). Further, although there has been considerable effort dedicated to health promotion interventions for individuals without disabilities, this has not been the case for individuals with intellectual disabilities (Havercamp and Scott 2015). Instead, they have generally poor knowledge of aspects of health such as substance use, exercise, and healthy eating (Jobling and Cuskelly 2006). As in other domains reviewed here, differences in effort paid to health promotion between those with and without intellectual disabilities can be related to more invisible aspects of stigma. That is, stigma can be actualized in policy decisions that simply fail to fully include or equally consider persons with intellectual disabilities.

Intimate Relationships and Reproductive Rights

Persistent beliefs that individuals with intellectual disabilities are child-like and asexual have had a negative impact on their opportunities for intimate relationships, procreation, and promotion of sexual health and safety (Scotti et al. 1996). They also limit access to reproductive health information, and youth and adults with intellectual disabilities are more likely to be excluded from sex education programs than their peers without disabilities (World Health Organization and World Bank 2011). Further, individuals with intellectual disabilities often lack private, safe places to engage in individual or partnered sexual activity (Di Giulio 2003).

Beliefs about the innocent and asexual nature of individuals with intellectual disabilities have also put them at risk of sexual exploitation. In some countries, a mix of a complete disregard for the humanity of persons with intellectual disabilities and beliefs in their asexual nature can place girls and women in particular at grave risk; for example, a belief that raping a girl with a disability because she is presumed to be a virgin will cure HIV/AIDS has been cited as a major challenge in some countries, such as Zimbabwe (Inclusion International 2006).

Individuals with intellectual disabilities becoming parents is often negatively viewed by health professionals, community members, and families (Aunos and Feldman 2002). Several legal cases in the USA have been brought against states that have removed children from their homes for the sole reason of the parents having an intellectual disability. These cases highlight concerns that child protection staff may lack the necessary training to perform their duties without discriminating on the basis of intellectual disability, as well as the need for meaningful assistance to support families with raising children. These issues are considered in greater depth in Chap. 6 of this book.

Self-determination

A far reaching and common belief about people with intellectual disabilities is that they lack the ability to make informed choices. This has led to the limitation of choice and autonomy in decision-making. Paternalistic attitudes and the infantilization of adults with intellectual disabilities stop them from being allowed to take risks in their lives and have experiences others take for granted. Reinforcing unwanted dependency on others can increase social vulnerability and limit opportunities to engage in self-determined behaviors and choices. Of note, youths with intellectual disabilities who report higher perceived self-determination also report better outcomes and higher quality of life (Wehmeyer and Palmer 2003).

The literature identifies attitudes of service professionals and their assumptions that people with intellectual disabilities are unable to consent to treatment or to make decisions on their own as a major barrier to self-determination and decision-making (Davison et al. 2015).

Such views can be motivated by benevolence and a desire to protect, as well as perceptions of ineptitude. Diminished expectations can be damaging to individuals with intellectual disabilities, and lead to subsequent discrimination through not offering them choices and opportunities for decision-making. Other barriers include insufficient time and resources to support self-determination, inadequate staff training, conflict between staff, families, and/or service users in relation to decision-making, and a service culture that is not supportive of the adoption of supported decision-making (Davison et al. 2015).

Future Directions

It is clear that people with intellectual disabilities face many inequalities related to key life areas. Continued research efforts are needed to more fully understand the impact of stigma across domains. This is not a simple task given the complexities inherent in the stigma process and the vast heterogeneity of cultures and countries in which people with intellectual disabilities live. We close with several suggestions for future research and continued considerations in this area.

First, documenting the full scope and reach of stigma across different settings is needed. Although stigma affects the lives of people with intellectual disabilities regardless of country or socioeconomic level, it is clear that individuals in lower income countries face some of the most difficult living conditions in the world and yet little research is conducted in these countries. Systemic discrimination and the absence of judicial protection perpetuate poor living conditions and violations of human rights. Additionally, reliable mechanisms for monitoring the well-being of people with intellectual disabilities across the globe are necessary to inform effective policy making (Fujiura et al. 2010). The role of cultural contexts in addressing stigma must be taken into consideration as well. For example, culture shapes how self-determination is understood, and more family-oriented cultures may not necessarily support independent decision-making by individuals, including those without disabilities (Lee et al. 2015). A challenge to continued research in this area will be recognizing and accounting for the vast differences in policies, practices, definitions of concepts such as disability or participation, and beliefs regarding intellectual disability across the globe.

Second, more research is needed to tease out the precise mechanisms and role of stigma in the context of well-documented educational, employment, and health inequalities facing people with intellectual disabilities. Such research must include attention to stigma as it plays out across multiple levels (*self, familial, structural,* and *public*) and conceptualization at all these levels in order to adequately inform intervention. For example, understanding the extent to which health outcomes are affected by provider attitudes over structural barriers (lack of provider training or inadequate resources) or self-stigma (decreased help seeking) can guide more efficient and focused approaches aimed at reducing inequalities. As our discussion of community integration demonstrates, tackling one piece of the stigma process (physical segregation) without simultaneously addressing others (societal rejection) can actually harm individuals with intellectual disabilities.

Third, as more research looks into stigma and its impact on the lives of people with intellectual disabilities, tough questions that have often been ignored in the stigma literature will need to be more adequately addressed. For instance, the balance between protecting the rights and safety of these individuals while not limiting their rights to self-expression and decision-making is complicated and not always clear. Generally, it can be easy to identify stigma based on fear or dehumanization, but often policies created with a benevolent intent also restrict the rights and ultimately quality of life of the individuals concerned. Segregated settings in many cases were set up to protect individuals with intellectual disabilities, yet they violate their human rights and limit the ability of the community to benefit from their contributions. Given that people with intellectual disabilities are at risk of exploitation and abuse, how do we adequately provide the resources and protection to minimize such risks while not unintentionally infantilizing them?

Similarly we need to wrestle with the question of the extent to which societies can express respect for people with disabilities—and value their contributions to social life while continuing with disability prevention efforts. This important issue often goes ignored in the stigma literature and is particularly relevant for people with intellectual disabilities, given that prenatal screening can lead to decisions as to whether to terminate pregnancies. These prevention efforts may well run counter to initiatives to revalue and fully include people with intellectual disabilities. At the same time, as key disability theorists have emphasized, it is always important to walk the line between devaluation and romanticization and resist the impulse to downplay negative aspects of disability, including physical pain and disability-linked physical health problems (Siebers 2013).

Finally, future research needs to do more to include people with intellectual disabilities as active participants in the research process. With adequate support, participatory research with these individuals is very much possible (Jurkowski 2008). However, the research world itself may be the last frontier of unrecognized stigma as it plays out in the often implicit assumption that those with intellectual disabilities cannot meaningfully participate (McDonald and Keys 2008). Through continued recognition of the impact of stigma and related research efforts, it is our hope that the disparities reviewed and questions posed in this chapter can be addressed and that improved quality of life and well-being for individuals with intellectual disabilities across the globe will be realized.

Key Learning Points

- Intellectual disability stigma affects a number of life domains associated with well-being and quality of life, including poverty, safety, education, employment, community integration and participation, health, intimate relationships and reproductive rights, and self-determination.
- Throughout the world, the vast majority of individuals with intellectual disabilities live in poverty and face human rights violations. The cycle of poverty and disability is influenced in part by stigma and institutional barriers to education, employment, and civic participation.
- A long history of segregation continues to shape the lives of those with intellectual disabilities even in the wake of deinstitutionalization.
- A major barrier to self-determination and decision-making by people with intellectual disabilities concerns attitudes of service providers and their assumptions that these individuals are not able to make informed choices.

Accessible Summary

- Negative attitudes can lead to poverty, health problems, threats to safety, and limited access to education, employment, and community life.
- People with intellectual disabilities are not usually given the support necessary to fully participate in the community.
- Many assume that people with intellectual disabilities cannot make their own decisions. This can lead to low expectations and lack of opportunities to make their own choices.
- People with intellectual disabilities should be included in research on stigma.

References

Anderson, L. L., Larson, S. A., & Wuorio, A. (2011). *2010 FINDS National Survey technical report part 1: Family caregiver survey.* Minneapolis, MN: University of Minnesota, Research and Training Center on Community Living.

Appelbaum, P. S. (2009). Law & psychiatry: Mental retardation and the death penalty: After Atkins. *Psychiatric Services, 60,* 1295–1297. doi:10.1176/ps.32.1.14.

Aunos, M., & Feldman, M. (2002). Attitudes towards sexuality, sterilization and parenting rights of persons with intellectual disabilities. *Journal of Applied Research in Intellectual Disabilities, 15,* 285. doi:10.1046/j.1468-3148.2002.00135.x.

Bach, M., & Burke, M. A. (2002). *Toward an inclusive approach to monitoring investments and outcomes in child development and learning.* North York, Canada: Roeher Institute.

Burge, P., Ouellette-Kuntz, H., Isaacs, B., & Lunsky, Y. (2008). Medical students' views on training in intellectual disabilities. *Canadian Family Physician, 54,* 568–569.

Burge, P., Ouellette-Kuntz, H., & Lysaght, R. (2007). Public views on employment of people with intellectual disabilities. *Journal of Vocational Rehabilitation, 26,* 29–37.

Buttimer, J., & Tierney, E. (2005). Patterns of leisure participation among adolescents with a mild intellectual disability. *Journal of Intellectual Disabilities, 9,* 25–42. doi:10.1177/1744629505049728.

Cummins, R. A., & Lau, A. L. (2003). Community integration or community exposure? A review and discussion in relations to people with an intellectual disability. *Journal of Applied Research in Intellectual Disabilities, 16*, 145–157. doi:10.1046/j.1468-3148.2003.00157.

Davison, G., Kelly, B., Macdonald, G., Rizzo, M., Lombard, L., Abogunrin, O., et al. (2015). Supported decision making: A review of the international literature. *International Journal of Law and Psychiatry, 38*, 61–67. doi:10.1016/j.ijlp.2015.01.008.

Di Giulio, G. (2003). Sexuality and people living with physical or developmental disabilities: A review of key issues. *The Canadian Journal of Human Sexuality, 12*, 53–68.

Disability Rights Commission (2004). *Hate crime against disabled people in Scotland: A survey report.* In *Stratford-upon-Avon.* UK: Disability Rights Commission.

Emerson, E. (2007). Poverty and people with intellectual disabilities. *Mental Retardation and Developmental Disabilities Research Reviews, 13*, 107–113. doi:10.1002/mrdd.20144

Emerson, E., & Baines, S. (2010). *Health inequalities and people with learning disabilities in the UK: 2010.* Durham, UK: Improving Health and Lives Learning Disabilities Observatory.

Emerson, E., & Hatton, C. (2014). *Health inequalities and people with intellectual disabilities.* Cambridge, UK: Cambridge Univ. Press.

Evenhuis, H., Henderson, C. M., Beange, H., Lennox, N., & Chicoine, B. (2000). *Healthy ageing adults with intellectual disabilities: Physical health issues.* Geneva, Switzerland: World Health Organization.

Fujiura, G. T., Rutkowski-Kmitta, V., & Owen, R. (2010). Make measurable what is not so: National monitoring of the status of persons with intellectual disability. *Journal of Intellectual and Developmental Disability, 35*, 244–258. doi:10.3109/13668250.2010.519330.

Hatton, C., Emerson, E., Glover, G., Robertson, J., Baines, S., & Christie, A. (2014). *People with learning disabilities in England 2013.* Durham, UK: Public Health England.

Havercamp, S. M., & Scott, H. M. (2015). National health surveillance of adults with disabilities, adults with intellectual and developmental disabilities, and adults with no disabilities. *Disability and Health Journal, 8*, 165–172. doi:10.1016/j.dhjo.2014.11.002.

Inclusion International. (2006). *Hear our voices: A global report. People with intellectual disability and their families speak out on poverty and exclusion.* Retrieved from http://inclusion-international.org/wp-content/uploads/2013/07

Jahoda, A., Kemp, J., Riddell, S., & Banks, P. (2008). Feelings about work: A review of the socio-emotional impact of supported employment on people with intellectual disabilities. *Journal of Applied Research in Intellectual Disabilities, 21,* 1–18.

Jobling, A., & Cuskelly, M. (2006). Young people with Down syndrome: A preliminary investigation of health knowledge and associated behaviours. *Journal of Intellectual and Developmental Disability, 31,* 210–218. doi:10.1080/13668250600999186.

Johnson, I., & Sigler, R. (2000). Forced sexual intercourse among intimates. *Journal of Interpersonal Violence, 15,* 95–108.

Jurkowski, J. M. (2008). Photovoice as participatory action research tool for engaging people with intellectual disabilities in research and program development. *Intellectual and Developmental Disabilities, 46,* 1–11. doi:10.1352/0047-6765.

Kersh, J. (2011). Attitudes about people with intellectual disabilities: Current status and new directions. *International Review of Research in Developmental Disabilities, 41,* 199–231. doi:10.1016/B978-0-12-386495-6.00006-0.

Kozma, A., Mansell, J., & Beadle-Brown, J. (2009). Outcomes in different residential settings for people with intellectual disability: A systematic review. *American Journal on Intellectual and Developmental Disabilities, 114,* 193–222. doi:10.1352/1944-7558-114.3.193.

Lee, E.-J., Lam, C., & Ditchman, N. (2015). Self-determination and cultural considerations: An Asian perspective. In P. W. Corrigan (Ed.), *Person-centered care for mental illness: The evolution of adherence and self-determination* (pp. 211–234). Washington, DC: American Psychological Association.

Lewis, S., & Stenfert Kroese, B. (2010). An investigation of nursing staff attitudes and emotional reactions towards patients with intellectual disability in a general hospital setting. *Journal of Applied Research in Intellectual Disabilities, 23,* 355–365. doi:10.1111/j.1468-3148.2009.00542.x.

Mai-Duc, C. (2014). 2 N.C. men wrongly convicted of murder freed after decades in prison. Retrieved from www.latimes.com/nation/nationnow/la-na-nn-death-row-inmates-released-mccollum-brown-20140903-story.html

McCarron, M., Swinburne, J., Burke, E., McGlinchey, E., Mulryan, N., Andrews, V., et al. (2011). *Growing older with an intellectual disability in Ireland 2011: First results from the intellectual disability supplement of the Irish longitudinal study on ageing.* Dublin, Ireland: School of Nursing & Midwifery, Trinity College Dublin.

McDonald, K. E., & Keys, C. B. (2008). How the powerful decide: Access to research participation by those at the margins. *American Journal of Community Psychology, 42*, 79–93. doi:10.1007/s10464-008-9192-x.

Mock, M., & Love, K. (2012). One state's initiative to increase access to higher education for people with intellectual disabilities. *Journal of Policy and Practice in Intellectual Disabilities, 9*, 289–297. doi:10.1111/jppi.12006.

Newman, L., Wagner, M., Knokey, A.-M., Marder, C., Nagle, K., Shaver, D., et al. (2011). *The post-high school outcomes of young adults with disabilities up to 8 Years after high school. A report from the National Longitudinal Transition Study-2 (NLTS2)*. Menlo Park, CA: SRI International.

Powers, L. E., & Oschwald, M. (2004). *Violence and abuse against people with disabilities: Experiences, barriers and prevention strategies*. Portland, OR: Oregon Institute on Disability and Development.

Rose, N., Rose, J., & Kent, S. (2012). Staff training in intellectual disability services: A review of the literature and implications for mental health services provided to individuals with intellectual disability. *International Journal of Developmental Disabilities, 58*, 24–39.

Ryan, T. A., & Scior, K. (2014). Medical students' attitudes towards people with intellectual disabilities: A literature review. *Research in Developmental Disabilities, 35*, 2316–2328.

Scotti, J. R., Slack, B. S., Bowman, R. A., & Morris, T. L. (1996). College student attitudes concerning the sexuality of persons with mental retardation: Development of the perceptions of sexuality scale. *Sexuality and Disability, 14*, 249–263. doi:10.1007/BF02590098.

Shaw, L., MacKinnon, J., McWilliam, C., & Sumsion, T. (2004). Consumer participation in the employment rehabilitation process: Contextual factors and implications for practice. *Work, 23*, 181–192.

Siebers, T. (2013). Disability and the theory of complex embodiment—For identity politics in a new register. In L. Davis (Ed.), *The Disability Studies Reader* (pp. 278–297). New York, NY: Routledge.

Siperstein, G. N., Norins, J., Corbin, S., & Shriver, T. (2003). *Multinational study of attitudes toward individuals with intellectual disabilities*. Washington, DC: Special Olympics, Inc..

U.S. Equal Employment Opportunity Commission (2014). *Charge statistics FY 1997 through FY 2014*. Retrieved from eeoc.gov/eeoc/statistics/enforcement/charges.cfm

UNESCO (2015). *Fixing the broken promise of education for all: Findings from the global initiative on out-of-school children*. Montreal, Canada: UNESCO Institute for Statistics.

United Nations (2007). *From exclusion to equality: Realizing the rights of persons with disabilities. Handbook for parliamentarians on the convention on the rights of persons with disabilities and its optional protocol.* Geneva, Switzerland: United Nations. Retrieved from www.un.org/disabilities/documents/toolaction/ipuhb.pdf

Verdonschot, M. M., de Witte, L. P., Reichrath, E., Buntinx, W. H., & Curfs, L. M. (2009). Impact of environmental factors on community participation of persons with an intellectual disability: A systematic review. *Journal of Intellectual Disability Research, 53,* 54–64. doi:10.1111/j.1365-2788.2008.01128.x.

Wehmeyer, M. L., & Palmer, S. B. (2003). Adult outcomes for students with cognitive disabilities three years after high school: The impact of self-determination. *Education and Training in Developmental Disabilities, 38,* 131–144.

Werner, S., & Stawski, M. (2012). Mental health: Knowledge, attitudes and training of professionals on dual diagnosis of intellectual disability and psychiatric disorder. *Journal of Intellectual Disability Research, 56,* 291–304. doi:10.1111/j.1365-2788.2011.01429.x.

World Health Organization & World Bank (2011). *World report on disability.* Geneva, Switzerland: World Health Organization.

Yalon-Chamovitz, S. (2009). Invisible access needs of people with intellectual disabilities: A conceptual model of practice. *Intellectual and Developmental Disabilities, 47,* 395–400. doi:10.1352/1934-9556-47.5.395.

Legislation

Fialka-Feldman v. Oakland University Board of Trustees, No. 08-14922 (E.D. Mich Feb 05, 2009).

Lane v. Brown (formerly Lane v. Kitzhaber), No. 12-CV-00138 (D. Or. 2012).

4

How Stigma Affects Us: The Voice of Self-advocates

Dana Roth, Dorit Barak, and Heli Peretz

Self-stigma or internalized stigma is shaped profoundly by how one believes one is seen by others (Lucksted and Drapalski 2015). Self-stigma occurs when individuals recognize negative attitudes that surround them and endorse these, believing and accepting that they apply to them (Corrigan and Watson 2002). Some have suggested that many people with intellectual disabilities do not identify with the label of "intellectual disability" ascribed to them (Cunningham et al. 2000; Davies 1998; Davies and Jenkins 1997) and have little awareness of their stigmatized status (Beart et al. 2005; Finlay and Lyons 1998). However, others suggest that people with intellectual disabilities do indeed understand that stigma and oppression are related to the label ascribed to them and therefore try to reject that label in the hope of avoiding the associated stigma (Jahoda and

D. Roth (✉) • H. Peretz
Beit Issie Shapiro, Ra'anana, Israel
e-mail: Danar@beitissie.org.il

D. Barak
Beit Issie Shapiro and Elwyn, Ra'anana, Israel

© The Editor(s) (if applicable) and The Author(s) 2016
K. Scior, S. Werner (eds.), *Intellectual Disability and Stigma*,
DOI 10.1057/978-1-137-52499-7_4

49

Markova 2004). Distancing themselves from others who ascribe the label of intellectual disability has negative implications in terms of sense of belonging and social isolation (Ali et al. 2012; Cunningham and Glenn 2004; Spassiani and Friedman 2014).

A systematic review on self-stigma among people with intellectual disabilities concluded that research should focus on the process by which stigma associated with the intellectual disability label is internalized and on the social and psychological factors associated with stigma (Ali et al. 2012). Accordingly, the study presented in this chapter sets out to investigate stigma and self-stigma as experienced by people with intellectual disabilities, to examine their actions in "dealing" with stigma, and the impact of participating in a self-advocacy group (SAG) on these perceptions of stigma and self-stigma.

Consulting Research Committee

Adopting a partial participatory research approach, our study recognized that people with intellectual disabilities are the experts on their lives while the researchers are the "technicians" in charge of planning, collecting, and analyzing the data and writing up the results. A partial participatory research approach was employed by forming a consulting research committee comprised of three individuals with intellectual disabilities, two professionals who are involved with SAGs, and the three researchers. The primary role of this committee was to oversee the research design and process. The tasks of data analysis and reporting of results were completed by the researchers without intellectual disabilities.

One key issue which was evident in the committee's discussions was that although people with intellectual disabilities themselves frequently use the terms "stigma", "negative attitudes", or "prejudice", these terms appeared to be unclear to the committee members and caused some confusion. Thus, it was necessary to provide an in-depth explanation in order to make sure that everyone understood these terms before progressing. Further, the discussions elicited many emotions such as frustration, anger, and sadness to the point of one member with an intellectual disability weeping.

The consultants with intellectual disabilities described experiencing ridicule, bullying, exploitation, and violence, which they attributed to being "disabled". Ahmed (all names used are pseudonyms), a 30-year-old man from the Bedouin Muslim Community in Southern Israel, described his feelings in relation to how others view him: "I feel ashamed to speak in front of people because I'm afraid they will laugh at me. I feel that they are talking behind my back." Uri, a young Jewish man from Jerusalem, added, "Sometimes I am laughed at, near my home they say to me 'you are retarded' and all sort of things. Today that I am already an adult, I understand. They think I am stupid, that I don't understand."

The consulting committee recognized that stigma was a very intense, difficult, shameful, and painful subject. Two committee members expressed concern that raising this topic "out of the blue" with other individuals with intellectual disabilities may cause them much distress. As one member said: "It's difficult, difficult to talk about it, difficult to think about." In order to avoid causing distress, it was decided only to recruit participants that had either raised the issue of stigma previously and/or were experienced in addressing painful issues. Further, in order to be able to provide ongoing support to participants, in the case that such a need would arise, it was decided to recruit the participants via SAGs.

Focus Group Study

A semi-structured interview guide was developed taking into consideration the issues raised by the consulting research committee. The following questions were included: Why are people afraid of us and reluctant to interact with us? Why do people think we are stupid? Why can't people accept us as we are? Why can't people believe in us? Are we really disabled? Why do people feel pity toward us? Why do people think we need charity? Why do our families and others tell us we cannot do things? These questions stemmed from committee members feeling violated by people around them and not understanding why they were treated so poorly. Additional questions were raised spontaneously during the focus group discussions, some by the participants themselves. For example, "How do you 'really' feel? What are you 'really' worth?"; "How do stigma and bad attitudes affect you?"; "How did self-advocacy change you?" The questions which included the word "really" were asked by individuals with intellectual disabilities and may imply that they perceived that some of the responses provided were perhaps not genuine.

Two groups took part in this study. First, a national Israeli SAG, made up of self-advocate leaders (or "guides" in Israeli SAG language) of seven different SAGs across Israel who have been meeting monthly for several years. The group included 12 guides and 5 "enablers" (SAG cofacilitators without intellectual disabilities). Second, a less well-established Tel-Aviv-based SAG that meets fortnightly took part. This group included one guide, nine self-advocates, and one enabler. In both groups there were a similar proportion of men and women, who ranged in age from 20 to 60 years. The majority of participants were Israeli Jews of different levels of religiosity and three Israeli Arab participants. One two-hour meeting was held with each group. The SAG members were familiar with the researchers, having met them on several previous occasions and felt comfortable in their presence.

The group discussion was opened by the researchers and one of the consulting committee members who outlined the purpose of the meeting. The meetings were audio recorded and transcribed. Further, field notes were taken by one of the researchers. Of note, rarely did focus group participants respond to questions or initiate responses spontaneously— most had to be directly asked and encouraged to participate. Further, participants who had difficulty expressing themselves were provided with support and adaptations necessary to help them participate, for example, rephrasing questions, waiting for a response, and asking questions which can be answered by yes/no responses.

The study was approved by Beit Issie Shapiro's Ethics Committee. All participants provided written consent from their parent or legal guardians as (is still) required by law.

Results

The following five themes represent concerns and responses to stigma raised most frequently by participants in both groups.

Emotional impact of stigma. Participants talked about being afraid of stigma, feeling ridicule, anger, shame, rejection, and pain related to others' reactions toward them. They described how their life experiences of negative societal attitudes had "taught" them to expect to be ridiculed and that people talked about them behind their backs. The statements that follow exemplify this: "they make a circus [make fun] of me"; "I feel exploited, they laugh at me"; "they think bad things of me"; "they laughed at me and said, this one is retarded"; "someone says to you that you are limited, it hurts, it pinched my heart"; "they think we are retarded." These statements clearly provide evidence of the negativity and pain these individuals experience, but it is unclear whether these stigmatic experiences were accepted and internalized by them. Some participants appeared not to internalize stigma but rather perceived it as unjust. They "swallowed" the insult, but did not accept it.

Not understanding why stigma occurs and is directed toward us. Many participants indicated that they did not understand why they were being treated negatively: "I don't know why they laugh at me ... we should be treated like everybody else..."; "I left my last job, they said I was too slow, but I worked as fast as possible exactly like the other worker." Another participant said: "I do all the work there is to do, I work harder than all the other workers, but they don't let me be the coordinator of the children in the kindergarten, despite the fact that I do things none of the other caregivers do." Some of the other participants said: "I am regular like everyone else"; "they think we are retarded and not normal"; "she said that I am a person with special needs, so I thought; what, I am retarded? So I asked her, and she said no." These findings can be explained in different ways. Firstly, it is possible that participants do not internalize the stigma associated with intellectual disability. Thus, they did not understand why they were being ridiculed, seen as unable to do what "normal" people do, or treated differently from those around them. This was reflected in answers to the question "why do you think you are treated like that", a question many participants were unable to answer. Instead, they elaborated on *how* they were treated and not *why* they were treated negatively. A second possible explanation is that no one had truly explained to them what it means to have an intellectual disability and its potential impact on them and their lives. It is possible that saying out loud "I have an intellectual disability" is too difficult, as society considers this term as derogatory. Yet, when listening closely to the participants, it was clear that there was a strong dissonance between their expressed denial of being different and their unspoken sense of being different and somehow deficient. This can be seen in statements made by participants when asked more directly: "we are different in our brain level"; "we cannot function alone"; "I work slower."

Confusion in self-concept and identity. Participants referred to themselves as having many titles and definitions: "special needs", "handicapped", "retarded", and "intellectually disabled". When asked how they would like their disability to be referred to, they suggested, "limited, this means that our brain is limited"; "intellectually disabled, this sounds nicer than limited or disabled"; "special needs because this will cause less people to laugh at me"; "mild retardation, so they understand that we have limitations in everything"; "a regular person, a person that does not have a problem".

Most of the participants felt very uncomfortable, especially in the national SAG, to address the issue of their identity related to being a person with an intellectual disability. They appeared more comfortable focusing on additional physical or sensory impairments that affected some of them. For example, in one of the groups there was a lively discussion about one of the participant's visual impairment, which the group was clearly more comfortable to discuss than intellectual disability.

Ignoring as a default response to stigma. Most participants described attempting to deal with the insults they faced by trying, in their words, "to ignore" them or avoid contact with people who had insulted them. Nevertheless, it seems that their attempts were not always fruitful. The behavioral response of ignoring carried with it an emotional cost. When asked how they responded to situations in which they were exposed to stigma, they said they were silent, looked down, and did not confront the offending person. Many shared situations in which they had chosen not to confront others: "They laughed at me, said I was limited, retarded, that I am a retarded one, 'that one, she has no brain'. I did not respond, I did not react, and I felt very bad." "If they laugh at me, I ignore it"; "if we will respond to them, they will burst at us"; "they will not listen to me … ignore … ignore …" "They told me 'you are from the retarded organization, you are limited'. I don't answer, I don't respond." (Researcher asked: "How did you feel?") "I feel sad. I cannot say anything."

Participants appeared hesitant to confront the people who hurt them because they feared they might encounter an even more negative reaction. By ignoring the situation they felt safer at the price of reinforcing negative reactions. Ignoring was a skill they were taught by their environment and those caring for them, who frequently gave them advice such as "ignore it, it is not true". While potentially well meaning, such advice encourages the person neither to stand up for themselves, nor to deal with their intellectual disability, and instead could be seen as being complicit in failing to challenge stigma.

The opportunity provided by self-advocacy. Participating in SAGs clearly provided participants with an alternative, an opportunity to be less fearful, talk, explain, and stand up for their rights, not ignore. The SAGs had an optimistic atmosphere where learning about self-advocacy provided a new and different way of being in the community. They were not focused on erasing or ignoring the disability but rather on increasing group members' understanding that having a disability and being different from others does not justify disrespect or hostility. Taking part in the SAG strengthened their sense of personal control: "I am responsible for myself"; "I am aware of my difficulties, but I am equal"; "I can explain what is difficult for me, but I still deserve fair treatment." Other statements illustrating this theme included: "I will talk to people so that they can listen to how people like us feel"; "SAG does good for me … gives me hope, I can stand on my own … if I see that things are not right I can say something"; "I can say in a nice polite way that they should treat us nicely and equally"; "I feel that I am doing something for myself and not for someone else"; "the group gives me the power, I am not afraid to tell people to treat me with a little more respect. Many times I was scared because I was treated like a child and today I am not afraid to say it"; "to know how to approach normal people … I also have the right to things." Other participants provided additional examples of how membership of a SAG helped them stand up for themselves: "If people in the community do not treat you nicely, argue with them and stand on your own in all cases, because people change their opinions." Or as another SAG member said: "You must stand on your own, if you do not stand on your own, you will not get what you want."

Members of the consulting committee also reported similar experiences related to being members of SAGs: "In the SAG I learned things and skills I succeeded in and it made me change how I think of myself." "Before the SAG I felt bad, I felt out of place, and then I changed. I did not think I had abilities, just suffer and go on." "I never heard of self-advocacy, I learned a lot, it changed my life. It gives me strength, it gives me power, and I have changed." "Our life has changed for the better."

Discussion and Conclusions

The findings of this study are consistent with previous studies in indicating that some individuals with intellectual disabilities do not identify with having an intellectual disability and prefer to refer to themselves as having other forms of disability. Further, individuals with intellectual disabilities who participated in this study described various difficulties that they faced due to holding a stigmatized status and being treated badly by others (Ali et al. 2012; Cunningham et al. 2000; Davies 1998; Davies and Jenkins 1997; Jahoda and Markova 2004). Accordingly, some individuals with intellectual disabilities feel frustrated about the label of "retardation" or "intellectual disability" ascribed to them (Dagnan and Waring 2004). They may respond by distancing themselves from other individuals with intellectual disabilities and ignoring and avoiding situations which may elicit stigmatic responses toward them, such as negative remarks and insults (Gibbons 1985; Jahoda and Markova 2004).

Self-stigma of individuals with intellectual disabilities is a very complex construct to measure. One question which remained unanswered in the current study is in what ways does self-stigma differ from public stigma? Is self-stigma a product of public stigma, that is, do all or most individuals who are prone to public stigma internalize this? On the one hand, the participants' descriptions of their behavior reflects that many internalized a sense of themselves as "inferior to others", along with a strong fear of society, and a tendency to avoid contact with those that impose stigma. On the other hand, participants had great difficulties saying "I have an intellectual disability." It seems that many participants had a sense that they "do not deserve such treatment", but did not understand why they are treated poorly or what to do about it.

The group discussions made it clear that ignoring, a strategy frequently chosen by participants, ultimately served to reinforce stigma. In contrast, self-advocacy provided a collective sense of strength and injustice. In listening to their voices, ideas, and experiences, it is clear that there is a need to support more self-advocacy, convince others of its importance and benefits, and support the development of different formats of self-advocacy, as regular discussion-based groups may not suit everyone. It is necessary to convince families, service providers, and policy makers of the importance and the necessity of self-advocacy and to encourage diverse forms of self-advocacy from a younger age as a possible method to mitigate the negative impact of stigma. Effort should be directed to examine how to promote the self-esteem of individuals with intellectual disabilities and provide them with skills to help them cope with their realities, alongside informing and educating communities at large to reduce and eliminate stigmatic beliefs.

Key Learning Points

- This chapter presents a study designed to hear the voices and investigate how people with intellectual disabilities experience stigma and self-stigma.
- The study was conducted using elements of the participatory research approach recognizing that people with intellectual disabilities are the experts on their lives.
- The participants were well aware of their stigmatized status within society, but did not understand why stigma is directed toward them. They preferred to ignore situations which raise stigma. Further, self-advocacy was described as an alternative approach to dealing with stigma.
- Efforts should be directed to examine how to promote individuals' self-esteem and provide them with skills to help them cope with their realities, and to inform and educate communities to reduce and eliminate stigmatic beliefs.

Accessible Summary

- We asked people with intellectual disabilities what other people without disabilities think about them.
- People with intellectual disabilities felt that others laugh at them. This made them feel bad about themselves. They didn't understand why others treat them this way. Many preferred to ignore situations in which people made fun of them or hurt them.
- Taking part in SAGs, they learned to speak for themselves and say what they want and feel. In these groups they are able to learn how to talk back and not let others treat them badly.
- People with intellectual disabilities should learn how to speak up for themselves and feel more confident. It is also very important to teach people without disabilities that people with intellectual disabilities are people just like them.

Acknowledgments We would like to thank the participants for taking part in this study and for teaching us so much about their lives. We clearly felt the difficulties, pain, and discomfort they experience in most walks of life and the great challenges they face in talking about these. They have taught us the importance of self-advocacy to empower them and enable them to develop skills to make changes in their lives.

References

Ali, A., Hassiotis, A., Strydom, A., & King, M. (2012). Self stigma in people with intellectual disabilities and courtesy stigma in family carers: A systematic review. *Research in Developmental Disabilities, 33*, 2122–2140. doi:10.1016/j.ridd.2012.06.013.

Beart, S., Hardy, G., & Buchan, L. (2005). How people with intellectual disabilities view their social identity: A review of the literature. *Journal of Applied Research in Intellectual Disabilities, 18*, 47–56. doi:10.1111/j.1468-3148.2004.00218.

Corrigan, P. W., & Watson, A. C. (2002). The paradox of self-stigma and mental illness. *Clinical Psychology: Science and Practice, 9*, 35–53. doi:10.1093/clipsy.9.1.35.

Cunningham, C. C., Glenn, S., & Fitzpatrick, H. (2000). Parents telling their offspring about Down syndrome and disability. *Journal of Applied Research in Intellectual Disabilities, 13*, 47–61. doi:10.1046/j.1468-3148.2000.00012.x.

Cunningham, C., & Glenn, S. (2004). Self-awareness in young adults with Down syndrome: Awareness of Down syndrome and disability. *International Journal of Disability, Development and Education, 51*, 335–361. doi:10.1080 /10349120042000295017.

Dagnan, D., & Waring, M. (2004). Linking stigma to psychological distress: Testing a social–cognitive model of the experience of people with intellectual disabilities. *Clinical Psychology & Psychotherapy, 11*, 247–254. doi:10.1002/ cpp.413.

Davies, C. A. (1998). Constructing other selves: Competence and the category of learning difficulties. In R. Jenkins (Ed.), *Questions of competence: Culture, classification and intellectual disability* (pp. 102–124). Cambridge, UK: Cambridge University Press.

Davies, C. A., & Jenkins, R. (1997). 'She has different fits to me': How people with learning difficulties see themselves. *Disability and Society, 12*, 95–110. doi:10.1080/09687599727498.

Finlay, M., & Lyons, E. (1998). Social identity and people with learning difficulties: Implications for self-advocacy groups. *Disability and Society, 13*, 37–51. doi:10.1080/09687599826902.

Gibbons, F. X. (1985). Stigma perception: Social comparison among mentally retarded persons. *American Journal of Mental Deficiency, 90*, 98–106.

Jahoda, A., & Markova, I. (2004). Coping with social stigma: People with intellectual disabilities moving from institutions and family home. *Journal of Intellectual Disability Research, 48*, 719–729. doi:10.1111/j.1365-2788.2003.00561.x.

Lucksted, A., & Drapalski, A. L. (2015). Self-stigma regarding mental illness: Definition, impact, and relationship to societal stigma. *Psychiatric Rehabilitation Journal, 38*, 99–102. doi:10.1037/prj0000152.

Spassiani, N. A., & Friedman, C. (2014). Stigma: Barriers to culture and identity for people with intellectual disability. *Inclusion, 2*, 329–341. doi:10.1352/2326-6988-2.4.329.

5

Rarely Seen, Seldom Heard: People with Intellectual Disabilities in the Mass Media

Rebecca Renwick

People with intellectual disabilities are remarkably underrepresented in the mass media such as newspapers, television, and film (Devotta et al. 2013; Saito and Ishiyama 2005). Thus, their images are rarely seen and their own voices seldom heard by the general public. Historically and currently, media representations of people with intellectual disabilities have frequently communicated stigmatizing messages based on negative stereotypes (Renwick et al. 2014; Special Olympics 2005). In combination, infrequent representation and stigmatizing messages communicated to vast audiences have considerable potential to detrimentally affect people with intellectual disabilities.

This chapter explores the nature of representations of people with intellectual disabilities in mass media. It considers how these representations are disseminated and their potential for influencing the thinking, feelings, and behavior of vast audiences. It focuses on representations in newspapers,

R. Renwick (✉)
Department of Occupational Science and Occupational Therapy,
University of Toronto, Toronto, Canada
e-mail: r.renwick@utoronto.ca

© The Editor(s) (if applicable) and The Author(s) 2016
K. Scior, S. Werner (eds.), *Intellectual Disability and Stigma*,
DOI 10.1057/978-1-137-52499-7_5

television, and film, which have the potential to reflect the voices of people with intellectual disabilities, but rarely do. It discusses the limited literature about people with intellectual disabilities in mass media to consider how these media have contributed to reproducing and counteracting stigma. Because this literature is sparse, relevant literature on other disabilities, such as physical and developmental disabilities, including autism, is included to help illuminate the context of media representations. The chapter concludes with a discussion of major gaps in the literature, future directions, and implications.

Nature of Media Representations and Stigma

Media representations refer to how particular people and groups are portrayed in media, as embodied in images, words/texts, language used, and tone. A particular perspective or set of assumptions, values, beliefs, and understandings, often grounded in dominant societal views, about those depicted typically frames such portrayals. In turn, these socially constructed representations, with their associated meanings and messages, are communicated to broad audiences (Hodgkinson 2011).

Dyer (1993) provides a complex definition of representations by distinguishing four meanings. These are highly relevant to media portrayals of people with disabilities (Hartnett 2000). The first meaning is *re-presenting* reality in the sense of conveying mediated portrayals of the 'real world' by mass media. A second is portrayal of individual persons as *typical* of groups in society or stereotypes rather than as individuals. The third is that media representations serve to *speak for* others rather than having those individuals speak for themselves. The fourth meaning refers to what the images and messages communicated *represent for audience members*.

Mass media representations are particularly powerful because they can evoke strong emotions and associations in audiences (Hodgkinson 2011). Although mass media, such as newspapers, television, and film, are often visual in nature, the representations they communicate are multimodal in that they also evoke other senses, such as hearing and touch, as well as thoughts, emotions, and mental imagery (Mitchell 2005).

Their multimodal nature affords extraordinary potential to disseminate powerful messages which reverberate across cultures and over time to exert far-reaching, long-lasting influence on vast audiences (Mitchell and Snyder 2001). For example, many mainstream films and television programs and some well-known newspapers have transnational circulation. Popular television programs may run for several seasons and then continue as reruns, including outside their countries of origin. Films shown in theaters may continue to be disseminated through DVD formats and/ or on Internet media sites accessible to international audiences.

Mass media are pervasive and have vast audiences, and thus are highly effective in communicating intentional and unintentional messages embodied in the socially constructed representations they disseminate. In the absence of direct contact, such media messages are often the primary sources of individuals' experiences with people with intellectual disabilities (Farnall and Smith 1999). Some of these representations include stigmatizing messages about people with disabilities (Renwick et al. 2014; Special Olympics 2005). Unfortunately, audiences often presume that such representations have elements of truth about them that may outweigh personal experiences (Garland-Thomson 2009).

What Constitutes Acceptable Representation?

Most analyses of media representations of intellectual and other disabilities point to the preponderance of unacceptable and potentially damaging stereotypes (Devotta et al. 2013; Lopez Levers 2001; Special Olympics 2005). However, mass media can also potentially communicate much more acceptable, enlightened portrayals (Lopez Levers 2001; Zhang and Haller 2013). It has been suggested that 'acceptable' representations of people with intellectual disabilities, or of people with disability in general, should portray, rather than conceal, experiences of people with disabilities that are related to their oppression by and struggles with disabling environments they encounter in society (Mitchell and Snyder 2001). Portrayals should depict these individuals as neither better nor worse than they are in real life. Media should portray individuals with disability frequently, realistically, and fairly, showing a range of functions, emotional expressions, and relationships with others

(Hartnett 2000; Special Olympics 2005). More acceptable representations should also depict disability as one aspect of the person rather than as the major characteristic or focus of portrayals. Presenting people with disabilities from their own perspectives has been identified as an optimal approach (Special Olympics 2005; Zhang and Haller 2013).

Process of Mass Media Communication

Hall's (1980) seminal Encoding/Decoding theory illuminates the process or circuit through which mass media communication occurs. It begins with encoding (creation) of verbal and nonverbal messages which are embodied in representations. These messages are typically based on dominant values, beliefs, and discourses in society and created by members of dominant, hegemonic societal groups that may have restricted views of disability (Zhang and Haller 2013). These messages are then circulated through mass media to receivers (audiences) who attempt to decode (interpret and understand) them. After audiences interpret the messages, they may reproduce them, that is, think, talk, and act on the basis of the messages such that they are fed back into the ongoing societal discourse.

Messages that influence audiences and are reproduced may or may not be the ones that were originally encoded by those creating them. Audiences may also interpret these messages in ways that negotiate, resist, or oppose the original meaning of the messages communicated (Hall 1980). However, the messages received are often interpreted in ways that are the same as or similar to the original meaning because audiences already agree with their content or do not know much about what is being communicated, for example, due to lack of exposure and personal experience with people with intellectual disabilities.

People with Intellectual Disabilities in the Mass Media

Research literature about people with intellectual disabilities in the mass media is sparse and appears in publications across diverse fields (communication, cultural studies, disability studies, media studies, psychology, occupational science, semiotics, and sociology). The following sections highlight some key findings across this literature, drawing upon recent research about portrayals within newspapers, television, and mainstream, Hollywood-style films. Only English-language publications since 2000 are considered. Hollywood-style films have fictional content and are rooted in North American culture. They are widely shown in public movie theaters and typically available in other formats (e.g., DVD), making them accessible to diverse viewers (Renwick et al. 2014). Except when they provide contextual information, studies that did not separate their findings by medium or distinguish findings for intellectual disabilities from other types of disabilities are excluded.

Newspapers

Recent research on newspaper representations of intellectual disability is scarce. One study of UK print media representations of people with developmental disabilities, including intellectual disabilities, compared articles published between 1983 and 2001 in *The Guardian*, a national newspaper (Wilkinson and McGill 2009). The number of articles more than doubled over that period, yet they continued to overrepresent children with autism. In 2001, articles were mainly about children with autism and Down syndrome while articles about adults typically referred to developmental disabilities generally rather than any specific condition. Articles from 1983 rarely distinguished specific types of developmental disabilities for any age group. In 2001, coverage reflected greater use of people first language, but continued to link developmental disabilities with other devalued groups, such as people with mental illness. Increasing differentiation among people with developmental disabilities, with greater attention to disabilities such as autism and Down syndrome and much less to individuals with more severe and complex needs, also featured.

A study of all major Taiwanese newspapers published in 2008 examined representations of people with intellectual disabilities (Chen et al. 2012). Most of the 355 articles identified appeared in local (77 %) rather than nationally circulated papers. Three key themes were identified in depictions of intellectual disabilities through the use of content analysis.

The first theme, *dispirited images* (45 % of articles), was consistent with social deviance models of disability (e.g., as victims of exploitation, lacking skills, and experiencing suffering or loss due to their disability). The second theme, *needy images* (33 % of articles), was congruent with a charity model of disability (e.g., emphasizing the need for professional supports, services, and interventions). The final theme, *affirmative images* (23 % of articles), was associated with a civil rights model of disability. These articles focused on 'normalcy' describing people with intellectual disabilities as doing things or having abilities characteristic of the general public or featured people with intellectual disabilities with supportive, caring families. The researchers concluded that, collectively, these newspaper portrayals emphasized the deficiency of people with intellectual disabilities and thus may support their social exclusion.

Another study examined and compared portrayals of individuals with intellectual disabilities in several mass media, including articles in newspapers published in four major American cities between 1995 and 2004 (Special Olympics 2005). Findings indicated that these individuals were presented as less competent (in reading, doing math, acting in a socially appropriate manner) in print than in television programs or films. Further, articles most frequently presented people with intellectual disabilities engaged in a narrow range of common activities related to sports, work, or school.

Television

Research on television portrayals of people with intellectual disabilities is rare. One study examined footage of first-time domestic coverage on British television of national Special Olympics games in 2009 (Carter and Williams 2012). It revealed 'relentless positivity' in the language and tone of the broadcasts, using exaggerated descriptors such as 'amazing', 'fantastic', 'inspiring', and 'incredible'. Positivity in the tone was evident in scenes featuring athletes and others smiling and waving very enthusiastically and in portraying social aspects of the games rather than their status as a competitive athletics event. Athletes were routinely and repeatedly referred to as 'them' and represented as different, with emphasis on their disabilities. Coverage included information about the nature of these disabilities and how the athletes were 'challenging existing barriers'. The focus on disability issues for individuals and human interest stories dominated the coverage, leaving larger, more important questions about political and social agendas linking sport and disability unaddressed. For instance, the issue of integration of sports for people with and without disabilities was not examined (Carter and Williams 2012).

A study on portrayals of people with disabilities, including intellectual disabilities, in prime-time television dramas in Japan (1993–2002) by Saito and Ishiyama (2005) found that their number increased over time but there was marked underrepresentation of individuals with all disabilities in all years. However, persons with intellectual disabilities were depicted second most often compared with other disabilities perhaps, the researchers suggested, because they are easier to portray on television. Children and young adults with intellectual disabilities were depicted disproportionately more compared to actual population statistics while adults over the age of 30 were not portrayed. These representations conveyed some basic misinformation suggesting that they can cultivate distorted perceptions, especially since many of the prime-time dramas featuring characters with intellectual disabilities were among those viewed most often.

Film

There is no research on films focused only on people with intellectual disabilities. Two studies examined Hollywood-style films presenting fictional portrayals of people with either developmental or intellectual disabilities. These films were released between 1968 and 2009, distributed widely to commercial movie theaters, and remain available on DVD or online.

Renwick et al. (2014) qualitatively analyzed portrayals of engagement in everyday and meaningful activities by adults with developmental disabilities in eight films (1999–2009). These films depicted mainly leisure (e.g., socializing, watching movies) and productive (e.g., volunteer or paid work, taking educational courses) activities which were typically safe and pleasurable, but not very challenging. Characters had restricted choices for participation in activities they found meaningful. Activities usually done by adults were performed in simplified ways and/or in a manner more characteristic of children and/or the activities were usually performed by children. These films conveyed many powerful, negative messages about what constitutes acceptable activities and social roles for people with intellectual and developmental disabilities and how they usually perform them. Nevertheless, closer examination revealed some other more complex portrayals, such as struggles with personal problems (alcoholism, job loss, death of a loved one) and ongoing challenges of dealing with a stigmatizing society. However, these were revealed only with careful, repeated viewing. Therefore, they would likely be missed by viewers watching the films for entertainment.

In an examination of nine films (1968–1997), Devlieger et al. (2000) found stereotypic portrayals of developmental disabilities, such as something to be hidden and a tragedy or burden. However, a few films included more complex representations, for instance, a person with an intellectual disability who was initially dependent on others but forged more reciprocal relationships with them and eventually learned to live independently. The study also found that few films featured voices of persons with intellectual disabilities as narrators, so that they are more often spoken for or about.

Discussion

Several recurring themes were identified across the literature examined. One is that these media consistently underrepresent people with intellectual disabilities. Another is their simplistic portrayals in all three media with frequently repeated stereotypes depicting childlike innocents who lack capabilities and are vulnerable, needy, passive, a burden to others, dangerous, and problematic. In addition, disability is the major focus such that individuality, complexity, nuance, and multiple social roles are not captured by these portrayals. Finally, negative and stigmatizing mass media messages are repeatedly emphasized, typically outnumbering and outweighing more acceptable ones. In general, such portrayals reinforce and cultivate stigmatizing beliefs, attitudes, and perspectives held by audience members, with potentially damaging implications for the identities and treatment of people with intellectual disabilities themselves.

The research examined offers important insights concerning people with intellectual disabilities in the mass media. One concern is what is typically included and what is excluded in mass media portrayals. This literature identifies what is most frequently included, for example, stereotyping, devaluation, stigmatization, and misinformation about people with intellectual and developmental disabilities. It also underscores Dyer's (1993) first and second meanings of representation, mediated presentations of reality and typified portrayals, respectively. However, several authors emphasized that what is not or rarely communicated equally influences audiences' beliefs and attitudes. For example, Carter and Williams (2012) pointed out that first-time television coverage of Special Olympics Games showcased the human interest angle and athletes' disabilities while neglecting overarching political and social issues concerning whether sports and sports events should be integrated or segregated. Renwick et al. (2014) noted that concerns people with developmental disabilities may grapple with (e.g., addiction, loss of employment) are portrayed infrequently and backgrounded in films.

Another issue is that the voices of people with intellectual disabilities themselves are seldom heard in mass media. Thus, what is portrayed is completely controlled by journalists, editors, experts, and others. This is not the preferred standard of journalistic reportage when individuals with intellectual disabilities may be readily available for interviews. Such findings are related to Dyer's (1993) third meaning of representation, being spoken for and about, rather than being allowed to speak for oneself.

It is essential to understand effects of specific media representations on the emotions, assumptions, beliefs, and behaviors of audience members with respect to people with intellectual disabilities, especially in terms of targeting changes in negative perceptions and behaviors. These issues, related to Dyer's (1993) fourth meaning of representation concerning what messages communicated by media mean for audience members, remain to be investigated.

Several significant gaps in knowledge exist in the literature. Very little is known about the strength of short- and long-term effects of different kinds of portrayals of intellectual disabilities on beliefs, attitudes, behaviors, and interpretations of audience members without disabilities. There is also no published research concerning effects on and responses to such portrayals on the part of people with intellectual disabilities themselves. Both studies with preexperimental and longitudinal designs may be effective in providing insights into such issues. Interventional studies could help illuminate what kinds of representations, frequency of exposure to more acceptable representations, and other factors, alone or in combination, can effectively shift attitudes, beliefs, and behaviors. Using media for stigma change interventions is touched on in Chap. 9.

Two critical areas requiring further illumination are what topics and issues media portrayals of people with intellectual disabilities are silent about and the absence of first person perspectives or voices of people with intellectual disabilities themselves. These are challenging areas to study because the focus is on missing information. However, this kind of research is likely to be very valuable in providing insights about how to construct more acceptable, nuanced, inclusive media portrayals of people with intellectual disabilities that can positively influence beliefs, attitudes, and behaviors of audiences and reduce stigma.

Studies of media representations by participatory research groups involving people with and without intellectual disabilities as coresearchers have not been reported in the literature. However, a media review coauthored by participatory research group members focused on findings from an in-depth analysis of one recent Hollywood-style film (*Defendor*) (Fudge Schormans et al. 2013). Currently, their larger participatory research study of multiple Hollywood-style films is still in progress. More participatory studies of media representations in films, television programs, and newspapers are needed to understand their effects and how to construct more inclusive representations from the perspective of people with intellectual disabilities.

Implications for Practice

Service professionals are exposed to the same media representations of intellectual disabilities as others in society and may also be influenced by them. Government policies regulating service delivery, practices, and procedures of organizations where professionals work and train may implicitly embody some of these stereotypical beliefs and assumptions about intellectual disability. People with intellectual disabilities whom they serve are also likely to encounter negative effects of such stereotypical beliefs and associated behaviors from people they interact with in everyday life. Therefore, attention to education of professionals using media as a learning vehicle could be a useful strategy for counteracting some of these stereotypical, stigmatizing assumptions and behaviors. Facilitated discussions after viewing of selected films could also stimulate new insights into the complexity of individuals with intellectual disabilities and their lives, such as their individual capabilities and struggles (Conn and Bhugra 2015). Involvement of self-advocates and advocates in such discussions could considerably enrich the learning process.

Implications for Advocacy

Advocacy strategies are needed to counteract stigmatizing representations and change the nature and quality of media portrayals. These could take the form of accessible and novel knowledge translation strategies and formats that could support self-advocates' efforts, such as short films and trailers that might be shown as a free community service on television, feature articles for mainstream and community newspapers, and free advocacy ads in community newspapers.

Education aimed at children may be especially valuable in counteracting and changing perceptions about people with intellectual disabilities. Educational vehicles such as short films for classroom viewing or short videos on YouTube featuring, and co-created by, people with intellectual disabilities could be used to stimulate discussion among younger students. A continuing emphasis on education implemented by advocates and self-advocates for older students in elementary and high schools could reinforce and promote media literacy (Englandkennedy 2008), stigma reduction, and acceptance of people with intellectual disabilities.

Given the power and pervasiveness of mass media and the representations they disseminate to broad audiences, changing the content of media portrayals will require considerable persistence and targeted strategizing.

Advocacy could take several forms, for instance, direct efforts to inform and educate newspaper editors and journalists (Jones and Harwood 2009), television executives and producers, and film makers (Hartnett 2000). Such advocacy should focus on potential harm done by stigmatizing portrayals that reproduce and perpetuate stereotypes, what constitute acceptable portrayals, and strategies for constructing more and better representations. Other strategies include employing more actors with intellectual disabilities to play such characters, and featuring characters with intellectual disabilities as narrators, instead of being spoken for and about. Creating more television programs and films focused on individuals with intellectual disabilities and having these individuals visible in many more programs and films in supporting roles and in the background could help normalize their natural presence in media and society. Newspapers could also feature more interviews that include these individuals themselves (with appropriate supports) such that their voices are reflected more often. All three mass media could benefit considerably from ongoing consultation with and feedback from self-advocates with intellectual disabilities, advocates, and their supporting organizations concerning construction and communication of more acceptable, nuanced, and inclusive representations.

The Long-Term Path to Change

Suggestions and recommendations for progressive changes to mass media representations are easily stated. Implementation is likely to be challenging and to require considerable time and persistence and multiple, innovative strategies by self-advocates and advocates working together at several levels (e.g., with individuals, schools, community organizations, and the media). Research has only begun to illuminate a path forward regarding what needs to change, how to change the fact that people with intellectual disabilities are rarely seen and seldom heard in the media, and how to construct portrayals that reduce, not reproduce, stigma. Researchers must continue to study mass media representations, especially their influence on audiences, including people with intellectual disabilities and professionals as audience members, and how this influence might be changed for the better. Strong research partnerships with self-advocates, advocates, and professionals collaborating to design and conduct studies grounded in real-world experiences will contribute significant new knowledge from multiple perspectives.

Key Learning Points

- People with intellectual disabilities are underrepresented in newspapers, television, and film.
- Stigmatizing stereotypes predominate in mass media portrayals while the complexity and individuality of people with intellectual disabilities are rarely represented.
- In the absence of other information sources, audiences can be influenced by such stigmatizing stereotypes.
- The voices of self-advocates must be central to more positive media portrayals.

Accessible Summary

- Stories that newspapers, television, and movies tell about people with intellectual disabilities often look mostly at the disability.
- These stories often give wrong information about what people with intellectual disabilities and their lives are really like.
- Stories about people with intellectual disabilities are getting a bit better but need to get much better.
- These stories can change what other people think and feel about people with intellectual disabilities, and how people with intellectual disabilities feel and think about themselves.
- We can work together to change the bad effects that newspapers, television, and movies have on people with intellectual disabilities.

Acknowledgments I am grateful to be part of a participatory research group that collaborates to study the stories that films tell about people with intellectual and developmental disabilities and present our findings in traditional and more accessible formats. I appreciate Matthew Devine's assistance with identifying diverse literature about mass media and disability.

References

Carter, N., & Williams, J. (2012). 'A genuinely emotional week': Learning disability, sport, and television—Notes on the Special Olympics GB National Summer Games 2009. *Media, Culture and Society, 34,* 211–227. doi:10.1177/0163443711430759.

Chen, C. H., Hsu, K. L., Shu, B. C., & Fertzer, S. (2012). The image of people with intellectual disability in Taiwan newspapers. *Journal of Intellectual and Developmental Disability, 17,* 35–41. doi:10.3109/13668250.2011.650159.

Conn, R., & Bhugra, D. (2015). The portrayal of autism in Hollywood films. *International Journal of Culture and Mental Health, 5,* 54–62. doi:10.1080/17542863.2011.553369.

Devlieger, P. J., Baz, T., & Drazen, C. (2000). Mental retardation in American film: A semiotic analysis. *Semiotica, 129,* 1–28. doi:10.1515/semi.2000.129.1-4.1.

Devotta, K., Wilton, R., & Yiannakoulias, N. (2013). Representations of disability in the Canadian news media: A decade of change? *Disability and Rehabilitation, 35,* 1859–1868. doi:10.3109/09638288.2012.760658.

Dyer, R. (1993). *The matter of images: Essays on representation.* London, UK: Routledge.

Englandkennedy, E. (2008). Media representations of attention deficit disorder: Portrayals of cultural skepticism in popular media. *Journal of Popular Culture, 41,* 91–117. doi:10.1111/j.1540-5931.2008.00494.x.

Farnall, O., & Smith, K. A. (1999). Reactions to people with disabilities: Personal contact versus viewing of specific media portrayals. *Journalism and Mass Communication Quarterly, 76,* 659–672. doi:10.1177/107769909907600404.

Fudge Schormans, A., Renwick, R., Barker, D., Chasi, E., Smith, B., McWilliam, L., et al. (2013). Why *can't* we be superheroes? Researchers' with and without intellectual and developmental disabilities thoughts on *Defendor.* Media Review. *Journal on Developmental Disabilities, 19,* 109–112.

Garland-Thomson, R. (2009). *Staring: How we look.* New York, NY: Oxford University Press.

Hall, S. (1980). Encoding/decoding. In S. Hall, D. Hobson, A. Lowe, & P. Willis (Eds.), *Culture, media, language* (pp. 128–138). London, UK: Hutchinson & Co..

Hartnett, A. (2000). Escaping the 'evil avenger' and 'the supercrip': Images of disability in popular television. *The Irish Communication Review, 8,* 21–29.

Hodgkinson, P. (2011). *Media, culture, and society: An introduction*. London, UK: Sage.

Jones, C., & Harwood, V. (2009). Representations of autism in Australian print media. *Disability and Society, 24*, 5–18. doi:10.1080/09687590802535345.

Lopez Levers, L. (2001). Representations of psychiatric disabilities in fifty years of Hollywood film: An ethnographic content analysis. *Theory and Science, 2*(2).

Mitchell, W. J. T. (2005). There are no visual media. *Journal of Visual Culture, 4*, 257–266. doi:10.1177/1470412905054673.

Mitchell, D., & Snyder, S. L. (2001). Representation and its discontents. The uneasy home of disability in literature and film. In G. L. Albrecht, K. D. Seelman, & M. Bury (Eds.), *Handbook of disability studies* (pp. 195–238). Thousand Oaks, CA: Sage.

Renwick, R., Fudge Schormans, A., & Shore, D. (2014). Hollywood takes on intellectual/developmental disability: Cinematic representations of occupational participation. *Occupational Therapy Journal of Research: Occupation, Participation, and Health, 34*, 20–31. doi:10.3928/15394492-20131118-01.

Saito, S., & Ishiyama, R. (2005). The invisible minority: Under-representation of people with disabilities in prime-time TV dramas in Japan. *Disability and Society, 20*, 437–451. doi:10.1080/09687590500086591.

Special Olympics (2005). *Changing attitudes, changing the world: Media portrayals of people with intellectual disabilities*. Retrieved from www.specialolympics. org/uploadedFiles/LandingPage/WhatWeDo/Research_Studies_ Desciption_Pages/Policy_paper_media_portrayal.pdf

Wilkinson, P., & McGill, P. (2009). Representation of people with intellectual disabilities in a British newspaper in 1983 and 2001. *Journal of Applied Research in Intellectual Disabilities, 22*, 65–76. doi:10.1111/j.1468-3148.2008.00453.x.

Zhang, L., & Haller, B. (2013). Consuming images: How mass media impact the identity of people with disabilities. *Communication Quarterly, 61*, 319–334. doi:10.1080/01463373.2013.776988.

6

Stigmatic Representation of Intellectual Disability and Termination of Parental Custody Rights

Hanna Björg Sigurjónsdóttir and James G. Rice

One objective of safeguarding, or 'child protection' as it is still referred to in many countries, is to aid and support parents to create a healthy environment within which to raise their children. However, in the case of parents with intellectual disabilities, the long-standing stereotypes, prejudice, and stigma associated with this label appear to influence the implementation and outcome of child protection work, creating a 'ripple effect' from the referral to the evaluation process (National Council on Disability 2012). The child custody removal cases we examine in this chapter in the Icelandic context, in addition to consulting the international literature, suggest that such cases proceed from an assumption that parents with intellectual disabilities are 'unfit' and that support measures will not work. Discriminatory practices can be detected throughout the process, and the various assessments used to evaluate parenting ability and custody adopt a narrow, restrictive, and almost obsessive view on the impairment-related 'flaws' of the individuals concerned, which come to

H.B. Sigurjónsdóttir (✉) • J.G. Rice
Center for Disability Studies, University of Iceland, Reykjavík, Iceland
e-mail: hbs@hi.is

© The Editor(s) (if applicable) and The Author(s) 2016
K. Scior, S. Werner (eds.), *Intellectual Disability and Stigma*,
DOI 10.1057/978-1-137-52499-7_6

play a more significant role in these cases at the expense of assessing the family's social and economic environment in order to determine their support needs. We conclude that intellectual disability stigma is very much alive and evident in contemporary child protection work.

Governing Sexuality

It has been argued that in the early twentieth-century European and American contexts, the tactics of governing the sexuality of people with intellectual disabilities, as well as the poor and in some cases immigrants and racial minorities, were rooted in the trans-Atlantic eugenic project of preventing the so-called undesirable members of the population from reproducing (Davis 2010; Mitchell and Snyder 2003; Stubblefield 2007). Mitchell and Snyder (2003) argued that the Nazi German regime during the Second World War only represented the most extreme application of existing eugenic ideologies. These ideas originated during an earlier cross-Atlantic collaboration between doctors, scholars, practitioners, policy makers, and eugenic societies and organizations which sought to prevent the birth of persons with traits perceived negatively (e.g., physical, intellectual, and sensory impairments, along with mental health problems) and encourage the birth of people with traits perceived positively and as beneficial to society.

Nazi German physicians and policy makers were influenced by the existing practices of sterilization and institutional segregation of people with disabilities that were already in place in Western Europe, the Nordic countries, and the USA and Canada (Mitchell and Snyder 2003). While these societies did not engage in murder as the solution to the 'problem' of populations deemed deficient, as did the Nazis, their responses, such as institutionalization (with the sexes firmly segregated) and involuntary sterilization, were nevertheless still very harsh. All these practices shared a common scientific and cultural language predicated on stigmatic views of people with disabilities, and people with intellectual disabilities in particular (Diekema 2003; Stefánsdóttir 2014).

While practices which seek to govern the sexuality and reproductive capabilities of people with intellectual disabilities continue in various forms in the present (World Health Organization 2014), it has been argued that the intent of current practices has shifted away to an extent from the concerns of the older eugenic ideologies. Using Iceland as an example of these ideologies in the Nordic context, Karlsdóttir (1998) argued that one focus of the eugenic project was the general 'improvement' of mankind and another the protection of society from the perceived social and economic threats from the so-called problematic populations. However, there were also concerns articulated about the welfare of individuals having to provide care for children when they were perceived by the authorities as incapable to perform the parenting role (Karlsdóttir 1998). Continuing these 'humanistic' concerns about the welfare of individuals and some of the consequences of their sexuality, contemporary concern is predominantly articulated as that of protecting children and adults seen as vulnerable to sexual abuse and exploitation (Series 2015). However, we contend that the desire to control, limit, and sometimes negate the reproductive capabilities of people labeled as having intellectual disabilities is still motivated by long-standing paternalistic concerns.

Research in Iceland (Karlsdóttir 1998; Stefánsdóttir 2014; Stefánsdóttir and Traustadóttir 2015) demonstrates that the governance of the reproductive capabilities of people with intellectual disabilities (primarily but not exclusively women) followed a similar pattern as Northern and North-Western Europe in general, with widespread use of sterilization that started to tail off in the 1970s and 1980s with the broadening acceptance of the principles of normalization. The practice of coerced sterilization as a condition for making the transition from institution to group homes (Stefánsdóttir 2014; Stefánsdóttir and Traustadóttir 2015; World Health Organization 2014) certainly reflects old eugenic fears about the reproductive capabilities of people with intellectual disabilities. However, the process of deinstitutionalization leading to community-based living arrangements has had the concomitant effect of leading to more people with intellectual disabilities becoming parents (McConnell and Llewellyn 2002; Park et al. 2006). Increasingly, these parents are coming to the attention of authorities that are concerned with the welfare of children. Research has demonstrated that one key assumption in child protection and custody proceedings is that parental intellectual disability itself is prima facie evidence of risk of harm to the child and in some states is legitimized by law. Another is that parents with intellectual disabilities are unfit parents *a priori* regardless of whatever interventions are undertaken (Llewellyn et al. 2010). The conditions under which custody is removed from parents with intellectual disabilities are illustrated in this chapter with evidence from the Icelandic context.

From Sterilization to Human Rights

Legal regulations concerning sterilization in Iceland generally followed the other Nordic countries. For example, a law enacted during the 1930s (nr. 16/1938) allowed for sterilization of both men and women deemed to be (or potentially at risk of being) an 'imbecile' (Is. *fáviti*), 'permanently mentally ill' (Is. *varanlega geðveikur*), as well as those who the medical authorities deemed at significant risk to bear children with a 'serious malformation' (Is. *alvarlegur vanskapnaður*), a mental or physical 'dangerous disease' (Is. *hættulegur sjúkdómur*), or 'idiocy' (Is. *fávitaháttur*). There were also apparent class biases interwoven with the Icelandic eugenic project as this law also allowed for sterilization or abortion due to a perceived 'disposition toward crime' (Is. *hneigð til glæpa*) and inability to support oneself or one's dependents. This law remained in force in Iceland until 1975. However, the legislation concerning abortion and sterilization, which replaced this and which remains in force (nr. 25/1975), still allows for sterilization under the authority of an appointed legal guardian, of those over the age of 25 on the basis of mental illness, 'significant mental deficiency' (Is. *mikils greindarskorts*), or 'other mental disturbances' (Is. *annarra geðtruflana*), where the individual is believed to be unable to appreciate the consequences of his or her actions.

The changes in Icelandic legislation detailed above coincided with a general international shift away from formal eugenic policy to that of human rights. However, such attitudinal changes were slow to develop as they had to contend with deeply entrenched views. One early example of this shift, explicitly focused on intellectual disability, was the United Nations Declaration on the Rights of Mentally Retarded Persons (1971). In many ways this declaration followed the principles of normalization with all of the expected caveats; for example, persons with intellectual disabilities were to live with their own families under circumstances 'as close as possible to those of normal life'. The declaration appeared to refer to the family in a guardianship role and no mention was made of the right (or expectation) of persons with intellectual disabilities to potentially form their own families and raise children. As such it was consistent with the notion that people with intellectual disabilities are simultaneously asexual and hypersexual, childlike, and in need of constant care and supervision, but never care providers or parents in their own right, which is long-standing, persistent, and exists in different national-cultural contexts over significant periods of time (Priestley 2003; Simpson 2011; Stefánsdóttir and Traustadóttir 2015).

A major piece of legislation concerning people with intellectual disabilities in Iceland was the 'Law on Assistance to the Retarded' (nr. 47/1979). In some ways this law reflected the ideology of normalization as seen in the 1971 UN declaration referred to above. The first article of this law sought to ensure for the 'mentally retarded' (Is. *proskaheftir*) equality with other citizens and to create conditions so they could live as normal a life as possible in the community. While this may seem progressive for the time, the rest of the text of the law discussed services that were to be provided in a variety of institutional settings and the home environment was generally envisioned to be small group homes (Is. *sambýli*), an improvement over large institutions but hardly a normative living arrangement compared with the general public, and one that often affords little privacy. The idea that people with intellectual disabilities might form intimate relationships, let alone become parents, and that such choices might be reflected in their living arrangements did not appear to be a consideration.

A key piece of modern legislation concerning people with disabilities in Iceland is the 1992 Act on the Affairs of Disabled People (nr. 59/1992, revised in 2010). Within this Act, people with intellectual disabilities are included along with people with other types of disabilities. The language is less ambivalent ('create conditions in which they are able to live a normal life'), and the Act includes a focus on human rights. However, the Act is silent on issues of sexuality or parenthood, and children are referred to in terms of the rights of children with disabilities, not as children of parents with disabilities. This stands in contrast with the latest international human rights convention concerning people with disabilities, the 2006 United Nations Convention on the Rights of Persons with Disabilities (CRPD), which clearly envisions people with disabilities as parents. Article 23.1 of the CRPD states that parties to the Convention (Iceland signed in 2007 but has not ratified the CRPD at the time of writing) are required to eliminate discrimination against people with disabilities 'in all matters relating to marriage, family, parenthood and relationships' as well as retaining their fertility.

However, the CRPD arguably reflects similar tensions as found within modern child protection in general, with a potential conflict between the rights of people with disabilities to raise children and the rights of children, which are argued to supersede those of parents. However, these rights do not necessarily have to be in conflict. Aunos and Feldman (2008) argue that while the protection of the child is paramount in international conventions, such as the UN Convention on the Rights of the Child, the violation of children's rights can also occur when children are removed from the home as the result of parents not being provided appropriate support. The rights of parents with disabilities, the rights of children, and the dual roles of child protection agencies in protecting children and supporting parents can clash when adequate supports to parents are not provided. Measures to support children as well as parents are, of course, necessary and child protection is by no means an easy task. Yet in our research we routinely encountered statements in case conclusions, which asserted that all possible forms of support had been tried, yet no evidence was provided that parents with intellectual disabilities had been provided with the specific kinds of support they required. The literature demonstrates that parents who are not provided such supports are at greater risk of losing custody of their children. This can be particularly problematic where efforts to support parents with intellectual disabilities intersect with long-standing prejudices, the historic role of professionals in assessing and governing people with intellectual disabilities, as well as the existence of legal tools that allow for the permanent removal of children on the basis of intellectual disability itself and the perceived 'risks' that this diagnosis entails.

Labeling 'Unfit' Parents

Iceland is a small nation and our analysis of a national sample of permanent custody removal cases during the period 2002 to 2014 identified only a small number of cases where parents had an intellectual disability. However, a number of findings from the international literature are worth presenting. One of the major themes that has emerged in the international literature concerns the overrepresentation of parents with intellectual disabilities in custody removal cases (Emerson and Brigham 2014; Gould and Dodd 2014; McConnell and Llewellyn 2000, 2002). While it is difficult to make similar assertions concerning custody removal rates in Iceland given the small sample size, it is obvious in our research that many of the other issues still resonate with the international literature. Here we will focus on two key assumptions identified in the international literature: parents who have been evaluated by professionals as having a low IQ, which serves as evidence of 'unfit' parenting in and of itself, and the assumption that parents with intellectual disabilities cannot benefit from education, training, and support measures.

Two particular cases caught our attention for the purposes of this chapter—they exhibit these assumptions and mirror some of the issues identified in the international literature, though other cases will be referred to in passing. Both were couples evaluated as having intellectual disabilities, or borderline intellectual functioning, and both cases involved parents with multiple children, the first of which was removed from custody shortly after birth and the remainder removed at a later date. Impairment labels figured prominently in these cases, often with little reference to how these impairment labels linked to abusive or negligent parenting. One couple was referred to as having 'significant intellectual impairments' ('*verulega proskaskerðingu*') and a number of other problems, such as assumed substance abuse, but it appeared that the low measured IQ was the main factor concerning the perception of their parenting and general competence. This was clearly stated in the case by a physician who referred to 'certain intellectual impairments' as the key issue in regard to why treatment programs for their alcohol and cannabis use would be ineffective—their 'treatment capacity' (Is. *meðferðarhæfni*) was posited to be 'below average'. It has been suggested that any use of alcohol or drugs, even mild or recreational, by someone with intellectual disabilities is perceived as problematic and as potentially a sign of addiction (Simpson 2012). Others have noted that the issue is a lack of access to treatment for addiction, if such is needed, not the inability to be treated (Slayter 2010); and if treatment fails, then the treatment methods need to be revised in conjunction with the service users to be effective (Taggart et al. 2007).

In another case, one weekend of alcohol misuse by the parents while they were being investigated by child protection services (CPS) was drawn upon repeatedly for the duration of the case as indicative of a pattern of alcohol abuse, when this specific weekend was the only reference we could find in the court documents to any alcohol use on the part of either parent. This was despite the fact that at one point the couple was under five and later seven day-a-week surveillance by CPS. This is typical, Simpson (2012) contends, of evidence of "an intrinsically pathologized and discrete pattern alcohol consumption being posited for adults with intellectual disabilities" (p. 186). In other words, the label of intellectual disability of itself colors and informs and perhaps distorts the interpretation of such behavior, including as well the perceived links between intellectual disability and poor parenting.

In the cases we examined, reference to the intellectual disability label was often made without an explicit connection to allegations of parental abuse or neglect. This mirrored patterns in other cases where disability was a factor. It was common to see references to parent(s) spending time under the care of psychiatric services, in which even voluntary attempts to seek treatment were consistently used as evidence to present parents in a negative light. Parents were often referred to as 'disability pensioners' (Is. *öryrkjar*), a heavily stigmatized label in Iceland (Rice 2010), with low disability pension rates used as evidence of the parents not being able to adequately support their children. In one case, a mother was referred to as having a history of epilepsy, without any explicit connection being made between epilepsy and parenting, as the case mainly focused on children neglected due to the mother working night shifts. As McConnell and Llewellyn (2000) note, in this type of situation, "intellectual disability *per se*, is treated as *prima facie* evidence of parental inadequacy" (p. 886). Tymchuk and Andron (1990) argue that while some intellectual capacity is obviously needed to parent, it is not at all clear what IQ level is adequate, nor is it clear what is meant by adequate parenting. IQ alone is not an adequate indicator of parenting ability and the literature has stressed for some time that parents with intellectual disabilities can be adequate parents with the proper support (Feldman 1994; Llewellyn et al. 2010; Wade et al. 2008), throwing into question the heavy reliance upon IQ tests for the purpose of parenting or custody assessment.

The importance of the intellectual disability label was so significant to all professionals involved in the cases we examined that in certain cases the parents' impairments were not only exaggerated but appeared to increase in the severity depicted over the duration of the investigative process. In one case, both parents were described in the opening of the court documents as having 'developmental deviations' (Is. *þroskafrávik*). In a report on a neurological assessment for a young mother who had come to the attention of CPS, she was described as being 'intellectually diminished' (Is. *vitsmunalegrar skerta*) in certain regards but 'normal' in others, and the report's author surmised that in sum she perhaps could be given a diagnosis of borderline intellectual disability. By the following year, the mother was described as having 'low intellectual ability' (Is. *lága greind*) and the father as 'mentally deficient' (Is. *greindarskertur*) as he was consistently referred to as having a lower IQ than the mother. Four years later both parents were referred to as having 'intellectual impairments' (Is. *þroskaskerðingar*). A further three years after this point, the term 'mentally deficient' (Is. *greindarskertur*) was used for the couple by the CPS, even though a psychological assessment earlier described the mother as having a 'lower-average' IQ. Toward the conclusion of the case, the diagnosis of dyslexia also entered the picture for the mother while her spouse continued to be described as a 'significantly intellectually impaired father' (Is. *verulega greindarskerðingu föður*). By the summation of the case, the lawyer for the CPS argued that both parents had intellectual disabilities (Is. *þroskaskert*).

Permanent custody removal was justified based primarily on a description of the parents' impairments and their alleged lack of cooperation with the CPS. Evidence of neglect remained ambiguous, as counterevidence of professionals asserting positive examples of parenting were disregarded in favor of their 'low intelligence' label and its negative associations.

The final justification for permanent custody removal was based primarily upon the potential risks the parents' impairments represented to their children. The main legal justification was Article 29, Section d of the *Child Protection Act* (nr. 80/2002), which provides that parents may be deprived of custody if the CPS believes 'that it is certain that the child's physical or mental health or his/her maturity is at risk because the parents are clearly unfit to have custody, due, for instance, to drug use, mental instability, or low intelligence, or that the behavior of the parents is likely to cause the child serious harm'.

Conclusions

We have argued that child protection is a necessary albeit difficult task and one fraught with difficulties in the case of parents with intellectual disabilities. One problem therein is that as our reading of these cases and the history of Icelandic legislation suggests—enhanced with a reading of the history of similar developments in Nordic countries and the trans-Atlantic region in general—that people with intellectual disabilities have long been viewed through the prism of stigmatic and prejudiced beliefs, rooted in older eugenic concerns and anxieties about their reproductive potential, and which in certain ways have been transposed to the area of child protection and custody. The role of stigma as an influence on the treatment of people with intellectual disabilities in these processes needs to be considered and critically reflected upon.

Key Learning Points

* Parents with intellectual disabilities face additional discrimination in custody cases due to persistent stereotypes and stigma associated with intellectual disability.
* Those involved in child protection share many of the same assumptions and stereotypes about disability that negatively influence how parents with intellectual disabilities are viewed and treated within the legal system.

- The label of intellectual disability acts as evidence in and of itself of parenting inability, despite research showing that it is a poor predictor of parenting ability.
- Parents with intellectual disabilities are perceived as unable to benefit from support measures, despite common claims made in custody proceedings that all support measures have been tried prior to custody removal.
- The multitude of diagnostic labels and disability categories applied to individual parents throughout custody cases call into question the scientific validity of these parenting and custody assessments.
- The cases we analyzed suggest the importance of reflexivity on the part of professionals in child protection work in order to question the influence of their views, assumptions, and knowledge and training in the development and outcomes of custody proceedings.

Accessible Summary

- Parents with intellectual disabilities are commonly believed to be unfit to raise children.
- Such beliefs are based on prejudice about people with intellectual disabilities.
- Prejudice can lead to children being removed from their parents.
- What others believe does not tell us how things are—it only tells us how they imagine things to be.

References

Aunos, M., & Feldman, M. (2008). There's no place like home: The child's right to family. In T. O'Neill & D. Zinga (Eds.), *Children's rights: Multidisciplinary approaches to participation and protection* (pp. 137–162). Toronto, Canada: University of Toronto press.

Davis, L. J. (2010). Constructing normalcy. In L. J. Davis (Ed.), *The disability studies reader* (5th ed., pp. 3–19). New York, NY: Routledge.

Diekema, D. S. (2003). Involuntary sterilization of persons with mental retardation: An ethical analysis. *Mental Retardation and Developmental Disabilities, 9*(1), 21–26. doi:10.1002/mrdd.10053.

Emerson, E., & Brigham, P. (2014). The developmental health of children of parents with intellectual disabilities: Cross sectional study. *Research in Developmental Disabilities, 35*, 917–921. doi:10.1016/j.ridd.2014.01.006.

Feldman, M. A. (1994). Parenting education for parents with intellectual disabilities: A review of outcome studies. *Research in Developmental Disabilities, 15*(4), 299–332. doi:10.1016/0891-4222(94)90009-4.

Gould, S., & Dodd, K. (2014). 'Normal people can have a child but disability can't': The experiences of mothers with mild learning disabilities who have had their children removed. *British Journal of Learning Disabilities, 42*, 25–35. doi:10.1111/bld.12006.

Llewellyn, G., Traustadóttir, R., McConnell, D., & Sigurjónsdóttir, H. B. (2010). Conclusion: Taking stock and looking to the future. In L. G. Llewellyn, R. Traustadóttir, D. McConnell, & H. B. Sigurjónsdóttir (Eds.), *Parents with intellectual disabilities: past, present and futures* (pp. 241–262). London, UK: Wiley-Blackwell.

Karlsdóttir, U. (1998). *Mannkynbætur: Hugmyndir um bætta kynstofna hérlendis og erlendis á 19. og 20. öld. [Eugenic ideas in Iceland and other countries in the 19th and 20th century]*. Reykjavík, Iceland: University of Iceland Press.

McConnell, D., & Llewellyn, G. (2002). Stereotypes, parents with intellectual disability and child protection. *Journal of Social Welfare and Family Law, 24*(3), 297–317. doi:10.1080/09649060210161294.

McConnell, D., & Llewellyn, G. (2000). Disability and discrimination in statutory child protection proceedings. *Disability & Society, 15*, 883–895. doi:10.1080/713662015.

Mitchell, D., & Snyder, S. (2003). The eugenic Atlantic: Race, disability, and the making of an international eugenic science, 1800–1945. *Disability and Society, 18*, 843–864. doi:10.1080/0968759032000012728.

National Council on Disability (2012). *Rocking the cradle: Ensuring the rights of parents with disabilities and their children*. Washington, DC: NCD.

Park, J. M., Solomon, P., & Mandell, D. S. (2006). Involvement in the child welfare system among mothers with serious mental illness. *Psychiatric Services, 57*, 493–497. doi:10.1176/ps.2006.57.4.493.

Priestley, M. (2003). *Disability: A life course approach*. Cambridge, UK: Polity Press.

Rice, J. G. (2010). Questions of disempowerment in disability specific entitlements in Iceland. In O. Ólafs & H. Proppé (Eds.), *Rannsóknir í félagsvísindum XI [Research in Social Sciences XI]* (pp. 99–105). Reykjavík, Iceland: Social Science Research Institute and the University of Iceland Press.

Series, L. (2015). Mental capacity and the control of sexuality of people with intellectual disabilities in England and Wales. In T. Shakespeare (Ed.), *Disability research today: International perspectives* (pp. 149–165). London, UK: Routledge.

Simpson, M. (2012). Alcohol and intellectual disability: Personal problem or cultural exclusion? *Journal of Intellectual Disabilities, 16*(3), 183–192. doi:10.1177/1744629512455595.

Simpson, M. K. (2011). Othering intellectual disability: Two models of classification from the 19th century. *Theory and Psychology, 22*(5), 541–555. doi:10.1177/0959354310378375.

Slayter, E. M. (2010). Disparities in access to substance abuse treatment among people with intellectual disabilities and serious mental illness. *Health and Social Work, 35*(1), 49–59. doi:10.1093/hsw/35.1.49.

Stefánsdóttir, G. V. (2014). Sterilisation and women with intellectual disability in Iceland. *Journal of Intellectual and Developmental Disability, 39*(2), 188–197. doi:10.3109/13668250.2014.899327.

Stefánsdóttir, G. V., & Traustadóttir, R. (2015). Life histories as counter-narratives against dominant and negative stereotypes about people with intellectual disabilities. *Disability and Society, 30*, 368–380. doi:10.1080/096875 99.2015.1024827.

Stubblefield, A. (2007). "Beyond the pale": Tainted whiteness, cognitive disability, and eugenic sterilization. *Hypatia, 22*(2), 162–181. doi:10.1111/j.15272001.2007.tb009-87.x.

Taggart, L., McLaughlin, D., Quinn, B., & McFarlane, C. (2007). Listening to people with intellectual disabilities who misuse alcohol and drugs. *Health and Social Care in the Community, 15*, 360–368.

Tøssebro, J., Bonfils, I. S., Teittinen, A., Tideman, M., Traustadóttir, R., & Vesala, H. T. (2012). Normalization fifty years beyond—Current trends in the Nordic Countries. *Journal of Policy and Practice in Intellectual Disabilities, 9*(2), 134–146. doi:10.1111/j.1741-1130.2012.00340.x.

Tymchuk, A. J., & Andron, L. (1990). Mothers with mental retardation who do or do not abuse or neglect their children. *Child Abuse and Neglect, 14*, 313–323.

Wade, C., Llewellyn, G., & Matthews, J. (2008). Review of parent training interventions for parents with intellectual disability. *Journal of Applied Research in Intellectual Disabilities, 21*, 351–366. doi:10.1111/j.1468-3148.2008.00449.x.

Wolfensberger, W. (1980). A brief overview of the principle of normalization. In R. J. Flynn & K. E. Nitsch (Eds.), *Normalization, social integration and community service* (pp. 7–30). Baltimore, MD: University Park Press.

World Health Organization (2014). *Eliminating forced, coercive and otherwise involuntary sterilization: An interagency statement.* Retrieved from http://apps.who.int/iris/bitstream/10665/112848/1/9789241507325_eng.pdf

Legislation

Barnaverndarlög, nr. 80/2002 [Child Protection Act, nr. 80/2002].

Lög um að heimila í viðeigandi tilfellum aðgerðir á fólki, er koma í veg fyrir, að það auki kyn sitt, nr. 16/1938. [Law setting out when surgery prevent procreation is appropriate], nr. 16/1938. Retrieved from http://www.althingi.is/lagas/137/1938016.html

Lög um aðstoð við þroskahefta, nr. 47/1979. [Law on assistance for 'the mentally retarded', nr. 47/1979]. Retrieved from http://www.althingi.is/thingstorf/thingmalalistareftirthingum/ferill/?ltg=100&mnr=270

Lög um málefni fatlaðs fólks, nr. 59/1992 með síðari breytingum. [Law on the affairs of people with disabilities, nr. 59/1992 with later amendments]. Retrieved from http://eng.velferdarraduneyti.is/acts-of-Parliament/nr/3704

Lög um ráðgjöf og fræðslu varðandi kynlíf og barneignir og um fóstureyðingar og ófrjósemisaðgerðir, nr. 25/1975. [Law on counselling, education on sex and family planning, abortion and sterilisation (nr. 25/1975 with later amendments]. Retrieved from http://www.althingi.is/lagas/124/1975025.html#G33

7

Self-stigma in People with Intellectual Disabilities

Rory Sheehan and Afia Ali

In this chapter we consider the concept of self-stigma, present a review of the relevant literature, and consider future directions for research in this area. Self-stigma can be defined as an internal experience whereby individuals perceive themselves (and others with intellectual disabilities) to be socially unacceptable (Vogel et al. 2007). Self-stigma is important as it is associated with a wide range of detrimental effects, including diminished self-esteem, shame, secrecy, and withdrawal (Ritsher et al. 2003).

Self-stigma, like public stigma, comprises stereotypes, prejudice, and discrimination. Stereotypes such as 'I am a weak person' or 'I am incapable' are endorsed by the individual and lead to self-prejudice in the form of negative emotional responses, such as low self-esteem or self-worth. These in turn can lead to self-discrimination through behavioral responses such as not seeking employment opportunities or avoiding social relationships. It has been proposed that self-stigma develops in a

R. Sheehan • A. Ali (✉)
Division of Psychiatry, University College London, London, UK
e-mail: afia.ali@ucl.ac.uk

© The Editor(s) (if applicable) and The Author(s) 2016
K. Scior, S. Werner (eds.), *Intellectual Disability and Stigma*,
DOI 10.1057/978-1-137-52499-7_7

stepwise manner (Corrigan and Rao 2012). Firstly, an individual (the person with intellectual disabilities) becomes aware of a negative stereotype. The negative stereotype is accepted uncritically by the individual who must also believe that it applies to them. Finally, the process of self-stigmatization results in deleterious outcomes. Self-stigma can occur in the absence of actual experiences of discrimination, due to the anticipation or fear of rejection or devaluation.

This stepwise model of self-stigma has limited empirical support. A study measuring public stigma and self-stigma among college students at two time points, three months apart, found that the strongest relationship was between public stigma at time point 1 and self-stigma at time point 2, suggesting that public stigma leads to the development of self-stigma as people internalize negative attitudes (Vogel et al. 2013). The stepwise model of self-stigma arises from research with other stigmatized groups and has not been applied in the intellectual disability field. However, the following sections demonstrate that it is possible to relate each step to this population.

Evidence for Self-stigmatization

Table 7.1 provides a summary of the research on self-stigma in people with intellectual disabilities.

Awareness of stigmatized status. Applying public stigma to oneself, or internalizing negative societal attitudes, lies at the heart of the process of self-stigmatization, see Fig. 7.1. This would appear to require an individual to have knowledge of their intellectual disability identity and the negative stereotypes associated with it. Indeed, evidence suggests that many people with intellectual disabilities are aware of the stigma associated with the condition. For example, in the early days of deinstitutionalization, Edgerton (1967) observed that individuals resettled from long-stay institutions into the community often attempted to hide their disability and distance themselves from peers with intellectual disabilities for fear of being stigmatized.

In a different study, individuals with mild intellectual disabilities attending an adult training center were found to be aware of their stigmatized

Table 7.1 Summary of studies on stigma in people with intellectual disabilities (ID)

Author (year)	Design	Sample	Method	Main findings
Ali et al. (2015)	Quantitative	229 adults with mild or moderate ID recruited from 12 sites/centers in England	Self-report measures of stigma (experiences of discrimination and reaction to discrimination), psychological distress, quality of life, adherence to treatment, and service use	Stigma was associated positively with psychological distress and service use and negatively with quality of life. Psychological distress mediated the relationship between stigma and quality of life and service use.
Chen and Shu (2012)	Qualitative	14 students with mild-moderate ID recruited from special educational program of a mainstream school	Semi-structured interviews examining experience of stigma, views, and responses to stigmatizing treatment; thematic analysis of responses	Students internalized the stigma of ID from a young age. Responses to stigma were avoidance, isolation, and attempts at self-promotion.
Cooney et al. (2006)	Cross-sectional	60 adolescents with mild-moderate ID recruited from mainstream and specialist schools	Interview including experiences of stigma, social comparisons, and future aspirations	Those in mainstream schools experienced more stigma inside school. Both groups had similar experience of stigma outside school. No relationship between self-report of stigmatized treatment and perception of likelihood of achieving future goals.

(continued)

Table 7.1 (continued)

Author (year)	Design	Sample	Method	Main findings
Craig et al. (2002)	Mixed methods	(1) 92 referrals to psychology service audited (2) 6 people with ID living in supported housing	(1) Audit of referrals (2) Focus group of people with ID covering their experience of the ID identity (3) Staff survey	No referrals to the psychology service mentioned coming to terms with the ID identity as pertinent. Discussions around ID identity were associated with discomfort and there was a tendency for participants to distance themselves from ID identity.
Cunningham and Glenn (2004)	Mixed methods	78 parents and 77 individuals with Down syndrome	Semi-structured interviews with parents; questionnaires administered to people with ID	Half of people with Down syndrome did not recognize their condition. One quarter were aware of the stigma associated with Down syndrome.
Dagnan and Sandhu (1999)	Cross-sectional	43 people with mild-moderate ID recruited from adult training centers	Self-report measures of self-esteem, social comparison, and depression	Social comparison was related to self-esteem and depression.

Emerson (2010)	Cross-sectional	1273 adults with ID living in private or supported accommodation	Interviews assessed self-reported health, well-being, and exposure to bullying and disablism	Self-reported exposure to bullying and acts of disablism were associated with worse self-reported health outcomes. Material or social resources can mitigate the effect of discrimination.
Finlay and Lyons (1998)	Mixed methods	28 people with mild-moderate ID recruited from ID services	Interviews assessing representations of ID, self-descriptions, self-esteem, group evaluation, and group identification	Two thirds of the group endorsed a label of ID, although none mentioned this spontaneously. Self-esteem was not correlated with group evaluation, even when the group was viewed negatively.
Finlay and Lyons (2000)	Qualitative	33 people with ID	Semi-structured interviews addressing descriptions of self and others and social comparisons	People with ID tended to present themselves in a positive light and view themselves as 'better' than others with ID and as 'as good as' those without ID.

(continued)

Table 7.1 (continued)

Author (year)	Design	Sample	Method	Main findings
Jahoda and Markova (2004)	Qualitative	28 people with mild ID moving to more independent living	Semi-structured interviews addressing participants' awareness, experience, and response to stigma associated with ID	Participants were aware of and had experienced discrimination and prejudice.
Jahoda et al. (1988)	Qualitative	12 adults with ID	Semi-structured interviews covering social life, autonomy, handicap, and stigma	All participants were aware of the stigma associated with ID. Only a minority endorsed negative stereotypes and viewed themselves as 'essentially different' from people without ID. The majority did not internalize their stigmatized status.
Paterson et al. (2012)	Cross-sectional	43 people with ID	Questionnaires measured perception of stigma, self-esteem, and social comparison	Perceived stigma negatively correlated with self-esteem and negative social comparisons.

Szivos-Bach (1993)	Cross-sectional	50 students with mild-moderate ID	Self-esteem and social comparison scales plus discussion of participants' perception of stigma and life aspirations	Stigma was negatively correlated with self-esteem and belief in fulfilling aspirations.
Szivos (1990)	(1) Cross-sectional (2) Qualitative	(1) 50 people with ID (2) 7 people with ID	(1) Self-esteem, including feelings of stigmatization, and aspirations and expectations measured by guided questionnaire (2) Discussion group over 13 weekly sessions	(1) 'Being different' subscale scores were negatively correlated with total 'expectation' score. (2) Those in discussion group expressed fear of being discredited by nature of their ID.

(continued)

Table 7.1 (continued)

Author (year)	Design	Sample	Method	Main findings
Zetlin and Turner (1984)	Qualitative	46 individuals with mild ID and their parents	Participant observations and in-depth interviews over 18 months about how individuals with ID and their parents viewed their ID identity	Identified four different attitudes to social identity: (1) Acceptance: parents and individuals accepted label; parents promoted self-sufficiency. Stigma was not salient. (2) Qualification: individuals rejected ID label but were aware of their limitations and stigma. Parents minimized difficulties and promoted self-sufficiency. (3) Vacillation: reluctance to discuss label; parents ambivalent or avoidant and overprotective. Most had experienced stigma/discrimination. (4) Denial: rejection of ID label and denial of stigma; parents ambivalent or avoidant and overprotective.

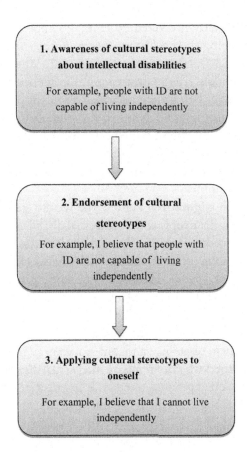

Fig. 7.1 The three-stage process of self-stigma

status and reported rejection and bullying from peers. Some individuals were aware that certain restrictions were imposed on them at home that did not apply to their siblings and were aware of the stigma attached to day services (Jahoda et al. 1988). Participants who had recently moved from an institution to the community described feeling 'cut off' from the outside world and described experiences of rejection and discrimination (Jahoda and Markova 2004). They were aware of the stigma attached to the hospital, wanted to distance themselves from it and other patients who had resided there, and were keen to develop a new identity. Those who had moved from the family home to residential community settings described feeling overly protected by family members, being considered incapable, and having their achievements go unrecognized.

Cooney et al. (2006) interviewed adolescents attending mainstream and segregated schools. The mainstream group reported more stigmatizing treatment such as being ridiculed, facing violent physical contact, or being ignored by other pupils. None of the students from the segregated school reported stigmatizing treatment within the school. However, outside the school setting, both groups reported stigmatizing treatment from people in the local area or their siblings calling them names and described being restricted at home.

Agreement with stigmatized status. The second step in the model of self-stigma requires that people with intellectual disabilities endorse negative attitudes relating to the disability. There is limited research on this topic. How people with intellectual disabilities view themselves has been investigated by Jahoda et al. (1988). Three of the 12 participants they interviewed regarded themselves as 'handicapped' and as essentially different from 'non-handicapped people'. They felt that they were not able to engage in activities that 'non-handicapped' individuals were able to do, accepted stereotypes associated with their disability, and did not expect to receive the same opportunities as others who did not have intellectual disabilities. These three participants, therefore, appeared to endorse negative stereotypes associated with intellectual disabilities. The other nine participants, however, did not endorse negative stereotypes associated with intellectual disabilities. They regarded themselves as 'essentially the same as non-handicapped individuals'. Two of these nine participants rejected the label of intellectual disability and wanted to distance themselves from others with the disability, but the remaining seven accepted the label and showed solidarity with peers.

Other studies have found little evidence that people with intellectual disabilities endorse negative stereotypes about themselves. Jahoda and Markova (2004) found that although their participants were aware of stigma, they did not agree with their stigmatized status and believed themselves to be the same as people without intellectual disabilities. Cooney et al. (2006) found that even though adolescents from mainstream and segregated schools had experienced stigmatizing treatment, they still compared themselves favorably to peers with and without disabilities. Both groups had positive aspirations about the future, such as getting a job, and this was not affected by their negative social interactions with others.

Application of negative stereotypes to oneself and harm. The final aspect of self-stigma is the translation of the internalized devalued identity into negative outcomes, in the form of loss of self-esteem and self-discrimination. One aspect of this has been termed the 'why try' effect, whereby self-stigma results in a loss of confidence and self-efficacy which in turn affects one's willingness to set and strive for life goals (Corrigan et al. 2009). In a study conducted in Taiwan, 14 school students with intellectual disabilities who had a 'handicapped identity card' that entitled them to have free access to additional educational support were interviewed. The possession of the card was found to be stigmatizing as these students realized that they were different from other students. Students endorsed and applied negative stereotypes to themselves. They viewed themselves as 'not good students', 'troublemakers', or 'odd' because of the reaction they received from others. Students felt ashamed and embarrassed about possessing the card. There was evidence that some of the students had internalized the stigma associated with their disability and responded by avoiding interactions with peers or trying to conceal the fact that they held the card. A few students used self-promotion to cope with stigma (Chen and Shu 2012).

Factors That Influence Whether People with Intellectual Disabilities Internalize Stigma

Research suggests that many people with intellectual disabilities may not be aware of their disability or attribute this label to themselves. Possible reasons for this finding include the cognitive development hypothesis, the use of denial as a defense mechanism, lack of awareness stemming from others' protection, and differentiating between awareness at the level of discourse and experience (Beart et al. 2005). A sufficient degree of cognitive development is required for an individual to be aware of one's disability and to understand one's limitations within a wider social context (Cunningham et al. 2000). It is perhaps not surprising, therefore, that a number of studies have found that many individuals lack awareness that they have a disability and even fewer are aware of the stigma associated with the label of intellectual disability. For example, Cunningham and Glenn (2004) interviewed

77 individuals with Down syndrome and found that only half of the sample were aware of having Down syndrome and only a quarter of the sample recognized the stigma associated with the condition.

Some individuals with intellectual disabilities may downplay their difficulties or frame their difficulties using phrases that are more socially acceptable, such as 'I have difficulties with reading and writing', or may emphasize their strengths. Studies of social comparisons suggest that when individuals with intellectual disabilities compare themselves with others with intellectual disabilities, they may regard themselves as 'better' and may even consider themselves to be 'as good as' people without intellectual disabilities (Finlay and Lyons 2000). This lack of identification with the stigmatized group may help some individuals avoid stereotypes associated with intellectual disabilities. However, Finlay and Lyons (1998) found that group identification was not associated with evaluating the group negatively. Even if people described themselves as having intellectual disabilities and evaluated people with intellectual disabilities more negatively compared to those without intellectual disabilities, this did not lead to a lowering of self-esteem. Some individuals did not believe that the label of intellectual disabilities was applicable to them. These issues are considered further in Chap. 14 of this book.

Lack of awareness of intellectual disability or of its stigmatized status may be influenced by how parents and carers disclose or discuss disability with their loved ones. For example, Todd and Shearn (1997) found that most parents avoided discussing their child's intellectual disability with them in order to protect them from stigma, and were complicit in agreeing with their child's unrealistic expectations of future jobs or marriage, even if they themselves did not believe this to be possible. In addition, carers who appeared overprotective or in denial about their child's difficulties were reluctant to disclose to their child that they had an intellectual disability. Zetlin and Turner (1984) found that parents who accepted their offspring's condition were more likely to disclose this to the individual, and, subsequently, the individual was more comfortable talking about their disability. In contrast, individuals who were uncomfortable talking about their disability had parents who were ambivalent about disclosing such information to their offspring. However, Cunningham et al. (2000) found that awareness of having an intellectual disability was not related to parental disclosure, indicating the difficulty of separating associations from cause and effect relationships.

Jahoda et al. (1988) found that carers who thought the individual with an intellectual disability was essentially different from people without disabilities provided them with less autonomy and choice than carers who thought that the individual was essentially the same as people without disabilities. Self-concept, or the way one views oneself, was not found to be determined by the way they were viewed or treated by significant others or according to whether they had more or less autonomy. Instead, individuals were capable of evaluating their own capability and actions.

Intellectual disability services may also play a role in perpetuating service users' lack of awareness or recognition of having intellectual disabilities. Referrals to a specialist psychology service for people disabilities were found to rarely make reference to helping an individual come to terms with their identity or stigmatized status (Craig et al. 2002). When professionals at a community intellectual disability service were surveyed, the researchers found that most thought that it was important to talk to individuals about their intellectual disability but many found it difficult to do so because they thought the topic was too sensitive and were worried about upsetting the individual or their family. Some professionals also perceived such discussions as stigmatizing.

Some researchers have argued that it is not mandatory that individuals understand the concept of intellectual disability in order to experience feelings of rejection or alienation by others through their social interactions (Beart et al. 2005). Individuals do not need to acknowledge that they have an intellectual disability in order to be aware that they are different as they experience stigma at the emotional level. Language that may be routinely used within services might not be accessible or understood by people with intellectual disabilities, which may explain why some may not internalize labels that are applied to them (Beart et al. 2005). Finally, Sinason (1992) proposed that denial of having intellectual disabilities may be a defense mechanism that enables individuals to cope with the pain associated with having a stigmatized status.

Coping with Self-stigma

Resilience and the ability to cope and make sense of stigmatizing and discriminatory treatment may influence whether individuals internalize stigma. Reframing experiences in a positive way, or focusing on strengths rather than limitations, can help individuals maintain self-esteem and protect against self-stigma. Having a number of meaningful roles such as being an employee, a mother, or a member of a club can help to act as a buffer against the emotional consequences of stigma (Dagnan and Sandhu 1999).

The possibility of utilizing experiences of stigma as a force for good has largely been overlooked in the intellectual disability literature, although other fields have shown that it is possible for members of a stigmatized group to be energized by experiences of discrimination and use their 'righteous anger' to drive positive change (Corrigan and Watson 2002).

The Effect of Stigma on Self-concept and Well-Being

There is limited empirical research that links self-stigma to reduced well-being in people with intellectual disabilities. Research has so far focused on the relationship between experiences of stigmatizing or discriminatory treatment and outcomes such as self-esteem, future aspirations, psychiatric symptoms, and quality of life.

College students with mild and moderate intellectual disabilities who reported more stigmatizing treatment were found to also have lower self-esteem (Szivos-Bach 1993). Similar findings have been reported by other researchers (e.g., Paterson et al. 2012). Students who reported higher levels of stigmatizing treatment were more likely to have lower aspirations in life (Szivos 1990; Szivos-Bach 1993). However, Cooney et al. (2006) found that experiences of stigma did not affect future aspirations, as many of the students they interviewed had high expectations about future employment prospects.

Four published studies have examined the impact of stigma on psychiatric symptoms. By far the largest study is by Emerson (2010) who carried out a secondary analysis of data from a population-based study of 1273 individuals with intellectual disabilities living in the community. Both bullying at school and incidents of bullying generally during the preceding 12 months were associated with symptoms of anxiety and depression and poorer self-reported health. In particular, access to social or material resources moderated the relationship between bullying and symptoms of anxiety and depression. Individuals who had poorer social or material resources were more likely to report depression or anxiety due to bullying, compared to those who had better access to resources. Paterson et al. (2012) found that higher levels of stigma were associated with more psychiatric symptoms and Dagnan and Sandhu (1999) found lower attractiveness and less perceived group membership to be associated with more depressive symptoms. More recently, Ali et al. (2015) concluded that higher levels of stigma are associated with higher levels of psychological distress (symptoms of depression and anxiety) and a lower quality of life. Participants reporting more stigmatizing treatment were more likely to use community intellectual disability services and make contact with the police. The relationship between stigma and quality of life and service use was found to be mediated by psychological distress.

Conclusions

There is a general lack of research on self-stigma as applied to people with intellectual disabilities. There is some limited evidence to support the three-stage process of self-stigma in people with intellectual disabilities, but more research on the validity and utility of applying this model to people with intellectual disabilities is required. Consideration should also be given to other models or approaches to understanding how stigma is internalized (or not) by people with intellectual disabilities, as this may differ from other stigmatized groups. For example, use of stigma research conducted with people affected by mental illness may provide a helpful framework to understand general principles, but several difficulties exist in extrapolating insights directly to individuals with intellectual disabilities (Ditchman et al. 2013). Stereotypes of people with mental illness and intellectual disabilities differ substantially, with the former more likely to be described as 'crazy' or 'dangerous' and the latter as 'dependent' or 'innocent'. In addition, people with intellectual disabilities are more likely to experience additional visible physical disabilities which can alter the public perception of their condition. Perceived attribution, or blame, may also differ between those with mental illness and those with intellectual disabilities, further influencing societal attitudes. Finally, the cognitive deficits of people with intellectual disabilities may mean that some are unaware of stigma and therefore the process of self-stigma may be altogether less relevant.

Many of the studies examining self-stigma in people with intellectual disabilities have included only a small number of participants and population-based prevalence studies have not been completed. Similarly, there is a lack of longitudinal studies which could help to explain the outcomes of self-stigma, and there are no trials of interventions that could disrupt the internalization of stigma and promote positive outcomes (Ali et al. 2012). Future research should focus on developing a model of self-stigma in people with intellectual disabilities. Longitudinal studies investigating the long-term consequences of stigma on health and social outcomes are also needed. Finally, the development of interventions that promote self-esteem and help individuals to develop coping strategies for managing self-stigma will play an important role in improving the quality of life of people with intellectual disabilities.

Key Learning Points

- There is limited research on the conceptualization of self-stigma in people with intellectual disabilities.
- Evidence suggests that people with intellectual disabilities are able to describe experiences of rejection, bullying, and discrimination. However, there is little research on whether people with intellectual disabilities internalize stigma.
- The ability of people with intellectual disabilities to internalize stigma may be affected by their level of cognitive development, disclosure, and overprotection from significant others, social interactions with others, and factors such as coping and resilience.
- Higher levels of stigmatizing treatment or bullying have been found to be associated with lower self-esteem, lower aspirations in life, and more psychiatric symptoms.
- Services for people with intellectual disabilities should recognize that stigma can have a negative impact on the well-being of people with intellectual disabilities and ensure that appropriate support is provided.

- Future research should focus on improving our understanding of whether people with intellectual disabilities internalize stigma and of the consequences of self-stigma on health and social outcomes. In addition, there is a need to develop evidence-based interventions that help individuals address self-stigma or cope with stigmatizing and discriminatory treatment.

Accessible Summary

- This chapter looks at research on how people with intellectual disabilities view themselves and how they are treated.
- We wanted to find out if people with intellectual disabilities believe that bad things that are said about them are true and how this affects them.
- Many people with intellectual disabilities say that they are treated badly or differently, such as being called names.
- Being treated badly by others can make people feel bad about themselves, depressed, and anxious.
- Services need to help people who have experienced bad treatment from others.

References

Ali, A., King, M., Strydom, S., & Hassiotis, A. (2015). Self-reported stigma and symptoms of anxiety and depression in people with intellectual disabilities: Findings from a cross sectional study in England. *Journal of Affective Disorders, 187*, 224–231. doi:10.1016/j.jad.2015.07.046.

Ali, A., Hassiotis, A., Strydom, A., & King, M. (2012). Self stigma in people with intellectual disabilities and courtesy stigma in family carers: A systematic review. *Research in Developmental Disabilities, 33*, 2122–2140. doi:10.1016/j.ridd.2012.06.013.

Beart, S., Hardy, G., & Buchan, L. (2005). How people with intellectual disabilities view their social identity: A review of the literature. *Journal of Applied Research in Intellectual Disabilities, 18*, 47–56. doi:10.1111/j.1468-3148.2004.00218.

Chen, C. H., & Shu, B. C. (2012). The process of perceiving stigmatisation: Perspectives from Taiwanese young people with intellectual disability. *Journal*

of *Applied Research in Intellectual Disability, 25,* 240–251. doi:10.111
1/j.1468-3148.2011.00661.

Cooney, G., Jahoda, A., Gumley, A., & Knott, F. (2006). Young people with intellectual disabilities attending mainstream and segregated schooling: Perceived
stigma, social comparison and future aspirations. *Journal of Intellectual Disability
Research, 50,* 432–444. doi:10.1111/j.1365-2788.2006.00789.

Corrigan, P. W., Larson, J. E., & Rüsch, N. (2009). Self-stigma and the "why
try" effect: Impact on life goals and evidence-based practices. *World Psychiatry,
8,* 75–81. doi:10.1002/j.2051-5545.2009.tb00218.

Corrigan, P. W., & Rao, D. (2012). On the self-stigma of mental illness: Stages,
disclosure, and strategies for change. *Canadian Journal of Psychiatry. Revue
Canadienne de Psychiatrie, 57,* 464–469.

Corrigan, P. W., & Watson, A. C. (2002). Understanding the impact of stigma
on people with mental illness. *World Psychiatry, 1,* 16–20.

Craig, J., Craig, F., Withers, P., Hatton, C., & Limb, K. (2002). Identity conflict
in people with intellectual disabilities: What role do service providers play in
mediating stigma? *Journal of Applied Research in Intellectual Disabilities, 15,*
61–72. doi:10.1046/j.1360-2322.2002.00101.

Cunningham, C., & Glenn, S. (2004). Self-awareness in young adults with
Down syndrome: I. Awareness of Down syndrome and disability. *International
Journal of Disability, Development and Education, 51,* 335–361. doi:10.1080
/1034912042000295017.

Cunningham, C. C., Glenn, S. M., & Fitzpatrick, H. (2000). Parents telling their
offspring about Down syndrome and disability. *Journal of Applied Research in
Intellectual Disabilities, 13,* 47–61. doi:10.1046/j.1468-3148.2000.00012.

Dagnan, D., & Sandhu, S. (1999). Social comparison, self-esteem and depression in people with intellectual disability. *Journal of Intellectual Disability
Research, 43,* 372–379. doi:10.1046/j.1365-2788.1999.043005372.

Ditchman, N., Werner, S., Kosyluk, K., Jones, N., Elg, B., & Corrigan, P. W.
(2013). Stigma and intellectual disability: Potential application of mental illness research. *Rehabilitation Psychology, 58,* 206–216. doi:10.1037/a0032466.

Edgerton, R. B. (1967). *The cloak of competence: Stigma in the lives of the mentally
retarded.* San Francisco, CA: University of California Press.

Emerson, E. (2010). Self-reported exposure to disablism is associated with poor
self-reported health and wellbeing among adults with intellectual disabilities
in England: A cross sectional survey. *Public Health, 124,* 682–689.
doi:10.1016/j.puhe.2010.08.020.

Finlay, M., & Lyons, E. (1998). Social identity and people with learning difficulties: Implications for self advocacy groups. *Disability and Society, 13,*
37–57. doi:10.1080/09687599826902.

Finlay, W. M., & Lyons, E. (2000). Social categorizations, social comparisons and stigma: Presentations of self in people with learning difficulties. *British Journal of Social Psychology, 39*, 129–146. doi:10.1348/014466600164372.

Jahoda, A., & Markova, I. (2004). Coping with social stigma: People with intellectual disabilities moving from institutions and family home. *Journal of Intellectual Disability Research, 48*, 719–729. doi:10.1111/j.1365-2788.2003.00561.

Jahoda, A., Markova, I., & Cattermole, M. (1988). Stigma and the self concept of people with a mild mental handicap. *Journal of Mental Deficiency Research, 32*, 103–115. doi:10.1111/j.1365-2788.1988.tb01396.

Paterson, L., McKenzie, K., & Lindsay, B. (2012). Stigma, social comparisons and self esteem in adults with an intellectual disability. *Journal of Applied Research in Intellectual Disability, 25*, 166–176. doi:10.1111/j.1468-3148.2011.00651.

Ritsher, J. B., Otilingam, P. G., & Grajales, M. (2003). Internalized stigma of mental illness: Psychometric properties of a new measure. *Psychiatry Research, 121*, 31–49. doi:10.1016/j.psychres.2003.08.008.

Sinason, V. (1992). *Mental handicap and the human condition: New approaches from the Tavistock*. London, UK: Free Association Books.

Szivos-Bach, S. E. (1993). Social comparisons, stigma and mainstreaming: The self esteem of young adults with a mild mental handicap. *Mental Handicap Research, 6*, 217–236. doi:10.1111/j.1468-3148.1993.tb00054.

Szivos, S. E. (1990). Attitudes to work and their relationship to self-esteem and aspirations among young adults with a mild mental handicap. *British Journal of Subnormality, 36*, 108–117.

Todd, S., & Shearn, J. (1997). Family dilemmas and secrets: Parents' disclosure of information to their adult offspring with learning disabilities. *Disability and Society, 12*, 341–366. doi:10.1080/09687599727218.

Vogel, D. L., Bitman, R. L., Hammer, J. H., & Wade, N. G. (2013). Is stigma internalized? The longitudinal impact of public stigma on self-stigma. *Journal of Counseling Psychology, 60*, 311–316. doi:10.1037/a0031889.

Vogel, D. L., Wade, N. G., & Hackler, A. H. (2007). Perceived public stigma and the willingness to seek counseling: The mediating roles of self-stigma and attitudes toward counseling. *Journal of Counseling Psychology, 54*, 40–50. doi:10.1037/0022-0167.54.1.40.

Zetlin, A. G., & Turner, J. L. (1984). Self perspectives on being handicapped: Stigma and adjustment. *Monograph of the American Association of Mental Deficiency, 6*, 93–120.

8

Intellectual Disability, Stigma, and Hate Crimes

Mark Sherry and Anna Neller

Disability hate crimes involve criminal victimization which is aimed at people specifically because of their disability. Using recent examples of disability hate crimes directed at people with intellectual disabilities in the UK and USA, the chapter highlights the magnitude of this problem, as well as the reasons why disability hate crimes usually go unreported. The time period 2011 to 2015 was selected largely because previous studies such as Sherry (2010) and Quarmby (2011) have outlined a number of crimes before this period, and with the increased awareness of disability hate crimes since then, it is important to examine whether there have been any significant cases since that time. Cases were selected on the basis of three criteria. First, they had to already be publicly reported (the authors were careful not to discuss cases where the victim/survivor did not want publicity). Second, they had to reflect a diverse range of locations, in order to give a sense of the global nature of this problem;

M. Sherry (✉) • A. Neller
University of Toledo, Toledo, OH, USA
e-mail: Mark.Sherry@utoledo.edu

© The Editor(s) (if applicable) and The Author(s) 2016
K. Scior, S. Werner (eds.), *Intellectual Disability and Stigma*,
DOI 10.1057/978-1-137-52499-7_8

111

this criterion was somewhat difficult because disability hate crimes are not officially recognized as a specific form of criminal activity in many countries. And third, the crimes had to range in severity; although a large number of disability hate crimes result in fatalities or serious injury, we deemed it important to include other examples of hate crimes as well.

Labels and Insults

Over time, terms once associated with the medical diagnosis of intellectual disability have morphed into the language of insult used in hate speech and in the commission of disability hate crimes. Historically, public health institutions often regarded those with intellectual disabilities as subhuman, relying on eugenic ideas which suggested that some lives are less worthy than others (Wolfensberger and Nirje 1972). The category of 'intellectual disability' was initially defined through a medical model replete with negative labels such as 'feebleminded', 'idiot', 'mental defective', 'subnormal', 'imbecile', 'moron', and 'retarded'. Such terms over time have trickled into common usage as generic slurs which take on extra layers of meaning when aimed at people with intellectual disabilities. For instance, the word 'retard' is widely used as an insult as well as a specific form of hate speech used in the commission of disability hate crimes.

Disability scholars consistently stress the importance of understanding intellectual disability in its social context (Gill 2015). This means that one cannot understand intellectual disability without noting the wider social context of disablism (prejudice and discrimination against disabled people) and ableism (processes and practices that privilege nondisabled minds, senses, or bodies) (Campbell 2009). Attitudes toward intellectual disability are not just characterized by stigma and prejudice; they may involve hostility and even hatred as well. The results of such attitudes include higher rates of violence, criminal victimization, and social exclusion. These experiences are framed by disablism and ableism—wider power systems that devalue and marginalize people with disabilities. The combined effects of stigma, disablism, ableism, and intolerance are seen most starkly in the violence of disability hate crimes.

In such a context, it may be easier to identify disablism because one can identify hurtful interpersonal experiences such as name-calling, teasing, and bullying—a commonplace and devastating experience in the lives of many people with intellectual disabilities (Robinson 2013). But it is equally important, and often harder, to examine ableist social dynamics which usually operate under the surface, creating situations of privilege or disadvantage, safety or harm, inclusion or exclusion. Both disablism and ableism operate in the context of stigma and intellectual disability, and both need to be addressed in order to challenge the connections between intellectual disability, stigma, and disability hate crime.

By situating disability hate crimes within a wider social content of prejudice and discrimination, it may seem that they are simply another manifestation of overall hostility to people with disabilities. Clearly, there is some weight to this suggestion. Disablist slurs are commonly used in the commission of disability hate crimes. But failing to distinguish these crimes from other beliefs, attitudes, and practices is not entirely satisfactory. There are distinct differences between prejudice (which is often unexpressed), disabling barriers (which are oftentimes legal), and criminal activity. Disability hate crimes are often felonies—serious actions which (if successfully prosecuted) result in imprisonment. Clearly, such actions and consequences are significantly different from other nonfelonious patterns of discrimination and prejudice.

People with intellectual disabilities experience more interpersonal abuse in schools, violence perpetrated by staff and other people with disabilities in institutional settings, and hate crimes (both from strangers and from people pretending to be friends) which are often brutally violent and hypersexual (Sherry 2010). They also experience higher rates of criminal victimization than the rest of the population (Petersilia 2001). Sexual abuse is also alarmingly common for both children and adults with intellectual disabilities (McCarthy 2014)—some cases have been considered disability hate crimes. The classification of such sexual and criminal acts—particularly whether they are labeled 'disability hate crimes' or not—varies from one jurisdiction to another. In some cases, they are immediately labeled as hate crimes; in others they may be given another classification, such as a 'crime against a dependent adult'. When crimes against a dependent adult are successfully prosecuted, they do involve serious consequences and enhanced penalties if the victim/ survivor receives serious injuries. Lesser crimes against dependent adults are usually not associated with the additional sentencing provisions of a disability hate crime. Such inconsistencies seem to be linked to prevalent attitudes and legislation about disability, care, crime, and victimization in a particular region.

The decision to prosecute a crime as a 'hate crime' is incredibly significant because when an act is labeled a 'hate crime', penalty enhancement occurs. Accordingly perpetrators often receive time and a half sentencing for their felonies. Such penalty enhancement is associated with hate crimes because the law recognizes that there are two victims in any hate crime: the individual victim and the community to which they belong. For instance, when a person with an intellectual disability is violently attacked in a hate crime, they are likely to avoid the area in future—but so too are other people with intellectual disabilities. Their freedom to travel in any area without fear has been taken away. This flow-on effect of a disability hate crime is the ultimate reason behind penalty enhancement.

People with intellectual disabilities may also suffer injustice in the legal system, particularly when it is assumed that they are considered 'unreliable witnesses' whose victim testimonies do not have sufficient credibility to be believed (Bottoms et al. 2003). This faulty assumption has meant that many cases of crime, including sexual assault, rape, violence, theft, maltreatment, abuse, and hate crimes against people with intellectual disabilities, have not been prosecuted (Henry and Wilcock 2013). This is particularly troubling because victims of crime who have intellectual disabilities may experience psychological distress at greater levels, and for longer periods, than nondisabled victims (Khalifeh et al. 2013). Additionally, when offenders feel that they will not be prosecuted for crimes against this population, they may feel encouraged to continue or escalate their crimes. A review of various forms of violence against children with disabilities published in *The Lancet* suggested that the social factors which result in lower prosecution rates include:

"… societal stigma and discrimination, negative traditional beliefs and ignorance within communities, lack of social support for carers, type of impairment (for example communication difficulties), and heightened vulnerability as a result of the need for increased care, including medical attention." (McCarthy and Thompson 1997, p. 1)

People with intellectual disabilities experience significant prejudice and social exclusion globally, including in Taiwan (Chen and Shu 2012), China and Hong Kong (Human Rights Watch 2013), and Africa (Njenga 2009). These attitudes and behaviors often result in a failure to take the testimonies of victims with intellectual disabilities and lack of access to the justice system. As well, responses to disability hate crimes differ greatly across the globe. Few countries formally recognize disability hate crimes, leaving victims with intellectual disabilities without legal recourse or protection. When disability hate crimes occur, few people know exactly what legal protection and redress is available (Scior et al. 2015). This failure to properly recognize and respond to disability hate crimes has been a major focus of the activism of disability rights campaigners in the UK.

UK Examples of Disability Hate Crimes 2011–2015

Personal stories of violent victimization put a human face on disability hate crimes. There are many well-known cases of crimes against people with intellectual disabilities. Some of these hate crimes were immediately recognized as hate crimes, but others were not, leading to campaigns by disability advocates (and sometimes prosecutors) to argue that they should have been identified in this way. In the UK, some of the horrific crimes against people with intellectual disabilities include the 2014 crimes against Craig Kinsella, who had been 'living like a slave' in a garage, sleeping on a piece of carpet, using an old curtain as a blanket, and eating scraps of food from a garbage bin (BBC Staff Reporter 2014); the 2011 murder of Gamma Hayter, who was locked in a toilet, forced to drink urine, beaten and left with a broken nose, and who choked on her own blood before she was stripped naked and dumped near a disused railway track (Slater 2011); the violent assaults on David Busby, who was beaten with a cricket bat and a metal dumbbell in 2012, sustaining 14 fractured ribs, a displaced breastbone, and a broken shoulder blade

(Cockerton 2012); and an (unnamed) woman in Oldham who in 2014 was kicked in the groin, punched, burned with a lighter, had her head and eyebrows shaved, and forced to eat dog food and raw sausages (Cox 2014). While disability rights campaigners immediately labeled these as 'hate crimes', law enforcement was often much more reluctant to use this term.

One problematic term which has been applied to certain hate crimes in the UK is the notion of 'mate crime'. This term suggests that people who pose as friends of the victim then use their position of trust to attack the person with an intellectual disability. While such a term has gained some currency in the press and among disability advocates, it is problematic because it risks biasing the understanding of disability hate crime in favor of male victims. Female victims also commonly know their attackers but are more likely to experience rape and assault in hate crimes (Sherry 2010). Rape and sexual assault are never considered 'mate crimes' (and often they are not considered 'hate crimes' either). So responses to the incidence of 'mate crime' tend to have an implicit masculinist bias.

Surprisingly, however, it is difficult to estimate the exact number of disability hate crimes against people with intellectual disabilities in the UK. Between 2007 and 2015, only 4,000 cases of disability hate crimes were prosecuted in the UK (Wheeler 2015). However, the UK Disability Hate Crime Network estimates the actual number of disability hate crimes to be much larger—'at least 30 times higher than official police records indicate' (Dodenhoff 2014). The Equality and Human Rights Commission also believes that police statistics vastly underestimate the actual numbers of disability hate crimes—they believe that there are approximately 72,000 incidents of disability hate crime per year in the UK (Coleman et al. 2013).

Unfortunately, despite widespread recognition of the problem of disability hate crime (Beadle-Brown et al. 2014), the response from the UK authorities has been disappointing overall. In 2013, a major report entitled *Living in a Different World: Joint Review of Disability Hate Crime* was published as a result of a collaboration between major institutions involved in the UK criminal justice system (HMCPSI, HMIC, and HMIC Probation 2013). It stated that disability hate crime was 'the hate crime that has been left behind' (p. 5) in comparison to other forms of hate crime, such as hate crime related to race, religion, or sexual orientation, and that there was significant underreporting of such crimes. Some of the problems the report specifically identified included lack of knowledge, misunderstanding, misclassification of crimes, and failure to record significant information at all levels of the criminal justice system. Specifically, the above report identified lack of training and lack of prioritizing disability hate crimes among police, prosecutors, witness care units, the probation service, and those involved in the postconviction process.

A 2015 follow-up report by the same institutions found that the problems identified in the *Living in a Different World* report are ongoing (HMCPSI, HMIC, and HMIC Probation 2015). There are still major problems in the way disability hate crimes are identified. The number of reports remains low; data handling errors persist; the information recorded is often inadequate; there are insufficient cases where penalty enhancements (referred to as 'uplifts') are applied to disability hate crimes; and training has been 'inconsistent and slow'.

US Examples of Disability Hate Crimes 2011–2015

The situation in the USA appears to be worse, because much smaller numbers of cases of disability hate crimes are prosecuted. For instance, despite the inclusion of disability hate crimes in federal legislation in 2009, only one case was prosecuted in the USA in the subsequent two years. This was the first time federal charges covering disability hate crimes had been laid under the 2009 Shepard-Byrd Hate Crimes Prevention Act. The fact that this was the first case to involve such charges is itself noteworthy, given that the Federal Bureau of Investigation (FBI) had reported 102 disability hate crimes in 2012, 58 in 2011, and 46 in 2010 (Federal Bureau of Investigation 2010–2013). The FBI does not provide details on the outcome of these other cases.

In the one case prosecuted between 2009 and 2011, in Philadelphia, disability hate crimes were allegedly inflicted upon four people with intellectual disabilities over a ten-year period. In January 2013, a federal indictment claimed that from 2001 to 2011, Linda Ann Weston kidnapped four people with intellectual disabilities, locked them in a tiny basement, beat them, starved them, and stole their disability benefit checks (Dolak 2013). Weston was allegedly assisted by four others who would confine, discipline, and transport the victims. She allegedly lured one of the victims, Maxine Lee (a woman with an intellectual disability), over the Internet, forced her into prostitution, beat her with sticks and bats, locked her in a cabinet under a kitchen sink, and left her in a basement where she died in a malnourished state, suffering from bacterial meningitis (Martin 2013).

In a later case, in 2014, three teens from Newark, New Jersey, were charged with a disability hate crime under State legislation after they allegedly kicked and punched a man with an intellectual disability in the head (Associated Press 2015). They were originally charged with offensive touching and assault of a vulnerable adult, but their charges were later upgraded to include a hate crime element. But throughout the USA, there seems to be no clear rationale behind the process of labeling some acts as 'disability hate crimes' and not labeling similar sadistic crimes in the same way. For instance, in May 2015, a Florida man was charged with using a walking stick he called the 'Stupid Stick' to perpetrate repeated physical abuse against his housemates, a disabled woman and her 15-year-old son with an intellectual disability and no verbal communication skills (WTSP10 News Staff 2015). The alleged perpetrator, Phillip Simons, was a 52-year-old former policeman. Simons allegedly threatened the crime victims with guns, beat them with his hands, and verbally abused them. He is also accused of grabbing the minor's genitals in order to traumatize and intimidate him (Fox 8 News Staff Winterhaven 2015). According to news reports, the woman reported his behavior to police only after he put a gun in her mouth and threatened to kill her, while her son and another boy watched (Wagner 2015). But his actions were never described in terms of 'disability hate crimes'.

Another US crime which arguably could have been identified as a disability hate crime occurred in Ohio in 2014. It involved a 14-year-old boy who was tricked into participating in the 'ice bucket challenge'—but in this case the bucket was drenched in classmates' feces, urine, and spit (Caulfield 2014). The crime was committed by multiple perpetrators—five teenagers aged between 14 and 16. All five were charged in juvenile court with disorderly conduct and three were also charged with delinquency and assault (Corcoran and Faberov 2014). However, another element of their actions deserves attention for those interested in the connection between stigma and disability hate crimes: the teenagers assumed that a crime against someone with an intellectual disability was socially acceptable, not shameful, and that it was funny or entertaining enough to share widely online.

Uploading such material online is becoming an alarmingly common feature of crimes against people with disabilities—four examples (of the many which are online) should demonstrate their nature. One video which was uploaded to the Internet by the perpetrators shows two men tormenting a 42-year-old woman with an intellectual disability outside a Sacramento donut store. They then push her, spit on her, and punch her in the face, laughing as they assault her (CBS13 Staff Reporters 2011a, b). Another video shows three teenagers in Winston-Salem, North Carolina, pushing a man with physical and intellectual disabilities down an embankment, chasing him, and continuing to attack him until he is motionless on the ground (Anthony 2015). A third video, uploaded to Facebook, shows six people attacking a 48-year-old woman with an intellectual disability with their fists and shoes, as well as kicking her (Pow and Staff Reporter Daily Mail 2013). A fourth video shows a group of girls beating a man with an intellectual disability in Caruthersville, Missouri, as he says 'Baby, leave me alone' (St. Amand 2012).

This small number of cases from the USA, alongside those discussed earlier from the UK, only scratch the surface of the global dimension of this problem. Reports from many other countries suggest that similar cases of violence, abuse, torture, murder, and kidnapping, as well as sexual assault, occur with alarming frequency—particularly for those people with disabilities who reside in institutions. Placement in segregated institutions, located far away from the rest of the population, adds to the stigma and prejudice experienced by people with intellectual disabilities. Their social isolation is compounded by the reluctance of other people to visit them in hospital-like institutions. Without external support and safeguards, institutionalized people become more vulnerable to victimization, violence, and abuse.

A horrifying case of institutional abuse (involving, among other things, severe physical abuse of people with intellectual disabilities) was uncovered by the BBC at the Winterbourne View care home in 2011. Because of their segregation from the rest of society, and the relative isolation of residents, institutions can be permeated by a culture of abuse. Often a country will claim that they have no institutions, because the label 'institution' has been removed from a facility, but many disability agencies nevertheless operate as de-facto institutions. Long-term residents have few alternative accommodation options and as a result, stay for many years. Demeaning attitudes that deny the rights of people with intellectual disabilities can flourish in such de-facto institutions. For instance, in many of these institutions, residents are dehumanized, devalued, and denied their right to choose the most basic things, such as when they will eat meals. In the aftermath of the Winterbourne exposé, many family members reported abuse in other UK institutions. Within a year, a joint report by two disability agencies reported another 260 cases of neglect or abuse identified by people who had family members with intellectual disabilities in institutions (Mencap and the Challenging Behaviour Foundation 2012). Instead of providing more statistics about this gruesome problem, we will now turn to ways of addressing disability hate crimes.

Tackling Disability Hate Crime

There are a number of effective strategies which have been developed to tackle disability hate crime. Some of these include the following:

- Establishing community education programs which address common misunderstandings (both among victims and law enforcement) about what constitutes a disability hate crime
- Involving families, friends, and other advocates in the process of safeguarding people with intellectual disabilities and emphasizing their key role in reporting abuse, neglect, and hate crimes
- Emphasizing accessible communication with people with intellectual disabilities and ensuring that they know they have the right to be safe,

that their experiences may be disability hate crimes, and that they can get support and seek justice through the legal system if they want

- Stressing to people with intellectual disabilities that such instances are not 'just a part of normal life' but do deserve police involvement
- Ensuring that disability hate crimes are appropriately identified and not mislabeled as something else
- Acknowledging and addressing disagreements among various parts of the legal system over the use of disability slurs during the commission of a crime, especially as to whether they are indicators of hate or simply generic insults
- Acknowledging the reluctance of victims to report the crimes (particularly their fears of retaliation or of not being believed) and putting in place meaningful safeguards which ensure that they are safe and protected and that their complaints are given a fair hearing
- Demonstrating to victims that making a complaint about a disability hate crime will not just involve reliving some of the worst experiences in their life without recourse to any real justice
- Community education programs which increase knowledge about the nature of disability hate crimes and teach people what they can do about them
- Partnerships between law enforcement agencies and disability groups to build trusting relationships which might lead to an increase in reporting of disability hate crimes
- Community education tools which involve personal accounts of disability hate crimes, discussing their physical and emotional effects
- Removing the stigma attached to intellectual disability so that people are not afraid of being publicly identified as someone with an intellectual disability
- Innovations that make it easier to report disability hate crimes, such as a reporting app for mobile phones, and the establishment of third-party reporting programs
- Enhanced education programs throughout the entire law enforcement system—from street-level policing to prosecutors, judges, parole officers, and so on
- Tracking the numbers of reported disability hate crimes which are successfully prosecuted

Conclusions

Disability hate crimes are a graphic reminder of the insult, abjection, and violence directed at people with intellectual disabilities. This chapter mainly focused on the UK and the USA, but the problem of violence, abuse, and disability hate crime is not confined to those countries, far from it. Disability hate crimes are a global problem. In challenging environments that produce such crimes, it is necessary to confront both ableism and disablism. Both create environments which devalue, segregate, marginalize, stigmatize, and endanger people with disabilities. But there are also specific responses to disability hate crimes which are necessary, for instance, community education, increased liaison between law enforcement and disability groups, improved training for people at all levels of the criminal justice system, and innovations in reporting processes such as the advent of third-party reporting systems and the development of reporting apps on telephones. But most importantly, there needs to be improved communication with people with intellectual disabilities, and their families and friends in order to ensure that they know what disability hate crimes are, and how they can seek justice when such crimes occur.

Key Learning Points

- The stigma attached to intellectual disability, combined with the wider power structures of ableism and disablism, create an environment which can be exclusionary, unsafe, and hostile for people with intellectual disabilities.
- Historical medical terms for intellectual disability are now being recirculated as terms of insult and hate, for instance, people are often called a 'retard' during disability hate crimes.
- Disability hate crimes are often directed at people with intellectual disabilities—both the size of the problem and the violence of the attacks are alarming.
- Such crimes are usually unreported.

Accessible Summary

- Sometimes people will hit you, kick you, or hurt you in some other way just because you have a disability. This is not okay. It is called a disability hate crime.
- You are not alone. This type of crime has happened to many other people and you can get support and help.
- You can report it to the police if you want to, or someone else can help you report it. They are less likely to hurt you, your family, or your friends again if you go to the police.
- You have the right to be safe.
- No one has the right to harm you or discriminate against you.

References

Anthony, C. (2015, January 13). Police: W-S teenagers recorded their attack on disabled man. Retrieved from http://www.wfmynews2.com/story/news/local/2015/01/12/wfmy-winston-salem-police-teens-record-attack/21621375/

Associated Press (2015, March 16). Teens sentenced after pleading guilty in videotaped assaults on mentally disabled man. Retrieved from http://www.foxnews.com/us/2015/03/16/teens-sentenced-after-pleading-guilty-in-videotaped-assaults-on-mentally/

BBC Staff Reporter (2014, January 7). Rooke family treated vulnerable man as 'slave'. Retrieved from http://www.bbc.com/news/uk-england-south-yorkshire-25642431

Beadle-Brown, J., Richardson, L., Guest, C., Malovic, A., Bradshaw, J., & Himmerich, J. (2014). *Living in fear: Better outcomes for people with learning disabilities and autism.* Tizard Centre, Canterbury, UK: University of Kent.

Bottoms, B. L., Nysse-Carris, K. L., & Tyda, K. (2003). Jurors' perceptions of adolescent sexual assault victims who have intellectual disabilities. *Law and Human Behavior, 27*(2), 205–227.

Campbell, F. K. (2009). *Contours of ableism.* Basingstoke, UK: Palgrave Macmillan.

Caulfield, P. (2014, September 9). Cops identify bullies who poured urine, feces on autistic teen in sick Ice Bucket Challenge. Retrieved from http://www.nydailynews.com/news/national/cops-id-bullies-poured-urine-feces-autistic-teen-sick-ice-bucket-challenge-prank-article-1.1933509

CBS13 Staff Reporters (2011a). Police arrest second suspect in viral video beating. Retrieved from http://sacramento.cbslocal.com/2011/11/13/police-arrest-second-suspect-in-youtube-beating/

CBS13 Staff Reporters (2011b). Video shows brutal attack at Sacramento strip mall. Retrieved from http://sacramento.cbslocal.com/2011/10/11/video-shows-brutal-attack-at-sacramento-strip-mall/

Chen, C. H., & Shu, B. C. (2012). The process of perceiving stigmatisation: Perspectives from Taiwanese young people with intellectual disability. *Journal of Applied Research in Intellectual disability, 25,* 240–251. doi:10.1111/j.1468-3148.2011.00661.

Cockerton, P. (2012, December 5). Bordering upon sadistic torture: Four locked up for "appalling" attacks on disabled man. Retrieved from http://www.mirror.co.uk/news/uk-news/four-locked-up-for-appalling-attacks-1474522

Coleman, N., Sykes, W., & Walker, A. (2013). *Crime and disabled people: Baseline statistical analysis of measures from the formal legal inquiry into disability-related harassment.* Manchester, UK: Equality and Human Rights Commission.

Corcoran, K., & Faberov, S. (2014, October 14). Five teens CHARGED over sickening Ice Bucket Challenge prank in which autistic boy was doused with urine, feces and cigarette butts. Retrieved from http://www.dailymail.co.uk/news/article-2793112/five-teens-charged-sickening-ice-bucket-challenge-prank-autistic-boy-doused-urine-feces-cigarette-butts.html

Cox, C. (2014). Ringleader jailed after gang tortured vulnerable housemate over rent debt 28 July. Retrieved from http://www.manchestereveningnews.co.uk/news/greater-manchester-news/lee-carter-jailed-torture-stacey-7522455

Dodenhoff, P. (2014). Challenging 'hate' within the UK–The disability hate crime network. Retrieved from http://www.disabled-world.com/disability/discrimination/dhcn.php

Dolak, K. (2013, January 23). Hate crime charges for allegedly stealing from mentally disabled. Retrieved from http://abcnews.go.com/US/hate-crime-charges-allegedly-stealing-mentally-disabled/story?id=18294194

Federal Bureau of Investigation (2010–2013). *Uniform crime reports for the United States 2010–2013.* Washington, DC: US Department of Justice.

Fox 8 News Staff Winterhaven (2015, May 21). Florida man beat woman with 'stupid stick'. Retrieved from http://myfox8.com/2015/05/21/police-florida-man-beat-woman-with-stupid-stick

Gill, M. (2015). *Already doing it: Intellectual disability and sexual agency.* Minneapolis, MN: University of Minnesota Press.

Henry, L., & Wilcock, R. (2013). Witnesses with intellectual disabilities. *International Journal of Disability, Development and Education, 60*(1), 1–2. doi:10.1080/1034912x.2013.757126.

HMCPSI, HMIC, & HMIC Probation (2013). *Living in a different world: Joint review of disability hate crime*. London, UK: HMCPSI, HMIC, HMI Probation.

HMCPSI, HMIC, & HMIC Probation (2015). *Joint review of disability hate crime follow-up*. London, UK: HMCPSI.

Human Rights Watch (2013). *'As long as they let us stay in class': Barriers to education for persons with disabilities in China*. Chicago, IL: Human Rights Watch.

Khalifeh, H., Howard, L. M., Osborn, D., Moran, P., & Johnson, S. (2013). Violence against people with disability in England and Wales: Findings from a national cross-sectional survey. *PLOS ONE, 8*(2), e55952. doi:10.1371/journal.pone.0055952.

Martin, J. P. (2013, January 25. Federal charges announced against Linda Ann Weston in Tacony basement case. Retrieved from http://articles.philly.com/2013-01-25/news/36529296_1_maxine-lee-tacony-basement-linda-ann-weston

McCarthy, M. (2014). Women with intellectual disability: Their sexual lives in the 21st century. *Journal of Intellectual and Developmental Disability, 39*(2), 124–131. doi:10.3109/13668250.2014.894963.

McCarthy, M., & Thompson, D. (1997). A prevalence study of sexual abuse of adults with intellectual disabilities referred for sex education. *Journal of Applied Research in Intellectual Disabilities, 10*(2), 105–124. doi:10.1111/j.1468-3148.1997.tb00012.

Mencap and the Challenging Behaviour Foundation (2012). *Stopping the abuse and neglect of people with a learning disability*. London: Mencap and the Challenging Behaviour Foundation.

Njenga, F. (2009). Perspectives of intellectual disability in Affrica: Epidemiology and policy services for children and adults. *Current opinion in psychiatry, 22*, 457–461. doi:10.1097/yco.0b013e32832e63a1.

Petersilia, J. R. (2001). Crime victims with developmental disabilities: A review essay. *Criminal Justice and Behavior, 28*(6), 655–694. doi:10.1177/009385480102800601.

Pow, H., & Staff Reporter Daily Mail (2013, February 1). Two teenage girls given prison terms after they pleaded guilty in shocking beating of mentally disabled woman captured on video. Retrieved from http://www.dailymail.co.uk/news/article-2272004/Jasmir-Womack-Rahmiiyah-Henderson-plead-guilty-shocking-beating-mentally-disabled-woman.html#ixzz3bElVTD4R

Quarmby, K. (2011). *Scapegoat: Why we are failing disabled people*. London: Portobello books.

Robinson, S. (2013). *Preventing the emotional abuse and neglect of people with intellectual disability: Stopping insult and injury.* London, UK: Jessica Kingsley Publishers.

Scior, K., Hamid, A., Hastings, R., Werner, S., Belton, C., Laniyan, A.,…,Kett, M. (2015). *Intellectual disabilities: Raising awareness and combating stigma— A global review.* London, UK: University College London. Retrieved from www.ucl.ac.uk/ciddr/documents/Global_ID_Stigma_Report_Final_July_15.pdf

Sherry, M. (2010). *Disability hate crimes: Does anyone really hate disabled people?* Surrey, UK: Ashgate.

Slater, R. (2011, July 31). The disabled woman abandoned to be murdered for fun by a gang of savages who she thought were her friends. Retrieved from http://www.dailymail.co.uk/femail/article-2020648/Gemma-Hayter-Disabled-woman-abandoned-murdered-fun.html

St. Amand, A. (2012, July 12. Teen girls accused of beating disabled Missouri man. Video posted on Facebook. Retrieved from http://www.stltoday.com/news/local/crime-and-courts/teen-girls-accused-of-beating-disabled-missouri-man-posting-video/article_477532c2-cc2b-11e1-bddd-001a4bcf6878.html#ixzz20bnmaksp

Wagner, M. (2015, May 21). Florida man arrested for allegedly beating disabled woman, teen with 'stupid stick'. Retrieved from http://www.nydailynews.com/news/crime/fla-man-disabled-woman-teen-stupid-stick-cops-article-1.2230860

Wheeler, C. (2015). Hate crimes on disabled up by 213 %. Retrieved from http://www.express.co.uk/news/uk/551327/EXCLUSIVE-Hate-crimes-on-disabled-rise-by-213

WTSP10 News Staff (2015). Man beats handicapped victims with "Stupid stick". Retrieved from http://www.wtsp.com/story/news/local/2015/05/21/physical-abuse-handicapped-phillip-simons/27707029/

Wolfensberger, W., & Nirje, B. (1972). *The principle of normalization in human services.* Toronto, Canada: National Institute on Mental Retardation.

Part III

Tackling Intellectual Disability Stigma

9

Interventions Aimed at Tackling Intellectual Disability Stigma: What Works and What Still Needs to Be Done

Shirli Werner and Katrina Scior

Throughout the years, changes in policies, service provision, and societal views of people with intellectual disabilities have led to their increased physical integration in society. Nevertheless, discrimination continues to be an everyday reality for many. The reluctance to interact with people with intellectual disabilities has been attributed to misconceptions that they have few capabilities, as well as discomfort related to lack of familiarity and insecurity about how to interact with them (Ouellette-Kuntz et al. 2010). Clearly more needs to be done to tackle stigma directed at

S. Werner (✉)
Paul Baerwald School of Social Work and Social Welfare, Hebrew University of Jerusalem, Jerusalem, Israel
e-mail: shirli.werner@mail.huji.ac.il

K. Scior (✉)
Division of Psychology & Language Sciences, University College London, London, UK
e-mail: k.scior@ucl.ac.uk

© The Editor(s) (if applicable) and The Author(s) 2016
K. Scior, S. Werner (eds.), *Intellectual Disability and Stigma*,
DOI 10.1057/978-1-137-52499-7_9

129

people with intellectual disabilities—this chapter provides an overview of such interventions and their outcomes. Because efforts in this area are very limited, where indicated, this chapter will draw on experience from other disability fields.

Levels of Stigma Change Interventions

We propose a multilevel model for combating intellectual disability stigma. This is informed by theories in the mental health field (Cook et al. 2014). However, our model incorporates the family as central force for stigma maintenance or conversely anti-stigma activism in the lives of persons with intellectual disabilities. This model provides a framework for exploring the range of stigma change interventions that have been employed within the intellectual disability field, as well as identifying where interventions are thin on the ground. It distinguishes interventions that target stigma at the intrapersonal, familial, wider interpersonal, and structural levels and emphasizes that efforts at different levels are related and reciprocally affect one another (Fig. 9.1).

The bulk of initiatives that have been attempted to date in the intellectual disabilities field, and which will constitute most of this chapter, have focused on the interpersonal level. Here we provide a brief overview of interventions at all levels.

Interventions at the Intrapersonal and Familial Levels

Interventions at the intrapersonal level focus on the persons affected by stigma, and aim to help them cope with the negative consequences of stigmatization, such as self-stigma. While cognitive behavior therapy is now widely used across a large range of presentations and populations to challenge unhelpful self-beliefs (Butler et al. 2006) and strategic self-disclosure has been utilized within the mental health field (Rüsch et al. 2014), to date these approaches have not been used explicitly to

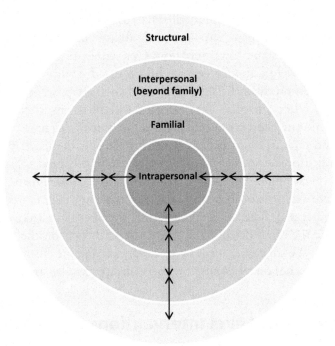

Structural

Interpersonal
(beyond family)

Familial

Intrapersonal

Fig. 9.1 Multilevel model of stigma change interventions

counter self-stigma affecting people with intellectual disabilities. Some authors have provided accounts of psychological group work interventions aimed at enabling individuals with intellectual disabilities to learn to cope with their stigmatized identity as a route to accepting the underlying impairment and developing a positive group identity (Szivos and Griffiths 1990). They label this process 'consciousness raising' but future work may wish to explore the impact of work of this kind on self-stigma. Others have noted the promise of narrative therapy, in which dominant stories are deconstructed and power relations that underpin them are examined (Scior and Lynggaard 2006). However, again the potential of such approaches to counter self-stigmatization has not been assessed. Of course, the potential value of individual and group self-advocacy in countering self-stigma cannot be underestimated but to our knowledge has not been formally tested.

Parents of individuals with intellectual disabilities have been central in improving perceptions of intellectual disability and in the fight against negative attitudes and discrimination. Conversely, negative family reactions, such as shame about having a child with a disability, can have detrimental effects on the individual concerned and may promote their social exclusion. While attention has been paid to how to ensure that families are well informed and supported around the time of diagnosis, such education and support is not available in many places or at different points of the family lifecycle, leaving families subject to widely held negative conceptions regarding intellectual disability. It may seem surprising that few reports are available on how to sensitively challenge stigmatizing beliefs that families may hold about their family member's intellectual disability despite the often detrimental effect of such beliefs on the individual concerned. We suggest that future research examine the effects of family-based approaches on all family members' ability to resist stigma.

Interpersonal-Level Interventions

Interpersonal-level interventions (beyond the familial level) target social interactions between stigmatized and non-stigmatized individuals (Cook et al. 2014). Two broad types of interventions have been employed at the interpersonal level: education and contact. Educational approaches are those that challenge inaccurate stereotypes by providing factual information (Seewooruttun and Scior 2014). Many disability organizations and NGOs in the intellectual disability field, either at national level (such as Mencap in the UK, AKIM and Keren Shalem in Israel, Community Living Association in Canada, or Lebenshilfe in Germany and Austria to name but a few) or at international level (Inclusion International and Special Olympics in particular), have provided education and messages designed to promote inclusion and more positive attitudes to children and adults in the general population via their programs, websites, leaflets, and social media. However, it is questionable to what extent their efforts reach audiences not already positively inclined toward people with intellectual disabilities. Further, the impact of these initiatives on attitude change has rarely been empirically studied, Special Olympics programs being an exception (Siperstein et al. 2003).

Educational interventions which have been more frequently evaluated have focused on students and convenience samples. They have attempted to challenge misconceptions and increase knowledge and awareness in order to improve attitudes through Internet-delivered brief films (Seewooruttun and Scior 2014), university-based lecture programs (Campbell et al. 2003), educational vignettes (MacDonald and MacIntyre 1999), and knowledge provision (Rae et al. 2011). For example, reading an educational vignette that emphasized skills, daily activities, and interests of an individual with an intellectual disability resulted in improved attitudes among university students (MacDonald and MacIntyre 1999).

Educational approaches have been frequently utilized among teachers, health and social service staff, and those training to enter relevant professions. For example, attempts have been reported to increase trainee teachers' understanding of intellectual disability, through a half-day training event (Rae et al. 2011). Elsewhere, a mix of formal teaching and experiential learning was provided through a semester-long course which improved teachers' knowledge of Down syndrome and their attitudes to teaching children with intellectual disabilities within inclusive environments (Campbell et al. 2003). As another example, a recent Scottish study examined student teachers' attitudes to inclusion at the beginning and end of a one-year diploma course which emphasized inclusion. Teachers' attitudes and beliefs toward the principles of inclusive education remained positive throughout the course and were largely undiminished by school experience. The researchers concluded that the teaching program helped sustain pro-inclusion attitudes despite students possibly being prone to conflicting messages within school settings in which they worked (Beacham and Rouse 2012).

A rather different approach to most other educational interventions was taken in a recent study that investigated the impact of human rights awareness training on support staff within an intellectual disability service (Redman et al. 2012). The training, not surprisingly, increased knowledge of human rights. However, it did not affect attitudes toward human rights or views on the relevance of human rights to support staff members' everyday work with individuals with intellectual disabilities.

Focusing on a different target group, attempts have been made to educate police officers about the needs of people with intellectual disabilities and improve their attitudes toward them. Such attempts employed an awareness-raising training event in which participants took part in role-play exercises as well as a debriefing knowledge provision explanation. Results showed a reduction in eugenic-based attitudes toward people with intellectual disabilities following training (Bailey et al. 2001).

While educational approaches have been found to be useful in increasing knowledge (Seewooruttun and Scior 2014), their impact on stigma change is frequently short-lived and of limited magnitude (Corrigan et al. 2012). Thus, researchers have advocated for interpersonal contact with members of stigmatized groups as the most effective stigma reduction strategy. In the mental health field, contact provided either in person (in vivo) or indirectly (e.g., through films) has been shown to result in positive shifts in attitudes and behavioral intentions, with more significant change following in vivo contact (Corrigan et al. 2012).

Some studies employed direct contact with people with intellectual disabilities as part of student training programs. For example, the impact of volunteering at sporting events, especially via the Special Olympics, on volunteers' attitudes was examined (Freudenthal et al. 2010). Elsewhere, interpersonal contact was provided by getting college students to house and entertain individuals with intellectual disabilities and their support staff over a 2.5-day period (Nosse and Gavin 1991). These contact-based interventions mostly showed positive effects on attitudes, because the target volunteers could be seen as 'preaching to the converted' (Seewooruttun and Scior 2014).

Recently, a study in Israel has examined stigmatic attitudes of soldiers without intellectual disabilities toward soldiers with intellectual disabilities. Unlike the above studies, as military service in Israel is mandatory, inclusion of individuals with intellectual disabilities into this setting brings about contact with young adults from various population groups and not solely volunteers. Findings from this study have shown that soldiers without intellectual disabilities who serve in units that are inclusive of soldiers with intellectual disabilities hold more positive attitudes toward individuals with intellectual disabilities than soldiers who lack such contact (Werner 2015).

In responding to concerns about inadequate healthcare delivered to people with intellectual disabilities, attempts have been made to increase knowledge of intellectual disability, increase skills in providing healthcare, and tackle negative attitudes among medical students. A positive effect was found for interventions that integrated didactic learning, discussions, disability awareness tasks, and workshop exercises facilitated by a tutor with intellectual disabilities (Tracy and Iacono 2008). In a different study, medical students had a two-hour meeting with the families of children with disabilities, including intellectual disabilities, during which they interviewed the parents about their experiences of parenting the respective child. The students subsequently wrote an account of the visit and their insights and showed increased understanding and empathy with these parents (Sharma et al. 2008).

An additional target group of contact-based interventions has been on neighbors. A study of neighbors' views of residential facilities for people with intellectual disabilities found that visiting the facility did not have a positive effect on attitudes across all participants, but only for some neighbors. Positive effects were observed, for example, on neighbors who had young children and visited the facility, perhaps because the visit alleviated fears they may have had for the welfare of their children (Schwartz and Rabinovitz 2001).

Given that in many instances it may be difficult to provide direct contact and control the quality of that contact, some attempts have been made to use indirect contact to improve attitudes. Such studies have simulated contact through the use of photographs and films delivered in a classroom or experimental site (Hall and Minnes 1999; Iacono et al. 2011), or via the Internet (Walker and Scior 2013).

For example, researchers compared the effects of showing a drama versus a documentary television program on college students' attitudes to people with Down syndrome. Greater comfort and more willingness to volunteer were associated with watching the documentary (Hall and Minnes 1999). More recently, the effect of brief film intervention within undergraduate healthcare education was examined (Iacono et al. 2011). In line with the social model of disability, the film highlighted the interests, activities, and relationships of the individual featured, as well as their health and social needs and everyday life, rather than focusing on their disability. Results of this study were mixed; quantitative evaluation did not show changes in level of comfort while qualitative data revealed increased awareness, insight, and knowledge.

Some studies have suggested that instead of providing each separately, it is most useful to combine contact-based approaches with education. The potential of combining between these can be seen in a recent UK-based pilot trial in which a convenience sample of adults were randomly exposed to one of two film-based interventions delivered via the Internet (Walker and Scior 2013). Both films featured people with intellectual disabilities, support workers, and professionals providing information on how intellectual disability is defined and noting inequalities faced by this population. One film stressed similarities between people with and without intellectual disabilities and showed both engaged as equal members of a band. The other film showed a man with an intellectual disability talk about his experiences of targeted violence and hostility while out alone in public. Both interventions resulted in positive, although modest, changes in inclusion attitudes and stigma, which were maintained after one month. The second film resulted in greater change, perhaps because it evoked stronger emotional responses.

With the growing awareness to disability hate crime, in many places police officers are receiving training related to the reporting of and responding to instances of possible disability hate crimes perpetrated against people with intellectual disabilities. One study evaluated the effects on police officers of a 45-minute didactic awareness training session, including indirect contact via video. Officers' self-rated knowledge and confidence in interacting with someone with an intellectual disability increased, but there was no change in their attitudes to people with intellectual disabilities (Raczka et al. 2014).

An additional type of interpersonal interventions are mass media campaigns which employ a means of communication intended to reach large audiences and are not reliant on person-to-person contact (Clement et al. 2013). Few such efforts have been made to change attitudes toward people with intellectual disabilities. One exception is a study by Russell and Ayer (1988), which attempted to influence attitudes toward people with intellectual disabilities among managers and bosses in industry through repeated information-based mail-outs.

In contrast to the lack of mass media campaigns within the intellectual disability stigma field, large mass media campaigns have been employed in other fields, such as *Beyond Blue* in Australia which aimed to raise awareness of depression and tackle stigma or the broader mental health anti-stigma campaigns *Time to Change* in England and *See Me* in Scotland. In the disability field, the recent UK campaign *End the Awkward* aimed to tackle discomfort rooted in lack of familiarity with people with physical and sensory disabilities and avoidance of talking to them. Such mass media campaigns have been found to result in small to medium reductions in stigma. Furthermore, those that included two or more of the following components tended to reduce stigma more than those with only one component: (1) Internet-based, such as interactive computer education programs, web-delivered newspaper articles, and email educational adverts; (2) audiovisual and audio recordings; and (3) print material, including magazine articles, brochures, written texts, and photographs (Clement et al. 2013).

The above-cited studies have been conducted with adult populations. However, fostering positive attitudes should start early with children and adolescents within the education system. Few would question that placing children with intellectual disabilities alongside their peers without disabilities within inclusive schools is important in principle and may also affect negative attitudes and discrimination. A recent study from Greece suggests that children in inclusive schools show more positive attitudes toward peers with intellectual disabilities than children in non-inclusive schools (Georgiadi et al. 2012). However, reports of bullying and feeling excluded within inclusive environments (Emerson 2015; Mencap 2007) indicate that physical inclusion alone is not enough and that more should be done to combat negative attitudes and behaviors and actively promote social interactions. Accordingly, children and young people in inclusive schools may receive interventions aimed at raising disability awareness and reducing bullying, including work targeting bullying of peers with disabilities, such as a current large program funded by the Department for Education in the UK (Anti-Bullying Alliance n.d.). However, one argument against such efforts, common among teachers, is that active interventions draw attention to the disability and enhance notions of difference (Beckett et al. 2009). Further, few efforts address negative attitudes to peers with intellectual disabilities specifically or tackle reluctance to engage closely with them.

Of note, more interventions have been reported in the literature that aim to educate or tackle negative attitudes toward peers with autism. One such example involved a six- to eight-session anti-stigma program that combined education with both direct and video contact with individuals with high functioning autism. The intervention was shown to have a positive effect on the knowledge and attitudes of adolescents but had no effect on their behavioral intentions toward peers with autism (Ranson and Byrne 2014; Staniland and Byrne 2013). In addition, a recent review of 42 disability awareness interventions that have targeted school-aged children concluded that multimedia and multicomponent approaches involving a range of activities are most likely to be effective in improving children and young people's attitudes and peer acceptance (Lindsay and Edwards 2013).

In summary, attempts to tackle intellectual disability stigma at the interpersonal level have focused on the general public, people more likely to have formal contact with the target population such as health and social care providers (or those in training), police and law enforcement personnel, and individuals who are likely to have informal contact with the target population such as neighbors, children, and young people in inclusive schools. Very few studies have focused on employers, which is of concern given the very low proportion of people with intellectual disabilities who are in some form of employment. This may reflect an institutionalized perception that people with intellectual disabilities really cannot work.

Structural-Level Interventions

Interventions at the structural level focus on social forces and institutions, through legislative action, mass media, governmental or organizational policies which aim to reach a large audience (Cook et al. 2014), and service delivery. Legislation such as the USA's Americans with Disabilities Act (1990), Australia's Disability Discrimination Act (1992), Israel's Disability Equality Act (1998), or the UK Equality Act (2010), to name just a few of many available acts, place a duty on public sector bodies to ensure that reasonable adjustments are made to public services to ensure that all sections of society, including people with disabilities, can access them.

Universal support for these rights, at least in principle, is reflected in the 161 nations (as of February 2016), which have ratified the 2006 UN Convention on the Rights of Persons with Disabilities (UN General Assembly 2007). The convention calls for the prevention of discrimination through increased awareness raising efforts to combat stereotypes and prejudice toward individuals with disabilities (Article 8). Other examples of legislation and policy aimed at decreasing discrimination toward individuals with intellectual disabilities can be seen in the widespread adoption of inclusive education as well as the naming of 'disability' as one of the categories motivating hate crime under legislation such as the UK's Criminal Justice Act (2003) and the USA's Matthew Shepard and James Byrd, Jr. Hate Crimes Prevention Act (2009).

The impact of legislation and policy by their very nature are very difficult to evaluate as their effects do not occur in isolation. Thus, not surprisingly, to the best of our knowledge, there is no evidence on what impact such structural-level interventions have had in reducing intellectual disability stigma.

Limitations of Research on Stigma Change Interventions

Numerous interventions from different parts of the world have been reported that aim to change stigma directed at people with (intellectual) disabilities, including disability awareness and disability equality training, and a host of mostly small-scale, isolated, contact-based interventions. Unfortunately, the utility of most of these interventions has not been evaluated in research, and many interventions that have been tested, despite showing promising results, have not resulted in wider implementation.

In addition, studies that have been conducted have methodological and conceptual limitations. Methodologically, existing studies have relied on small samples of mainly students and volunteers. Many studies were retrospective in nature rather than employing a before and after design. Finally, most studies have failed to test the impact of attitude change interventions on actual behavior. Furthermore, many interventions have not been based in a coherent fashion on theories of attitude and attitude change, despite these being abundant in the field of social psychology. Without clear theoretical underpinnings that guide intervention design, that is, a statement of how attitude change is expected to happen, any changes observed are vulnerable to unconvincing, post hoc explanations.

Conclusions and Recommendations for Action

The overview presented here suggests that there is a need to do more to tackle attitudinal barriers within society at large and among groups that are more likely to have contact with people with intellectual disabilities. The available evidence on interventions designed to improve attitudes and reduce discrimination in relation to people with intellectual disabilities is not sufficiently robust to recommend one type of intervention over another at the present time.

Given the rather piecemeal nature of interventions and research reported to date, several recommendations for research can be made. We suggest that a greater emphasis on collaboration between those delivering interventions and researchers is needed to develop a strong evidence base, as well as collaboration with individuals with intellectual disabilities themselves. Where such collaboration involves multinational efforts, close attention should be paid to exploring universal change processes alongside the influence of local and national circumstances, demands, and resources, as evident in a recent study by McKenzie et al. (2013).

With regard to general population attitudes to intellectual disability, more research is needed to decipher which specific components of interventions are effective drivers for change, which make best use of limited resources and which are most capable of reaching large audiences, while being effective. To achieve this understanding, interventions and awareness projects should have carefully designed evaluation built in from the outset. Further, the effects of direct and indirect contact both through face-to-face and e-learning should be tested to advance our understanding of the conditions under which contact with individuals or groups of people with intellectual disabilities leads to positive attitude change. More research is also called for on the effects of interventions on real-life behaviors.

In addition, more interventions are needed that focus on the stigma experienced by parents and family members of persons with intellectual disabilities, an area that, as noted, has found limited attention to date (Ali et al. 2012). Research should also advance our understanding of the impact of intellectual disability stigma on its targets and examine interventions designed to reduce the impact of internalized stigma. These issues are discussed in depth in Chap. 7 of this book.

Several recommendations can be made in terms of priorities for interventions. In view of apparent widespread confusion about what an intellectual disability is, and misconceptions about the capabilities of people with intellectual disabilities, attempts to educate the general public should be part of efforts to counter prejudice and discrimination. The media clearly have a role to play in providing more positive portrayals that refrain from depicting people with intellectual disabilities as incapable, childlike, or pitiable victims. Also, as the media are frequently a big cause of stigma, there is a need to establish reporting criteria for how to refer to individuals with intellectual disabilities. Nevertheless, it is important to acknowledge that it is unclear by how much we need to increase people's understanding about intellectual disability and what type of understanding of intellectual disability would generate more positive attitudes. Furthermore, efforts to educate the public should draw on a range of terms in use nationally and internationally and should not rely on any one specific label, such as 'intellectual disability', not least as labels are changeable.

Lack of direct contact with or exposure to people with intellectual disabilities may leave many feeling uncomfortable and unsure how to interact with someone with an intellectual disability. To counter the risk that such discomfort prompts avoidance, more exposure to people with intellectual disabilities is called for. Research fairly consistently points to the role of contact with individuals with intellectual disabilities as one of the most promising routes to improving attitudes. While direct personal contact has been found to be most useful, recent evidence (Walker and Scior

2013) suggests that indirect contact (e.g., through films featuring persons with intellectual disabilities) may also be beneficial and their integration into more wide-ranging efforts to change attitudes should be considered.

With regard to the need to challenge stereotypes, evidence from other fields suggests that exposing people to individuals who moderately or strongly disconfirm common stereotypes, and who vary in terms of their backgrounds, life roles, and the challenges they face (Clement et al. 2012), is likely to be most effective. These suggestions should be tested in relation to intellectual disability stigma. There is clear scope for exposure to individuals who challenge common stereotypes of people with intellectual disabilities as childlike, dependent, and in need of protection. This will need balancing, carefully though, without denying the needs of people with severe and profound intellectual disabilities who may be at risk of being further marginalized.

Contact-based interventions need to be carefully planned to minimize the risk of unintended, adverse consequences. For example, negative contact experiences, especially in childhood, may in fact increase social distance (Tachibana 2005), while a moderate amount of contact, as opposed to no or ample contact, appears to have the strongest association with more positive attitudes and willingness to interact (Freudenthal et al. 2010).

For the general public, contact is most likely to be facilitated by the media. Efforts to educate and challenge the formation of prejudice directed at individuals with intellectual disabilities should start at an early age. For children and young people, contact can be provided through inclusive activities and inclusive education. For those more likely to be in regular contact with people with intellectual disabilities, contact should be provided as part of training and continuing professional development.

In addition, fighting for the right of people with intellectual disabilities to have increased access to community resources must be an integral part of efforts to change attitudes. Equal participation in education, employment, and social and leisure pursuits not only respects the rights of people with intellectual disabilities but also gives the general public increased opportunities for, and benefit from, direct contact.

Finally, involving people with intellectual disabilities in delivering attitude change interventions is important, as first person narratives have been found to have greater impact than narratives by family members or carers (Walker and Scior 2013). Although the utility of such interventions needs to be explored further, reliance on first person narratives rightly privileges the experiences of individuals with intellectual disabilities.

Key Learning Points

* More needs to be done to tackle attitudinal barriers among children and adults in the general population and among groups that are more likely to have contact with people with intellectual disabilities.
* Collaboration is needed between those implementing interventions and researchers, and between research teams, in order to develop a strong evidence base.
* To counter discomfort in interacting with people with intellectual disabilities resulting from lack of contact, more exposure to and contact with individuals with intellectual disabilities is of high importance.
* Contact-based interventions, along with knowledge and education provision, are recommended for stigma reduction. However, these must be carefully planned and evaluated in order to minimize risk of unintended, adverse consequences.
* Involving people with intellectual disabilities in delivering attitude change interventions is likely to lead to more positive outcomes while also respecting their right to voice their own concerns and relate their experiences first hand.

Accessible Summary

* More should be done to fight negative attitudes toward individuals with intellectual disabilities.
* Research is needed so we learn how to fight negative attitudes.
* People without intellectual disabilities should meet more frequently with people with intellectual disabilities.
* People should also learn more about intellectual disability.
* People with intellectual disabilities should tell their life stories to help change negative attitudes.

References

Ali, A., Hassiotis, A., Strydom, A., & King, M. (2012). Self-stigma in people with intellectual disabilities and courtesy stigma in family carers: A systematic review. *Research in Developmental Disabilities, 33,* 2122–2140. doi:10.1016/j.ridd.2012.06.013.

Anti-Bullying Alliance SEN and Disability. n.d. *Developing effective anti-bullying practice.* Retrieved from http://www.anti-bullyingalliance.org.uk/send-programme

Bailey, A., Barr, O., & Bunting, B. (2001). Police attitudes toward people with intellectual disability: An evaluation of awareness training. *Journal of Intellectual Disability Research, 45,* 344–350. doi:10.1046/j.1365-2788.2001.00339.

Beacham, N., & Rouse, M. (2012). Student teachers' attitudes and beliefs about inclusion and inclusive practice. *Journal of Research in Special Educational Needs, 12,* 3–11. doi:10.1111/j.1471-3802.2010.01194.

Beckett, A. E., Buckner, L., Barrett, S., Ellison, N., & Byrne, D. (2009). *Promoting positive attitudes towards disabled people—The views of schools and teachers.* DEEPS Project Working Paper 2. University of Leeds, UK: School of Sociology & Social Policy.

Butler, A. C., Chapman, J. E., Forman, E. M., & Beck, A. T. (2006). The empirical status of cognitive-behavioral therapy: A review of meta-analyses. *Clinical Psychology Review, 26,* 17–31. doi:10.1016/j.cpr.2005.07.003.

Campbell, J., Gilmore, L., & Cuskelly, M. (2003). Changing student teachers' attitudes towards disability and inclusion. *Journal of Intellectual and Developmental Disability, 28,* 369–379. doi:10.1080/13668250310001616407.

Clement, S., Lassman, F., Barley, E., Evans-Lacko, S., Williams, P., Yamaguchi, S., et al. (2013). Mass media interventions for reducing mental health-related stigma (Review). *The Cochrane Database of Systematic Reviews, 7.* doi:10.1002/14651858.cd009453

Clement, S., van Nieuwenhuizen, A., Kassam, A., Flach, C., Lazarus, A., de Castro, M., et al. (2012). Filmed versus live social contact interventions to reduce stigma: Randomised controlled trial. *British Journal of Psychiatry, 201,* 57–64. doi:10.1192/bjp.bp.111.093120.

Cook, J. E., Purdie-Vaughns, V., Meyer, I. H., & Busch, J. T. (2014). Intervening within and across levels: A multilevel approach to stigma and public health. *Social Science and Medicine, 103,* 101–109. doi:10.1016/j.socscimed.2013.09.023.

Corrigan, P. W., Morris, S. B., Michaels, P. J., Rafacz, J. D., & Rüsch, N. (2012). Challenging the public stigma of mental illness: A meta-analysis of outcome studies. *Psychiatric Services, 63*, 963–973. doi:10.1176/appi.ps.201100529.

Emerson, E. (2015). *The determinants of health inequities experienced by children with learning disabilities*. Durham, UK: Public Health England.

Freudenthal, J. J., Boyd, L. D., & Tivis, R. (2010). Assessing change in health professions volunteers' perceptions after participating in Special Olympics healthy athlete events. *Journal of Dental Education, 74*, 970–979.

Georgiadi, M., Kalyva, E., Kourkoutas, E., & Tsakiris, V. (2012). Young children's attitudes toward peers with intellectual disabilities: Effect of the type of school. *Journal of Applied Research in Intellectual Disabilities, 25*, 531–541. doi:10.1111/j.1468-3148.2012.00699.

Hall, H., & Minnes, P. (1999). Attitudes towards persons with Down's syndrome: The impact of television. *Journal of Developmental and Physical Disabilities, 11*, 61–76. doi:10.1023/A:1021812702337.

Iacono, T., Lewis, B., Tracy, J., Hicks, S., Morgan, P., Recoche, K., et al. (2011). DVD-based stories of people with developmental disabilities as resources for inter-professional education. *Disability and Rehabilitation, 33*, 1010–1021. doi:10.3109/09638288.2010.520802.

Lindsay, S., & Edwards, A. (2013). A systematic review of disability awareness interventions for children and youth. *Disability and Rehabilitation, 35*, 623–646. doi:10.3109/09638288.2012.702850.

MacDonald, J. D., & MacIntyre, P. D. (1999). A rose is a rose: Effects of label change, education and sex on attitudes towards mental disabilities. *Journal of Developmental Disabilities, 6*, 15–31.

McKenzie, J. A., McConkey, R., & Adnams, C. (2013). Intellectual disability in Africa: Implications for research and service development. *Disability and Rehabilitation, 35*, 1750–1755. doi:10.3109/09638288.2012.751461.

Mencap (2007). *Bullying wrecks lives: The experiences of children and young people with a learning disability*. London, UK: Mencap Publications.

Nosse, L. J., & Gavin, K. J. (1991). Influence of direct contact on college students' attitude towards adults with mental handicaps. *College Student Journal, 25*, 201–206.

Ouellette-Kuntz, H., Burge, P., Brown, H. K., & Arsenault, E. (2010). Public attitudes towards individuals with intellectual disabilities as measured by the concept of social distance. *Journal of Applied Research in Intellectual Disabilities, 23*, 132–142. doi:10.1111/j.1468-3148.2009.00514.

Raczka, R., Theodore, K., & Williams, J. (2014). *Can brief training have an impact on police attitudes towards people with intellectual disabilities?*

Presentation for the British Psychological Society. Retrieved from https://www.bps.org.uk/system/files/user-files/Faculty%20for%20Learning%20Disabilities%20CPD%20event/paper_can_brief_awareness_training_impact_on_police_attitudes_towards_people_with_intellectual_disabilities.pdf

Rae, H., McKenzie, K., & Murray, G. (2011). The impact of training on teacher knowledge about children with an intellectual disability. *Journal of Intellectual Disabilities, 15*, 21–30. doi:10.1177/1744629511401168.

Ranson, N. J., & Byrne, M. K. (2014). Promoting peer acceptance of females with higher-functioning autism in a mainstream education setting: A replication and extension of the effects of an autism anti-stigma program. *Journal of Autism and Developmental Disorders, 44*, 2778–2796. doi:10.1007/s10803-014-2139-1.

Redman, M., Taylor, E., Furlong, R., Carney, G., & Greenhill, B. (2012). Human rights training: Impact on attitudes and knowledge. *Tizard Intellectual Disability Review, 17*, 80–87. doi:10.1108/13595471211218811.

Rüsch, N., Abbruzzese, E., Hagedorn, E., Hartenhauer, D., Kaufmann, I., Curschellas, J., et al. (2014). Efficacy of Coming Out Proud to reduce stigma's impact among people with mental illness: Pilot randomised controlled trial. *British Journal of Psychiatry, 204*, 391–397. doi:10.1192/bjp.bp.113.135772.

Russell, T., & Ayer, F. E. (1988). The effects of a direct-mail informational campaign on attitudes of industrial managers toward the mentally retarded population. *Journal of Mental Deficiency Research, 32*, 183–191. doi:10.1111/j.1365-2788.1988.tb01404.

Schwartz, C., & Rabinovitz, S. (2001). Residential facilities in the community for people with intellectual disabilities: How neighbours' perceptions are affected by the interaction of facility and neighbour variables. *Journal of Applied Research in Intellectual Disabilities, 14*, 100–109. doi:10.1046/j.1468-3148.2001.00060.

Scior, K., & Lynggaard, H. (2006). New stories of intellectual disabilities: A narrative approach. In S. Baum & H. Lynggaard (Eds.), *Intellectual disabilities: A systemic approach* (pp. 100–119). London, UK: Karnac.

Seewooruttun, L., & Scior, K. (2014). Interventions aimed at increasing knowledge and improving attitudes towards people with intellectual disabilities among lay people. *Research in Intellectual Disabilities, 35*, 3482–3495. doi:10.1016/j.ridd.2014.07.028.

Siperstein, G. N., Norins, J., Corbin, S., & Shriver, T. (2003). *Multinational study of attitudes toward individuals with intellectual disabilities*. Washington, DC: Special Olympics.

Sharma, U., Forlin, C., & Loreman, T. (2008). Impact of training on pre-service teachers' attitudes and concerns about inclusive education and sentiments about persons with disabilities. *Disability and Society, 23*, 773–785. doi:10.1080/09687590802469271.

Staniland, J. J., & Byrne, M. K. (2013). The effects of a multi-component higher-functioning autism anti-stigma program on adolescent boys. *Journal of Autism and Developmental Disorders, 43*, 2816–2829. doi:10.1007/s10803-013-1829-4.

Szivos, S. E., & Griffiths, E. (1990). Group processes involved in coming to terms with a mentally retarded identity. *Mental Retardation, 6*, 333–341.

Tachibana, T. (2005). Attitudes of Japanese adults toward persons with intellectual disability: An exploratory analysis of respondents' experiences and opinions. *Education and Training in Developmental Disabilities, 40*, 352–359.

Tracy, J., & Iacono, T. (2008). People with developmental disabilities teaching medical students: Does it make a difference? *Journal of Intellectual and Developmental Disabilities, 33*, 345–348. doi:10.1080/13668250802478633.

UN General Assembly (2007). *Convention on the rights of persons with disabilities: Resolution*. Adopted by the General Assembly, 24 January 2007.

Walker, J., & Scior, K. (2013). Tackling stigma associated with intellectual disability among the general public: A study of two indirect contact interventions. *Research in Developmental Disabilities, 34*, 2200–2210. doi:10.1016/j.ridd.2013.03.024.

Werner, S. (2015). Equal in uniform: Its impact on attitudes of soldiers without disabilities towards soldiers with intellectual disabilities. *Beit Issie Shapiro's 6th International Conference on Disabilities: Unity and Diversity in Action*. Tel-Aviv, Israel.

.

10

Relationships Matter: Addressing Stigma Among Children and Youth with Intellectual Disabilities and Their Peers

Erik W. Carter, Elizabeth E. Biggs, and Carly L. Blustein

Conversations about effective schooling often pivot around providing students with access to strong instruction and learning experiences marked by their *rigor* and *relevance*. But if one were to ask most students to reflect on their own school experiences, one would be quite likely to hear first about the ways in which their *relationships* mark their memories and shape their sense of self. Attention to relationships right alongside rigor and relevance is central to strong schooling for all students, but particularly for children and youth with intellectual disabilities. Supportive and satisfying relationships can enhance their engagement in school, contribute to a sense of belonging, and create rich contexts for learning within and beyond the classroom. The absence of such relationships, however, can lead to loneliness, isolation, marginalization, and stigma (Kersh et al. 2013).

E.W. Carter (✉) • E.E. Biggs • C.L. Blustein
Department of Special Education, Vanderbilt University, Nashville, TN, USA
e-mail: erik.carter@vanderbilt.edu

© The Editor(s) (if applicable) and The Author(s) 2016   **149**
K. Scior, S. Werner (eds.), *Intellectual Disability and Stigma*,
DOI 10.1057/978-1-137-52499-7_10

This chapter focuses centrally on the contributions of peer relationships to reducing stigma during elementary through secondary school. Numerous studies affirm the strong influence peer relationships can have on the lives and learning of any student, as well as their special salience for students with intellectual disabilities (Carter et al. 2014; Kersh et al. 2013). In many schools, hundreds of students navigate the same classes, hallways, cafeterias, and extracurricular activities each day as their schoolmates with intellectual disabilities. Whether and how the lives of these students intersect with one another throughout the week can either contribute to or counter stigma. In this chapter, we review various indicators of stigma in schools, address elements comprising successful efforts to promote relationships and reduce stigma, review promising school-based intervention approaches, and offer recommendations for future research in this area.

Indicators of Stigma in Schools

The social experiences and stigma of school-age children and youth with intellectual disabilities can vary widely within and across schools, communities, and countries. Some students report being warmly welcomed within the classrooms, clubs, and cafeterias of their school; others attend school each day feeling wounded or invisible. Available studies suggest that peers without disabilities hold a broad range of attitudes toward their schoolmates with intellectual disabilities—from negative to positive and all points in between. For example, Siperstein et al. (2007) found that middle school students in the USA held varied views regarding the capabilities of their schoolmates with intellectual disabilities, the types of activities they would be willing to do with them, and the benefits they attributed to inclusion. Studies conducted in other countries reveal similarly heterogeneous portraits (Scior 2011; Siperstein et al. 2011). Peers also can hold inaccurate knowledge about the origins and outcomes of having an intellectual disability, which in turn contribute to negative stereotypes and actions (Carter et al. 2001). Studies have highlighted the ways in which students with intellectual disabilities are frequently avoided, ostracized, teased, or bullied (e.g., Christensen et al. 2012).

Such collective encounters may lead some students with intellectual disabilities to adopt a type of 'self-stigma', in which reluctance to participate in school activities is driven by a belief that one's own social identity is devalued (Ditchman et al. 2013).

These various forms of stigma contribute in part to the paucity of peer relationships and friendships in the lives of many students with intellectual disabilities. According to a large-scale study involving parents of children with intellectual disabilities (ages 6–13) in the USA, 17 % of parents reported their child with an intellectual disability never visited friends during the previous year and 50 % reported their children never or rarely received telephone calls from friends (Wagner et al. 2003). The scarcity of social relationships becomes even more apparent when focusing on high school students with intellectual disabilities: according to their parents, only 22 % frequently saw any friends outside of school, 42 % never or rarely received telephone calls from friends, and only 54 % got together with friends outside of school and took part in organized activities at least once each week.

Important Intervention Elements

Creating opportunities for students with and without intellectual disabilities to meet, learn alongside, and get to know one another may be among the most promising pathways for fostering relationships and reducing stigma within schools. The published literature provides ample evidence that increased awareness, knowledge, interactions, and friendships can be addressed through well-designed, school-based interventions (see reviews by Carter et al. 2010; Lindsay and Edwards 2013). In this section, we cull from this literature five core elements that may substantially increase the likelihood that students with and without intellectual disabilities will develop positive relationships with one another within the school environment. Each element may represent a key consideration in the design and delivery of school-based interventions.

Shared experiences. One primary barrier to peer relationships is the limited extent to which students with and without intellectual disabilities are present in the same places at the same times and engaged in the same activities. The absence of students with intellectual disabilities from regular classes, extracurricular activities, and other school events severely restricts or altogether precludes students with and without intellectual disabilities from ever encountering one another. Given the influential role of personal contact in shaping attitudes, ensuring students with intellectual disabilities have the opportunities, encouragement, and support to be part of the breadth of social and learning opportunities taking place in schools can reduce stigma and provide the foundation for most other intervention efforts. Moreover, such shared experiences must be sustained—rather than episodic and time-limited—to best position students to develop new relationships.

Common connections. Shared interests, backgrounds, and experiences can provide the catalyst for new friendships. Connecting students on the basis of these commonalities may create opportunities for new friendships within shared experiences. This could involve inviting peers who have hobbies, sports, or music interests in common with the focus student; planning activities that incorporate the student's interests; or helping students develop age-appropriate interests and activities (Koegel et al. 2013). When students discover such connections, lasting relationships may be more likely to maintain when formal expectations to spend time together end.

Valued roles. The roles students are assigned within shared activities also matters. When the students with intellectual disabilities are always the recipients of support—or have minimal involvement in inclusive activities—they may be viewed only in terms of their differences and deficits. Giving all students valued roles in activities may enable peers to see them in light of their talents, strengths, and contributions. Having a leadership role, volunteering within a service project, or being assigned interdependent roles within a group activity all reflect high-status roles.

Relevant information. What peers know and think about disability may affect their receptivity toward developing friendships with students with intellectual disabilities. Reluctance to spend time with these students can stem from limited knowledge, uncertainty about how to interact, or questions about someone's capabilities. Providing relevant information and training may help peers feel more confident in their interactions. Targeted curricula, media, personal contact, and/or simulations have all been part of efforts to promote awareness (Lindsay and Edwards 2013). However, such training may have more of an impact within individualized interventions when it focuses on individualized information about a particular student and the expectations of a particular activity (Carter et al. 2015a).

Balanced support. The presence and support of paraprofessionals, special educators, and other professionals can help—or inadvertently hinder—positive peer relationships among students. The persistent presence of adults can be particularly problematic in adolescence, limiting peer interactions and leading to greater stigmatization. At the same time, the facilitative role of staff can be instrumental in creating connections among students and supporting inclusive involvement. Finding just the right balance between providing sufficient adult support to promote participation—but not too much to hinder new relationships—is critical to consider within any intervention effort.

Promising Intervention Approaches

Although few school-based interventions have been framed as reducing stigma directed at children and youth with intellectual disabilities, hundreds of studies have addressed avenues for improving the interactions, relationships, attitudes, and knowledge of students with and without disabilities. Our selective review focuses on intervention approaches with particular promise for creating contexts in which relationships might flourish and stigma might fade. We highlight six categories of intervention approaches that have been implemented individually or in combination with one another.

Inclusive educational experiences. Involvement in inclusive classroom and school activities maximizes opportunities for students with and without intellectual disabilities to spend time together in shared experiences throughout the school day. Numerous comparative studies have documented social advantages associated with involvement in typical versus specialized school settings for students with intellectual disabilities (see reviews by Jackson et al. 2008; Ryndak et al. 2013). Most of this research has focused on students in elementary and middle school settings. However, the specific sources of these social advantages are multifaceted and complicated to pinpoint. Enrollment alone (i.e., physical presence) may be necessary, but insufficient, for promoting social connections and improving attitudes. Indeed, students can be further stigmatized when insufficient or inappropriate supports are provided in inclusive settings. Instead, the available literature suggests *how* the participation of students with intellectual disabilities is supported is as essential to consider as *where* these students spend their school day (Feldman et al. 2015). Inclusive education is a powerful intervention only when accompanied by well-planned efforts to equip, connect, and support students with and without intellectual disabilities.

Awareness and informational interventions. A number of disability-related awareness and informational interventions have been evaluated as avenues for improving knowledge about, attitudes toward, and acceptance of peers with disabilities (see reviews by Leigers and Myers 2015; Lindsay and Edwards 2013). These interventions have varied widely in their length (e.g., single session, year-long program), format (e.g., presentations, multimedia, activities, role-playing), setting (e.g., classroom, school-wide), level (e.g., elementary, secondary), and scope (e.g., general categorical information, individualized information about a student). The outcomes associated with these interventions have been mixed and few studies have focused narrowly on students with intellectual disabilities. However, multicomponent interventions that combine informational content with personal contact may be the most promising. Moreover, it is important to consider what information is shared with peers so it reflects what students would want to be shared, introduces them in a positive light, and protects confidential information.

Social competence interventions. Many students with intellectual disabilities have social, communication, and behavioral difficulties that may make interactions with peers challenging to navigate. Effective interventions for teaching communication strategies, strengthening social skills, enhancing self-advocacy, and decreasing socially inappropriate behaviors among students with intellectual disabilities across the age span have been well documented in the literature (e.g., Carter et al. 2010; Rispoli et al. 2010). Such skill-building interventions may enhance how students with intellectual disabilities are viewed by others. Students with such difficulties are equally deserving of respect, positive interactions, and membership as students who do not experience such difficulties.

In advocating for social competence interventions we are not suggesting that students themselves are at fault for the stigma they experience. Instead, we assert that skills-focused interventions may serve an important role in improving the quality and frequency of students' interactions by building their strengths and capabilities.

Peer interaction training. Peers may themselves benefit from receiving instruction on specific social skills and strategies for conversing with students who have complex communication needs. When peers are uncertain of what to say or how to sustain a conversation, they may be likely to avoid interactions altogether. Numerous studies demonstrate that peers can learn to implement a variety of targeted conversational skills that contribute to higher-quality interactions with students with intellectual disabilities. Peers have been taught strategies for sustaining conversations during group activities (Hughes et al. 2011), for inviting students who appear socially isolated to participate in play leisure activities (Kasari et al. 2011), and for interacting socially with students with severe and multiple disabilities (Brady et al. 1991). While the research in this area is promising, very few studies have isolated the specific impact of peer training from larger multicomponent interventions.

Adult facilitation. Equipping and encouraging paraprofessionals and other school staff to actively facilitate social interactions and collaborative learning among students with and without intellectual disabilities also has research support across grade levels, both on its own and as a component of other packaged interventions (Brock and Carter 2015; Causton-Theoharis and Malmgren 2005). Educators might adapt activities to include a clear role for the student with disabilities, highlight shared interests, provide interpretation of unconventional or unfamiliar behaviors, redirect conversation away from adults and toward other classmates, or model ways for peers to initiate and maintain conversations. Such active efforts call attention to and capitalize on interaction opportunities that might be inadvertently overlooked. Although less empirical attention has focused on the more subtle influences of adults, the ways in which educational professionals talk about and to students with intellectual disabilities often serves as the primary role model for pupils. When adults model respectful interactions, use affirming language, and communicate high expectations for students with intellectual disabilities, other students may be more likely to engage in similar behaviors.

Peer-mediated interventions. Peer-mediated interventions create individualized, supported opportunities for students with intellectual disabilities to interact with and learn alongside their peers within or beyond the classroom. They involve equipping one or more peers to provide targeted social, behavioral, or academic assistance to students with disabilities with guidance and support from teachers, paraprofessionals, counselors, or other school staff (Carter et al. 2015b). These interventions can be mutually beneficial. Short-term increases in social interactions, skill acquisition, and engagement have been documented in numerous studies (see reviews by Carter et al. 2010; Chung et al. 2012). Moreover, peers often report substantial changes in their attitudes toward and expectations of students with disabilities, speak about their enjoyment and the friendships they formed, and report becoming stronger advocates in their schools (Carter et al. 2015a; Hochman et al. 2015). We provide an overview of four categories of peer-mediated interventions, each of which incorporates some of the intervention approaches previously described.

Peer support arrangements. Within peer support arrangements, one to three classmates without disabilities are taught to provide ongoing social and academic support to a student with intellectual disabilities within an inclusive classroom (Carter et al. 2011, 2015a). Peers are selected from the same classroom to maximize natural interaction opportunities. Peers participate in an initial orientation and receive ongoing support from a special educator or paraprofessional on how to work collaboratively with their classmate during various instructional activities (e.g., small-group activities, whole-group instruction, and independent seatwork). Peers might initiate conversations, encourage the student to contribute to class discussions, or make introductions to other peers in the class. Similarly, they might promote academic participation by sharing materials, partnering together on assignments, or providing assistance. An educator or paraprofessional provides facilitation to students as necessary to ensure they are successful and confident in their work together. Within peer support arrangements, peers without disabilities gain opportunities and support to work alongside and interact with their classmate with intellectual disabilities that may replace stigma with positive attitudes and experiences. Additionally, supporting a student with intellectual disabilities to become a more valued member of the classroom may promote an overall climate in the class of acceptance, respect, and belonging. Empirical support for these interventions is most prominent among adolescents with severe intellectual disabilities; less is known about their efficacy with students in earlier grades or who have less extensive support needs.

Peer networks. Peer network interventions focus on increasing social connections outside of the classroom, such as during lunch, in the playground, in hallways, within extracurricular groups, or before and after school. Peer networks involve three to six peers and the student with the disability meeting both formally and informally as a social group (Carter et al. 2013; Hochman et al. 2015; Koegel et al. 2013). The network meets weekly or biweekly to participate in an enjoyable shared activity such as playing a game, eating a meal, or completing a service project together. School staff (a coach, teacher, or guidance counselor) facilitate the network meetings to ensure all students actively participate. Outside of each formal meeting, students plan other ways to connect with one another between classes, such as eating lunch together or meeting for an activity outside of school. As with peer support interventions, peer networks have primarily been evaluated in secondary schools. Moreover, much of this research has involved students with autism.

Peer tutoring. Peer tutoring interventions involve pairs or groups of students working with one another to practice, review, and master academic content. These instructional interventions have been widely evaluated among students with mild intellectual disabilities. They can involve peers of similar or different ages and can be established for a single student or carried out on a whole class basis. Although peer tutoring promotes both interactions and academic skill development, static roles involving peers as 'helpers' and students with intellectual disabilities as the recipients of assistance may inadvertently perpetuate deficit-based views of students. Although there is an important place for this type of academic support, promoting opportunities for students with and without disabilities to provide reciprocal support may reduce stigma by highlighting the strengths of students with intellectual disabilities.

Peer partner programs. Peer partner programs are formal, group-based initiatives to connect students with and without intellectual disabilities during the school day. Although referred to by a variety of names (e.g., peer buddy programs, peer mentoring programs, Best Buddies), these programs similarly build into the school day regularly occurring opportunities for students to spend time together while receiving guidance and support from special educators or other school staff. Many programs involve having peers spend time with students in special education classrooms (reverse mainstreaming). However, they can also serve as a platform for planning new inclusive activities at a school, carrying out school-wide awareness efforts, or equipping peers to later provide support in general education classrooms (Hughes and Carter 2008). Although formal evaluations of these programs have been limited, available research suggests that they may draw in peers who already have positive attitudes (Carter et al. 2001).

Implications for Research

The pervasiveness of segregated service delivery models highlights the need for high-quality research to push policy and practice in new directions. We highlight five areas of particular importance. First, little attention has focused on the broader or longer-term impact of the interventions described in this chapter, including the ways in which each might shape the attitudes, expectations, career pathways, and future behaviors of peers who had the opportunity to get to know fellow pupils with intellectual disabilities while in school. The few studies that have explored the impact of interventions that continued beyond a single school term suggest that some newly formed friendships are maintained and that positive attitudes may endure (Carter et al. 2015a; Kishi and Meyer 1994). Recognizing that the peers of present are the civic, corporate, congregational, and community leaders of tomorrow, well-designed school-based interventions hold potential to shape broader societal attitudes over time. Longitudinal studies are needed to explore these possible pathways. The spread of these interventions should also be considered more closely to learn whether and how other students who are not directly involved in these interventions may be affected by what they observe.

Second, much of the existing literature has emphasized student-level interventions, with only modest attention dedicated to classroom-level efforts. Scaling up these interventions to be delivered throughout an entire school in intentional and coordinated ways is a continued need. What might it take for schools to prioritize addressing stigma amidst the numerous other priorities school leaders may view as competing or more pressing? How might schools shift from a reactive to a proactive posture, in which these interventions are viewed to be an important investment in creating a safe and inclusive school? Such questions need strong answers.

Third, the intersection of policy and practice warrants much closer consideration. Policies addressing educational placement, school staffing patterns, discipline, and service delivery all have implications for how students with intellectual disabilities are received and perceived in their schools. While much attention has focused on how these policies affect the academic and behavioral outcomes of students, how they shape attitudes and stigma should be explored more fully.

Fourth, the limited extent to which the voices of students have permeated this literature is striking. Relatively few studies have focused on how students with disabilities view the issue of stigma and the recommendations they have for the design and delivery of school-based interventions. Likewise, the perspectives of participating peers have not been prominent. The input and 'buy-in' of participating students with and without intellectual disabilities are especially important to understand when designing interventions aimed at addressing stigma.

Fifth, much of the research described in this chapter has taken place in Western contexts. Because countries and cultures differ in their priorities, policies, resources, and prevailing attitudes, additional investment is needed to replicate and extend available research across diverse educational and community contexts. The biggest obstacles to ensuring students with intellectual disabilities are seen as valued members of schools and communities—as well as the most effective efforts to eliminating these barriers—may be different across various contexts. Moreover, international conversations about these issues can identify important cultural influences and promote opportunities to learn from other contexts.

Summary

Although substantial changes in the participation and perceptions of young people with intellectual disabilities have taken place over the past three decades, far too many students remain on the periphery of everyday school life and are the focus of considerable stigma. In this chapter, we highlighted important elements and research-based interventions that put students in the best position to learn alongside and develop positive relationships with their peers without disabilities in inclusive school experiences. The importance of this investment to the long-term outcomes of young people with intellectual disabilities is hard to overestimate.

Key Learning Points

- The prominence of peers in the lives of children and youth makes them an essential entry point for intervention efforts aimed at reducing stigma.
- Although peers hold varying views and attitudes about their classmates with intellectual disabilities, many are willing to play an active role in promoting shared learning and relationship opportunities.
- Fostering supportive peer relationships should focus adequate attention on shared experiences, common connections, valued roles, relevant information, and balanced support.
- Peer-mediated interventions—such as peer support arrangements, peer networks, and peer partner programs—are effective and feasible approaches for promoting social connections and participation in inclusive activities.
- Key research needs include investigating the breadth and long-term impact of these interventions, pursuing the perspectives of students, and exploring intervention applications across cultures and contexts.

Accessible Summary

- Some of your classmates at school may think of you differently because you have a disability.
- You should not allow negative experiences with your peers to change the way you feel about yourself or make you feel any less of a person.
- Friendships are very important in life. There are many people around you who want to be your friend or help you make friends.
- Participating in activities inside and outside of school with your classmates can give you an opportunity to get to know each other and become friends.
- Teachers and researchers are always coming up with new ideas to support you in school and help you make friends easier. There are many ways adults can help you connect more with your classmates.

References

Brady, M. P., Martin, S., Williams, R. E., & Burta, M. (1991). The effects of fifth graders' socially directed behavior on motor and social responses of children with multiple handicaps. *Research in Developmental Disabilities, 12*, 1–16. doi:10.1177/105381519301700301.

Brock, M. E., & Carter, E. W. (2015). Efficacy of teachers training paraprofessionals to implement peer support arrangements. *Exceptional Children. Advance online publication.* doi:10.1177/0014402915585564.

Carter, E. W., Asmus, J., Moss, C. K., Cooney, M., Weir, K., Vincent, L., et al. (2013). Peer network strategies to foster social connections among adolescents with and without severe disabilities. *TEACHING Exceptional Children, 46*(1), 51–59. doi:10.1352/0895-8017(2005)110[366:FISIAH]2.0.CO.

Carter, E. W., Asmus, J., Moss, C. K., Amirault, K. A., Biggs, E. E., Born, T. L., et al. (2015a). Randomized evaluation of peer supports arrangements to support the inclusion of high school students with severe disabilities. *Exceptional Children. Advance online publication.* doi:10.1177/0014402915598780.

Carter, E. W., Bottema-Beutel, K., & Brock, M. E. (2014). Social interactions and friendships. In M. Agran, F. Brown, C. Hughes, C. Quirk, & D. Ryndak (Eds.), *Equity and full participation for individuals with severe disabilities: A vision for the future* (pp. 197–216). Baltimore, MD: Paul H. Brookes.

Carter, E. W., Hughes, C., Copeland, S. R., & Breen, C. (2001). Differences between high school students who do and do not volunteer to participate in peer interaction programs. *Journal of the Association for Persons with Severe Handicaps, 26*, 229–239. doi:10.2511/rpsd.26.4.229.

Carter, E. W., Moss, C. K., Hoffman, A., Chung, Y. C., & Sisco, L. (2011). Efficacy and social validity of peer support arrangements for adolescents with disabilities. *Exceptional Children, 78*, 107–125. doi:10.1352/2008.46:346-363.

Carter, E. W., Moss, C. K., Asmus, J., Fesperman, E., Cooney, M., Brock, M. E., et al. (2015b). Promoting inclusion, social relationships, and learning through peer support arrangements. *TEACHING Exceptional Children, 48*, 9–18. doi:10.1177/0040059915594784.

Carter, E. W., Sisco, L. G., Chung, Y., & Stanton-Chapman, T. (2010). Peer interactions of students with intellectual disabilities and/or autism: A map of the intervention literature. *Research and Practice for Persons with Severe Disabilities, 35*, 63–79. doi:10.2511/rpsd.35.3-4.63.

Causton-Theoharis, J. N., & Malmgren, K. W. (2005). Increasing peer interactions for students with severe disabilities via paraprofessional training. *Exceptional Children, 71*, 431–444. doi:10.1177/001440290507100403.

Christensen, L. L., Fraynt, R. J., Neece, C. L., & Baker, B. L. (2012). Bullying adolescents with intellectual disability. *Journal of Mental Health Research in Intellectual Disabilities, 5*, 49–65. doi:10.1080/19315864.2011.637660.

Chung, Y., Carter, E. W., & Sisco, L. G. (2012). A systematic review of interventions to increase peer interactions for students with complex communication challenges. *Research and Practice for Persons with Severe Disabilities, 37*, 271–287. doi:10.2511/027494813805327304.

Ditchman, N., Werner, S., Kosyluk, K., Jones, N., Elg, B., & Corrigan, P. W. (2013). Stigma and intellectual disability: Potential application of mental illness research. *Rehabilitation Psychology, 58*, 206–216. doi:10.1037/a0032466.

Feldman, R., Carter, E. W., Asmus, J., & Brock, M. E. (2015). Presence, proximity, and peer interactions of adolescents with severe disabilities in general education classrooms. *Exceptional Children.* doi:10.1177/0014402915585481.

Hochman, J. M., Carter, E. W., Bottema-Beutel, K., Harvey, M. N., & Gustafson, J. R. (2015). Efficacy of peer networks to increase social connections among high school students with and without autism. *Exceptional Children, 82*, 96–116. doi:10.1177/0014402915585482.

Hughes, C., & Carter, E. W. (2008). *Peer buddy programs for successful secondary school inclusion.* Baltimore, MD: Brookes.

Hughes, C., Golas, M., Cosgriff, C., Brigham, N., Edwards, C., & Cashen, K. (2011). Effects of a social skills intervention among high school students with intellectual disabilities and autism and their general education peers. *Research and Practice for Persons with Severe Disabilities, 36*, 46–61. doi:10.2511/rpsd.36.1-2.46.

Jackson, L. B., Ryndak, D. L., & Wehmeyer, M. L. (2008). The dynamic relationship between context, curriculum, and student learning: A case for inclusive education as a research-based practice. *Research and Practice for Persons with Severe Disabilities, 33*, 175–195. doi:10.2511/rpsd.33.4.175.

Kasari, C., Rotheram-Fuller, E., Locke, J., & Gulsrud, A. (2011). Making the connection: Randomized controlled trial of social skills at school for children with autism spectrum disorders. *Journal of Child Psychology and Psychiatry, 53*, 431–439. doi:10.1111/j.1469-7610.2011.02493.

Kersh, J., Corona, L., & Siperstein, G. (2013). Social well-being and friendship of people with intellectual disability. In M. Wehmeyer (Ed.), *The Oxford handbook of positive psychology and disability* (pp. 60–81). New York, NY: Oxford University Press.

Kishi, G. S., & Meyer, L. H. (1994). What children report and remember: A six-year follow-up of the effects of social contact between peers with and without severe disabilities. *Research and Practice for Persons with Severe Disabilities, 19*, 277–289. doi:10.1177/154079699401900404.

Koegel, R., Kim, S., Koegel, L., & Schwartzman, B. (2013). Improving socialization for high school students with ASD by using their preferred interests. *Journal of Autism and Developmental Disorders, 43*, 2121–2134. doi:10.1007/s10803-013-1765-3.

Leigers, K. L., & Myers, C. T. (2015). Effect of duration of peer awareness education on attitudes toward students with disabilities: A systematic review. *Journal of Occupational Therapy, Schools, & Early Intervention, 8*, 79–96. doi:10.1080/19411243.2015.1021067.

Lindsay, S., & Edwards, A. (2013). A systematic review of disability awareness interventions for children and youth. *Disability and Rehabilitation, 35*, 623–646. doi:10.3109/09638288.2012.702850.

Rispoli, M., Franco, J., van der Meer, L., Lang, R., & Carmargo, S. (2010). The use of speech generating devices in communication interventions for individuals with developmental disabilities: A review of the literature. *Developmental Neurorehabilitation, 13*, 276–293. doi:10.3109/17518421003636794.

Ryndak, D., Jackson, L. B., & White, J. M. (2013). Involvement and progress in the general curriculum for students with extensive support needs: K-12 inclusive-education research and implications for the future. *Inclusion, 1,* 28–49. doi:10.1352/2326-6988-1.1.028.

Scior, K. (2011). Public awareness, attitudes and beliefs regarding intellectual disability: a systematic review. *Research in Developmental Disabilities, 32,* 2164-2182. doi:10.1016/j.ridd.2011.07.005.

Siperstein, G. N., Parker, R. C., Bardon, J. N., & Widaman, K. F. (2007). A national study of youth attitudes toward the inclusion of students with intellectual disabilities. *Exceptional Children, 73,* 435–455. doi:10.1177/001440290707300403.

Siperstein, G. N., Parker, R. C., Norins, J., & Widaman, K. F. (2011). A national study of Chinese youths' attitudes towards students with intellectual disabilities. *Journal of Intellectual Disability Research, 55,* 370–384. doi:10.1111/j.1365-2788.2011.01382.

Wagner, M., Cadwallader, T., Marder, C., Cameto, R., Cardoso, D., Garza, et al. (2003). *Life outside the classroom for youth with disabilities. A report from the National Longitudinal Transition Study-2 (NLTS2),* (Retrieved from www.nlts2.org/reports/2003_04-2/nlts2_report_2003_04-2_complete.pdf.

11

Empowering People with Intellectual Disabilities to Challenge Stigma

Sian Anderson and Christine Bigby

Many people with intellectual disabilities remain on the social and economic margins of society, in our country Australia as much as elsewhere, living in a 'distinct social space' made up of family, paid staff, and other people with disabilities, without employment or engagement in meaningful activities or social relationships (Clement and Bigby 2010; Productivity Commission 2011). More than three decades of social policies promoting equal rights and social inclusion have failed to generate the social conditions or deliver the individual support necessary to enable people with intellectual disabilities to lead full lives of their own design. Disability discrimination legislation, for example, has achieved far more for people with physical and sensory disabilities than those with intellectual disabilities. Having an intellectual disability remains a powerful and stigmatized social identity (Beart et al. 2005). A 'fear

S. Anderson (✉) • C. Bigby
Living with Disability Research Centre, LaTrobe University, Melbourne, Australia
e-mail: Sian.Anderson@latrobe.edu.au

© The Editor(s) (if applicable) and The Author(s) 2016   **165**
K. Scior, S. Werner (eds.), *Intellectual Disability and Stigma*,
DOI 10.1057/978-1-137-52499-7_11

of difference' obstructs the engagement of the broader community with people with intellectual disabilities as a means of overcoming prejudice (Goffman 1961; Hubert 2000). For example, both leaders and members of mainstream community groups are often reluctant to countenance the inclusion of a person with an intellectual disability in their group. One study that investigated processes that support inclusion found a pattern of group leaders offering only 'conditional' group membership to a potential member with an intellectual disability and anxiety on the part of members without disabilities about the person's capacity to 'fit in' and 'be manageable' by the group (Craig and Bigby 2015). Even inclusion in the disability rights movement has proven problematic for people with intellectual disabilities given the need to embrace a stigmatized disability identity to join, and if they do, they are frequently placed at the bottom of the 'disability hierarchy' (Byrne 2010; Dowse 2001). Finding ways to reject stigmatized labels, build more positive identities, and locate comfortable places to 'belong' (Bauman 1996) poses a significant challenge to people with intellectual disabilities, their allies, and policy makers.

The Social Model, Disability Rights Movement, and People with Intellectual Disabilities

Conceptualizing the distinction between impairment and disability, the social model of disability has focused on the way people with impairments are disabled by social structures and processes. It grew out of the lived experiences of people with physical disabilities and some commentators have claimed that people with intellectual disabilities have been left out of subsequent social model theorizing and the disability rights movement. Goodley (2004, p. 49), for example, writes that people with intellectual disabilities

> have been only partially included in major theoretical developments in disability studies; their activism is not given the same weight as that of their physically impaired comrades; the leaders of the People First movement are too easily ignored and the policies and practices that impact upon their lives remain in the hands of the nondisabled policy makers who created them.

This latter point has been glaringly evident in the new Australian National Disability Insurance Scheme; the design of the scheme reflected an attendant care model, and during its first 12 months of operation, it failed to have any formal advisory structures which included people with intellectual disabilities or their representative organizations (Bigby 2015b).

The lack of social model theorizing about people with intellectual disabilities has meant neglect of social processes and structures more specifically disadvantaging to them, such as societal reliance on complex written or spoken communication or replacement of staff with technology in systems such as public transportation. A drawback of diverting attention away from impairment has been the seemingly unproblematic acceptance of intellectual disability as a biological given. More recent work in disability studies on psychosocial and political views of impairment holds promise for greater attention both to the social construction of impairment and more nuanced action about the complex interactions between different types of impairment and social processes (Goodley and Roets 2015).

Inclusion in collective action and the disability rights movement has held a problematic contradiction for people with intellectual disabilities. The difficulties posed by the presumption that to be part of the movement one must adopt a 'disabled identity', and thus embrace an ascribed label, have not been acknowledged (Dowse 2001). The label 'intellectual disability' carries with it a level of stigma and negativity not generally ascribed to those with other disabilities which may explain a lack of willingness to openly adopt such an identity. 'Passing' rather than identifying with a stigmatized label is the preferred option for many people with intellectual disabilities (Edgerton 1993; Rapley 2004). The choice 'not to identify' is seen by some disability activists as a rejection of the social model, an 'internalized oppression' (Shakespeare and Watson 2002). Yet if the common identity to be embraced is highly stigmatized, it seems unreasonable to pathologize people with intellectual disabilities by accusing them of 'internalizing oppression'. As noted in Chap. 14, for many, rejecting the identity of someone with an intellectual disability is one way to deal with stigma. If an individual is willing to take on the label and join a group for people with intellectual disabilities advocating change in social attitudes toward people with stigmatized identities, there remains the question of the willingness of the broader disability rights movement to be inclusive enough to support their wearing of the 'badge' of an activist.

Narratives About Self-advocacy

Independent self-advocacy groups and networks, such as People First, have been the main avenue for collective action of people with intellectual disabilities and their connection with the broader disability rights movement. The dominant narrative about self-advocacy has been political, seeing it as a 'countervailing force, questioning the devalued status, oppression and discrimination experienced by people with intellectual disability' (Frawley and Bigby 2015, p. 2). Self-advocacy groups have been seen as a means for people with intellectual disabilities to speak out, have a say and develop skills in empowerment (Goodley 2000; McNally 2002; Nind and Seale 2009). Run by and for adults with intellectual disabilities, it is claimed that groups enable feelings of being powerful and strong (Beresford 2012), providing opportunities for their members to engage with ideas about rights and empowerment and to share and celebrate their personal resilience. There may however be another narrative about self-advocacy, which frames it as a 'self-authored space' and is more subtly radical.

In this chapter we draw on our research about social identity and inclusion conducted in Australia to illustrate the 'subtle radicalism' of independent self-advocacy groups as one route to combating stigma and furthering the social inclusion of people with intellectual disabilities. While this research is based mainly on the Australian experience, it is relevant to most (Western) societies. The study 'Self-advocacy and inclusion: What can be learned from "Speaking Up" over the years' was a collaboration between academics and members of Reinforce, the oldest self-advocacy group in Melbourne. Group members wanted to write their history and the academics wanted to explore links between self-advocacy and social inclusion. The project investigated the history of Reinforce, through interviews and document reviews using inclusive research methods. Additionally, a PhD study of independent self-advocacy groups in the UK and Australia investigated the impact of group membership on individual social identity (Anderson 2013; Anderson and Bigby 2015; Bigby 2015a; Bigby et al. 2014; Frawley and Bigby 2015, Frawley et al. 2013).

During the 1980s Reinforce reflected the more radical political narrative of self-advocacy. It was a vibrant and radical organization that could get things done. As one member said, 'in the early days like in the '80s, well, if we wanted to see a particular person we'd just go up there and sit outside their office, wait for them'. 'We achieved so much', one self-advocate observed, 'fighting for rights more, getting somewhere, letting the people out there know that we're not as dumb, as stupid, as what they think we are'. And indeed, by the end of the decade, self-advocacy had been included in the broader advocacy sector and recognized by government policy as integral to the disability service system. The state government continued to embrace Reinforce as a representative body, thus giving the voice of people with intellectual disabilities a place alongside parents and professionals. For example, in the late 1980s, several Reinforce members were part of consultations about plans for the redevelopment of the disability service system and members of various government advisory committees. Some members were sought out by the first Public Advocate, Ben Bodna, to take on voluntary roles as community visitors to group homes. These were significant milestones in the engagement of people with deeply stigmatized identities in political activities around issues which had very real impacts on their quality of life.

However, the face of self-advocacy has changed since the 1980s, influenced by conservative political climates and the conditions that came with dependence on governments for funding (Frawley et al. 2013). For many organizations like Reinforce, staying afloat in times of retrenchment and just keeping the doors open have become a more dominant theme than radical action. As one of the founding members of Reinforce talking about the early years reflected, 'we were more radical, when we first started'.

Milner and Kelly's (2009) conceptualization of 'self-authored spaces' as places where people with intellectual disabilities come together to create communities and celebrate their individuality provides an alternative, less radical narrative about self-advocacy groups, perhaps more reflective of current political climates. Self-authored spaces, such as a drama group for people with intellectual disabilities described by Hall and Wilton (2011), act as a vehicle for inclusion through creating a strong sense of belonging within the group, friendships, and social connections with the wider community. Such groups provide opportunities to challenge entrenched stigma and exclusion but do so in subtle ways, through their influence on members' self-identities and social participation, and, in turn, the public's perception of people with intellectual disabilities. Our study of Reinforce found, for example, that membership of the group had been a means of social inclusion, providing a sense of belonging and social connection to the wider community, as well as an occupation for some members (Frawley and Bigby 2015).

While self-authored spaces, such as independent self-advocacy groups, are segregated, they mimic the social spaces in the mainstream community where people with common interests come together and through which people find identity and belonging: the football club, the community choir, the self-help group. Indeed there are signs throughout accounts of the experiences of self-advocates of the potential of groups to positively change the social identities of people with intellectual disabilities (Anderson and Bigby 2015; Beart et al. 2005; Caldwell 2010). By enabling people with intellectual disabilities to see themselves differently and for others to see them 'in a new light', independent self-advocacy groups and other self-authored spaces may counter some of the negativity, labeling, and entrenched stigma attached to their identities.

New Positive Identities Through Self-Advocacy

Anderson (2013) investigated these ideas further among self-advocates in Australia and the UK, finding that engagement with self-advocacy groups affected members' social identities in highly positive ways. The six independent self-advocacy groups involved in the study (four in the UK and two in Australia) were characterized by collegiality, which contributed to members' feelings of being affirmed as individuals. Respectful relationships were the norm and groups offered a wide range of interesting activities providing opportunities to members for recreation, skill development, and paid and voluntary employment. Members had a strong sense of ownership and being in control of their group, even in groups where supporters played a significant role in directing the agenda. Membership of a self-advocacy group had opened up a range of previously new, unimagined, and more positive social identities, including being an expert, a businesslike person, an independent person, and a self-advocate. Most importantly, these identities, outlined below, challenged the stigmatized notions of incapacity and dependency so often attached to the social identities of people with intellectual disabilities.

Being an expert. Self-advocates talked about becoming 'experts' about their own lives and had used this expertise in powerful ways: sharing experiences with other group members, talking to community groups, or participating in research. The idea that a person with an intellectual disability could be an 'expert' was an important shift in their social identity. For many, this shift occurred after a lifelong identity as a service user, a client, or a patient in services, treatment, or rehabilitation. It was not difficult to see the impact of being regarded by others as having important knowledge on the self-confidence and esteem of these self-advocates. One of the interviewees said that he loved going to schools and speaking and that the children enjoyed hearing him speak. He felt affirmed as a person and as an expert about his own life.

Being a 'businesslike' person. Many self-advocates gave examples of deriving a 'businesslike' or worker identity from their involvement in a group. The enormous pleasure and satisfaction gained from participating in the 'business' of self-advocacy stood out as a highlight for many, whether they did so on a paid or voluntary basis. The trusted self-determination implicit in the assigning of tasks in an office context was important to the self-advocates in many ways. It signified the positive regard in which they were held by both the group's support staff and by fellow members. The tasks, such as answering the phone, passing on messages, and buying tins of coffee and stamps, were all examples of 'work' of the kind the self-advocates recognized. Their participation in these tasks gave them the identity of 'worker', an identity many had been told (or had understood) that they could never attain. One member described a meeting with a former teacher from his early school days and the pride he felt in being able to say to him that he had a job and that he worked at Green Group, saying 'I told him I've been working down in [city], like, and he was surprised and he said; '[Frank], I am surprised that you've got a job'. The office-based nature of the tasks marked them as white collar jobs perhaps mimicking the work environments of some of the disability professionals with whom many of the self-advocates would have had prolonged contact.

Being an independent person. Some of the self-advocates had embraced the social identity of an 'independent person'. For two, this was evidenced by having their own front door keys and their own flats. They felt pride and pleasure at their ability to live with confidence in a new setting with limited support, making choices about daily living and activities such as what to watch on television or whether to invite friends or family around for a meal. For others developing the identity of an independent person was evidenced through their participation in activities in the broader community. Greater personal confidence gained from the group meant people felt more comfortable about being 'out and about' in the community, more able to travel and to participate in a greater range of activities, and be in social spaces like pubs and cafes.

Being a self-advocate. For the self-advocates, the self-advocacy group offered a safe place to take risks and build skills in articulating opinions and choices which drew on rather than detracted from individual resilience. There was some acknowledgment of the stigma attached to their identities outside the group alongside an emphasis on individuals showing to themselves and others that they were capable and engaged. The identity of 'self-advocate' encompassed both speaking up for oneself and acting in ways which supported and enabled peers to understand their rights and to deal with the negative consequences of a disabling society, such as exclusion and bullying. Group members spoke as much about 'helping' as they did about 'speaking out' in describing what they understood to be 'self-advocacy'. It is this insight which reveals a great deal about the potential that membership of such groups has to change the lived experience of people with intellectual disabilities. Seeing themselves as capable and skilled in bringing about change in the lives of their peers radically altered their stigmatized social identity. The negative identity attached to a person who is a client, patient, or service user is underpinned by an assumption that they are passive recipients—of advice, of treatment, of therapy or control.

For these self-advocates, the disability activism in which they were engaged took them beyond negative social identities ascribed by the broader community to embracing multiple (more) positive and included identities. These newer identities were highly individual and demonstrated that many people with intellectual disabilities were not interested in wearing *either* the 'label or the badge' of disability (Shakespeare 2006), but in being recognized as themselves. These new identities involved occupying different kinds of social space, both within their group and in the broader community, which raised their visibility and changed their public image.

Subtle Radicalism of Self-Advocacy and Self-Authored Spaces

The self-advocacy group members who participated in Anderson's (2013) study did not feel 'left out' of the broader disability movement. Those who had sought to engage with other advocacy organizations had not found the shared understanding and experiences which were such a positive feature of their own self-advocacy groups and decided not to remain involved. Their engagement with activism was highly personal and for the most part enacted within the self-advocacy group setting. Nor did they adopt the 'assimilation' approach described by Szivos and Griffiths (1990), whereby individuals in stigmatized or disadvantaged groups seek to 'pass' into the mainstream. What emerged from the findings was a modulated version of 'consciousness raising', as described by Szivos and Griffiths (1990), that built positive social identity based both on difference and on shared humanity.

These self-advocacy groups rarely engaged in overtly political acts such as staging protests, signing petitions, or participating in street marches; instead, their activities could be described as subtle radicalism. The voluntary nature of engagement in groups and the range of activities and roles offered provided a framework for individuals to build on and demonstrate their skills, capacity, and confidence. The groups were places in which people were valued as individuals and experienced a positive social environment unlike any other in their lives. The groups were 'self-authored' (Milner and Kelly 2009), with a culture and character created by members and supporters, representing a social environment quite different from that experienced by many adults with intellectual disabilities in the wider community. While it is difficult to measure the impact of this on challenging the stigma attached to intellectual disability among those outside the group, it is important to acknowledge the significant positive impact this engagement with self-advocacy had on the self-perception of those involved.

Empowering people with intellectual disabilities to challenge stigma is complex. When stigma is deeply entrenched, people who are viewed by others in negative ways may choose to reject the label and seek to 'pass' (Edgerton 1993; also see Chap. 14). In so doing, they reject the focus on a shared disability identity and risk losing support to improve their quality of life. Self-advocacy groups appear to offer a middle way for people with intellectual disabilities. They empower individuals to challenge stigmatized identities but in a subtly radical way. The low-key nature of their political activity may frustrate some commentators, but it is clear that they are working to challenge stigma in ways which have significant positive personal impact for their members. It is troubling that opportunities for people with intellectual disabilities to engage with such groups remain so limited. In both Australia and the UK, limited funding and a lack of explicit policy support threaten their sustainability. In other countries, there are no self-advocacy groups and where advocacy organizations exist, they are often led by parents whose activism is unlikely to constitute as overtly a challenge to intellectual disability stigma as the voices of self-advocates themselves.

Key Learning Points

- In many Western countries including Australia and the UK, decades of social policy promoting equal rights and social inclusion for people with intellectual disabilities have not delivered the social conditions or support arrangements necessary to enable individuals to live full, engaged lives of their own design.
- The broader disability rights movement's focus on the social model has to a great extent left out the voices of people with intellectual disabilities.
- Self-advocacy groups have a long history of offering a unique social space for people with intellectual disabilities.
- Self-advocacy groups are subtly radical in challenging the stigma attached to the identity of members and offer them occupation, peer support, recreation, and friendship.

Accessible Summary

- In Australia and the UK, governments have tried for many years to make it easier for people with intellectual disabilities to make their own choices. But many people are still not living how they would like.
- Sometimes, people with intellectual disabilities have not been included in groups that fight for better rights for people with disabilities.
- Self-advocacy groups are really important. They challenge some of the negative ideas people have about people with intellectual disabilities. They offer different activities which can make people feel more confident and independent. They are also places where people can enjoy support from friends.

References

Anderson, S. (2013). 'We just help them be them really'—Building positive, included identities: engagement in self-advocacy groups by adults with intellectual disabilities (Unpublished PhD thesis). LaTrobe University, Melbourne, Australia.

Anderson, S., & Bigby, C. (2015). Self-advocacy as a means to positive identities for people with intellectual disability: "We just help them, be them really". Journal of Applied Research in Intellectual Disability. Advance online publication. doi:10.1111/jar.12223.

Bauman, Z. (1996). From pilgrim to tourist—Or a short history of identity. In S. Hall & P. du Gay (Eds.), Questions of cultural identity (pp. 18–36). London: SAGE.

Beart, S., Hardy, G., & Buchan, L. (2005). How people with intellectual disabilities view their social identity: A review of the literature. Journal of Applied Research in Intellectual Disabilities, 18, 47–56. doi:10.1111/j.1468-3148.2004.00218.x.

Beresford, P. (2012). The theory and philosophy behind user involvement. In P. Beresford & S. Carr (Eds.), Social care, service users and user involvement (pp. 21–37). London, UK: Jessica Kingsley.

Bigby, C. (2015a). Self-advocacy and inclusion: A summary of the study 'What can be learned from speaking up over the years'. La Trobe University, Melbourne, Australia: Living with Disability Research Centre. Retrieved from https://engage.dss.gov.au/wp-content/uploads/2015/07/Final-self-advocacy-and-inclusion-what-can-be-learned-from-speaking-up-over-the-years-Bigby-21-07-2015.pdf

Bigby, C. (2015b). Is the national disability insurance scheme taking account of people with intellectual disability (Editorial). *Research and Practice in Intellectual and Developmental Disabilities, 1*, 93–97. doi:10.1080/23297018 .2014.974484.

Bigby, C., Frawley, P., & Ramcharan, P. (2014). A collaborative group method of inclusive research. *Journal of Applied Research in Intellectual Disability, 27*, 54–64. doi:10.1111/jar.12082.

Byrne, M. (2010). Levelling the disability hierarchy. *Eureka Street, 20*, 23.

Caldwell, J. (2010). Leadership development of individuals with developmental disabilities in the self-advocacy movement. *Journal of Intellectual Disability Research, 54*, 1004–1014. doi:10.1111/j.1365-2788.2010.01326.

Clement, T., & Bigby, C. (2010). *Group homes for people with intellectual disabilities: Encouraging inclusion and participation.* London, UK: Jessica Kingsley.

Craig, D., & Bigby, C. (2015). 'She's been involved in everything as far as I can see': Supporting the active participation of people with intellectual disability in community groups. *Journal of Intellectual and Developmental Disability, 40*, 12–25. doi:10.3109/13668250.2014.977235.

Dowse, L. (2001). Contesting practices, challenging codes: Self-advocacy, disability politics and the social model. *Disability and Society, 16*, 123–141. doi:10.1080/09687590020020903.

Edgerton, R. (1993). *The cloak of competence* (Revised and updated ed.). Berkeley, CA: University of California Press.

Frawley, P., & Bigby, C. (2015). Reflections on being a first generation self-advocate: Belonging, social connections and doing things that matter. *Journal of Intellectual and Developmental Disability, 40*, 254–264. doi:10.3109/1366 8250.2015.1028910.

Frawley, P., Bigby, C., Banfield, D., Blythman, N., Rosengrave, J., Hiscoe, A., et al. (2013). *Reinforce self-advocacy: Speaking up over the years.* Melbourne, Australia: La Trobe University.

Goffman, E. (1961). *Asylums: Essays on the social situation of mental patients and other inmates.* London, UK: Penguin Books.

Goodley, D. (2000). *Self-advocacy in the lives of people with learning difficulties.* Maidenhead, UK: Open University Press.

Goodley, D. (2004). The place of people with 'learning difficulties' in disability studies and research: Introduction to this special issue. *British Journal of Learning Disabilities, 32*, 49–51. doi:10.1111/j.1468-3156.2004.00279.

Goodley, D., & Roets, G. (2015). The (be)comings and goings of 'developmental disabilities': The cultural politics of 'impairment. *Discourse: Studies in Cultural Politics of Education, 29*, 239–255. doi:10.1080/01596300801966971.

Hall, E., & Wilton, R. (2011). Alternative spaces of 'work 'and inclusion for disabled people. *Disability and Society, 26,* 867–880. doi:10.1080/09687599 .2011.618742.

Hubert, J. (2000). The social, individual and moral consequences of physical exclusion in long-stay institutions. In J. Hubert (Ed.), *Madness, disability and social exclusion. The archaeology and anthropology of 'difference'* (pp. 196–207). London, UK: Routledge.

McNally, S. (2002). A survey of self-advocacy groups for people with learning disabilities in an English region. *Journal of Intellectual Disabilities, 6,* 185–199. doi:10.1177/14690047030073004.

Milner, P., & Kelly, B. (2009). Community participation and inclusion: People with disabilities defining their place. *Disability and Society, 24,* 47–62. doi:10.1080/09687590802535410.

Nind, M., & Seale, J. (2009). Concepts of access for people with learning difficulties: Towards a shared understanding. *Disability and Society, 24,* 273–287. doi:10.1080/09687590902789446.

Productivity Commission (2011). *Disability support and care.* Canberra, Australia: Productivity Commission.

Rapley, M. (2004). *The social construction of intellectual disability.* Cambridge, UK: Cambridge University Press.

Shakespeare, T. (2006). *Disability rights and wrongs.* London, UK: Taylor and Francis Routledge.

Shakespeare, T., & Watson, N. (2002). The social model of disability: An outdated ideology? *Research in Social Science and Disability, 2,* 9–28. doi:10.1016/ S1479-3547(01)80018.

Szivos, S., & Griffiths, E. (1990). Group processes involved in coming to terms with a mentally retarded identity. *Mental Retardation, 28,* 333–341. doi:10.1111/j.1468-3156.2008.00507.

12

Tackling Stigma in Developing Countries: The Key Role of Families

Roy McConkey, Callista Kahonde,
and Judith McKenzie

Intellectual disability occurs in every nation on earth, although it is not uniformly understood or perceived across the world. Likewise this disability, as with other bodily impairments, has existed through the generations but our understanding and perceptions of it have changed especially during the last 100 years (Parmenter 2001). But the extent to which these changes have occurred differs across nations. More developed nations of the 'North' with their long-established educational, health and social care systems founded on industrial and technological economies present a very different social context for persons with an intellectual disability than do poorer countries of the 'South', which were reliant on agrarian economies but are rapidly urbanizing with poorly developed education, health and social services. Yet despite the economic and social disparities

R. McConkey (✉)
University of Ulster, Northern Ireland, Coleraine, UK
e-mail: r.mcconkey@ulster.ac.uk

C. Kahonde • J. McKenzie
University of Cape Town, Cape Town, South Africa

© The Editor(s) (if applicable) and The Author(s) 2016   **179**
K. Scior, S. Werner (eds.), *Intellectual Disability and Stigma*,
DOI 10.1057/978-1-137-52499-7_12

across the nations, people with intellectual disabilities and their families still encounter stigma and discrimination from their fellow citizens. Thus, the lessons learnt of tackling stigma in the developed world and described in the earlier chapters of this book may well be applicable to less developed countries. And the converse is equally true: the methods that have proved effective in less affluent nations can inform and guide actions that need to be taken in more affluent countries if full equality of opportunity is to be obtained for all their citizens. In that sense, this chapter is well placed to challenge and extend our current understanding of the roots of stigma within human society and to offer tangible strategies to reduce, if not remove, the stigmatizing impact of disability in every nation.

An Impossible Dream?

It certainly will be a struggle to attain the aspiration of removing the stigmatizing impact of disability in every nation because three main factors may work against us. First, disability never exists in a pure form; rather, reactions to it are compounded by other societal attitudes, such as to women, ethnic and religious minorities and by the impact of poverty—the link between disability and poverty is long established globally (Eide and Ingstad 2011). Thus, the stigma that families and people with intellectual disabilities experience can be an expression of attitudes that go beyond those relating to disability and strategies to counter discrimination must take this into account.

A second consideration is that every nation is an amalgam of different cultures and communities with diverse beliefs and values. Thus, we should expect, as research confirms, variations in public understanding and perceptions of disability within and between countries (Siperstein et al. 2003). This suggests that a range of approaches will be needed often tailored to 'sub-cultures' rather than relying on national strategies.

The third challenge is arguably the most daunting: how do we move beyond changing attitudes to changing people's behavior? Some would say we have placed too much reliance on giving people 'head knowledge' about disability and insufficient opportunity for them to experience 'heart knowledge' that engages their emotions because that is a more effective motivator for people to change their behavior. Our change strategies need to be focused on people getting to know one another personally (McConkey et al. 2009).

Although it might appear like an impossible dream to remove from human society the stigma of intellectual disability, it is far too early to be despondent because in the great scope of human history we have barely begun to try.

The Key Role of the Family

In this chapter, we want to focus on the key role that families have in perpetuating and also in reducing stigmatizing attitudes to people with an intellectual disability. This is not to excuse others, such as professionals, from their responsibilities in this regard. Rather in low-income countries in particular, families arguably have the greatest influence due to the dearth of professional advocates (McKenzie and Muller 2006), which incidentally was true throughout the developed world over the past two generations and some would argue is still the case. But more significantly it is within the family that the child first experiences acceptance or rejection and if families offer positive experiences they will do a great deal to build the resilience of the child to bolster their identity in the face of stigma. By 'family' we refer to all those in parenting roles such as grandmothers and siblings and other relatives living as extended families in a shared habitat.

Figure 12.1 illustrates the mediating role that all families play between the affected person and the wider society. This is especially true throughout the childhood years, but for persons with an intellectual disability this may extend long into adulthood because of their ongoing need for support, which in developing countries most families provide without any external assistance (McKenzie et al. 2013).

We focus on two sets of influences. As the arrows indicate, these operate as mutual influences between society and family and between the family and the person. Thus, societal attitudes impact on the family but equally the reactions of families contribute to and confirm society's attitudes. Likewise the family response to the person affects the person but

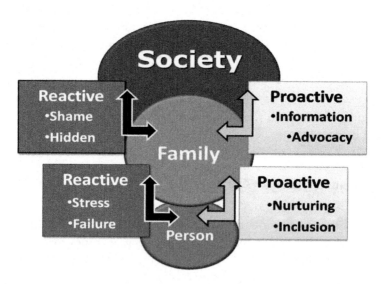

Fig. 12.1 Family influences on society and the person with an intellectual disability

equally the person affects the family. These are dynamic influences that become ever more entwined over time.

We distinguish between reactive and proactive influences. By reactive we mean the passive acceptance of prevailing reactions to intellectual disability that are reinforced within the community and contribute to the self-stigma of the family and of the person. Four common reactions are detailed in the following section. In contrast, proactive influences challenge prevailing attitudes and perceptions of intellectual disability. These too are mutual so that families can influence their community and also the person, while also being open to proactive influences coming to them from the community and from the person. Four examples of proactive influences will be presented.

It is likely that these two cycles of influence are present in varying degrees within families, with the balance possibly changing over time and in relation to certain issues, for example, the availability of support for the family and varying characteristics of the child/adult with an intellectual disability. Moreover, intrafamilial differences in reactions to the disability are a further source of tension between these two cycles that can result in the affected child's nuclear family 'splitting away' from the reactive influences of the wider family. Sometimes the tension happens within the nuclear family whereby one of the parents, usually the mother, gets blamed for the occurrence of a disability (Haihambo and Lightfoot 2010). Such tensions invariably add to maternal stress. However, international experience suggests that all families are capable of becoming more proactive and that this is an essential component in reducing the self-stigmatization of families and that of their relative with an intellectual disability, as well as challenging stigmatizing attitudes and behaviors in their community and wider society.

Reactive Influences

We begin by highlighting the strength of negative reactions in the community and in families to people with an intellectual disability as uncovered in our ongoing research in South Africa (Kahonde 2015; McKenzie and McConkey 2015) and in various recent studies undertaken in other developing countries such as Ghana, Tanzania, Namibia and Pakistan (Aldersey 2012; Haihambo and Lightfoot 2010). A much more extensive literature exists in more affluent countries yet it is broadly supportive of the dominant reactions described here. However, comparisons should be made cautiously as there have been few well-controlled, cross-cultural studies. Further research is needed not only to define the issues facing families in different countries but also to provide a yardstick against which change can be measured within cultures.

The stigma of shame. One clear message emerges from past research: intellectual disability brings shame on families. A common response is then to hide the person from the community and even the wider family (Essop 2012; Haihambo and Lightfoot 2010). This response further reinforces the shamefulness associated with this disability that is still prevalent in many societies. Intellectual disability is often interpreted as misfortune befalling the family because of their misdeeds. Other families may prefer to hide children or adults with intellectual disabilities because of physical deformities or behavioral challenges (Ingstad 2001). Such reactions negatively affect the growing child. A woman with Down syndrome in Cape

Town described how her mother reacted to the birth of a child with a disability (quotations are from McKenzie and McConkey 2015):

> My mother was in shock when they told her I was Down Syndrome. She did not know how to handle me and so my mother cried for days. She locked herself in a dark room and cried because she was in shock because her child was disabled.

Zimbabwean mothers explained how their shame was reinforced when they turned to traditional healers for a 'cure'. These healers attributed the cause of disability to the evil spirits that possessed the child because of the mother's misdeeds or breaking of taboos and used traditional rituals to cast out these spirits (Tarusarira 2015).

The burden on families. Caring for a child or adult with an intellectual disability places additional burdens on the family. Some of this comes from the physical demands of looking after a child with mobility, feeding, or behavioral difficulties (Mirza et al. 2009). Financial pressures often add to the stress on mothers as they have limited time for tending to the family farm or obtaining other sources of income and there is no one else to relieve them of their caring responsibilities. The toll on mothers' health and well-being due to stress can be great and in turn affects the growing child or adult. On one hand, it can lead to neglect and abuse within the family, while at the other extreme, it may be expressed as 'over-protectiveness' on the part of mothers especially and a reluctance to expose the person to opportunities outside the home.

The burden of care is further exacerbated by poor living conditions as this example illustrates of a mother living in an informal settlement near Cape Town:

> It is not easy to wash them, you have to lift her up, I suffered from backache. I think they need to have separate bathroom that is equipped with standing frame which will make easier for us to wash them. It is worse for us staying in the shacks because we do not even have decent toilets.

All these burdens accumulate in a sense of failure on the part of parents as this mother noted: 'I don't know that we are doing him any favors to just keep him at home unable to access companionship and so forth.' Parents dwelling overly on their child's vulnerabilities to abuse from others may impair the self-confidence and self-esteem of their children (Ali et al. 2015).

> She does not like to go out, always watch television. If I go to Eastern Cape, I took her with me; wherever I go she is always next to me. I do not want anything happened to her.

The reactive influences described here if left unchallenged only serve to perpetuate the negative perceptions and misunderstandings about disability that persist in many countries around the world. But just as the family is central to this self-fulfilling prophecy of hopelessness and despair, so can it provide the stimulus for change.

Proactive Influences

The relationship between parents, especially mothers/grandmothers, and the child with the disability is the engine that drives a proactive challenge to existing attitudes. Oftentimes this is expressed when parents proclaim that they will treat the child just like their other children. This is not to deny their child's additional needs, but rather it is recognition that the label of disability need not alter a 'normal' relationship with their child (Essop 2012). Indeed, this distinction between the person and the label is fundamental to reshaping societal responses to disability. Four main strategies have proved effective in challenging negative perceptions of intellectual disability.

Nurturing development. Treating the child as any other sibling means actively nurturing their development so as to assist them to gain developmental milestones in mobility, communication and self-care, albeit at a later age than their peers without disabilities (Einfeld et al. 2012). It also means taking the child outside the home and participating in family and community events despite the inevitable criticism and disdain of others. Children who are nurtured in such supportive family environments will hopefully escape most of the self-stigma that can be associated with intellectual disability. Equally as they acquire the competencies that others thought impossible, they in turn further convince their families that disability need not constrain their child's abilities, talents and personality.

Nonetheless much resolve and resilience is needed by parents to persist in their beliefs and not to be defeated. In the African context mothers frequently draw on their faith in God as their greatest support in coping with their child's disability (Essop 2012).

> So I go down on my knees still every night and I believe, if you are sincere, God would provide. Before I used to be a different person but, today without Him I am lost. Every step I take is in His name.

Meeting other parents of children with disabilities also provides much needed emotional support along with the informational and practical supports that can make life easier. Thus, parent associations, such as Down Syndrome South Africa, can play a crucial role in making families proactive change agents for their children.

Inclusion. One immediate, but crucial, outcome of family proactivity is the child's presence and participation in the life of the family and in due course in the life of the community. No longer hidden away, the child has the opportunity to gain from interacting with others and they with him or her. Yet the courage of parents to break the time-honored conventions within families and communities around disability can be met with rejection and hostility. Once again they need support from allies and the discernment to choose with care the challenges they take on. Of primary importance is the child's opportunity to join in formal and informal education through crèches, playgroups, schools and religious communities. The potential developmental gains for the child are manifold, but it also confirms for families the validity of their aspiration for the child to have the same opportunities as their other children. Yet families in rural areas can face formidable challenges given the long distances children have to walk to school or community events.

Information. Family proactivity needs to extend into the wider community in other ways. Foremost of which is the provision of information regarding the causes of intellectual disability. Myths and superstitions persist because they are left unchallenged. That is why many parent associations place such an emphasis on giving families information about disabilities so that parents themselves become better informed and can in turn pass on this knowledge to others, especially in relation to their own child. Sympathetic professionals in positions of authority are crucial allies in educating families and the wider community (Kelly et al. 2012), but even so their efforts are made all the more effective when they are applied to particular individuals: a task that parents can fulfill.

Advocacy. International Declarations of Rights have been supported by governments in poor and rich countries alike, yet the realization of those rights is far from complete, particularly in low-income countries that face competing demands on their limited resources. Moreover, the voices of people with disabilities are usually drowned out by more strident groups arguing for their rights. Here too families have taken the lead in speaking up for their children both as individuals and collectively as local and national associations of parents. Parental advocacy has brought the needs of people with intellectual disabilities to the attention of politicians and officials and ensured that they got a fair deal when it comes to the provision of support services (Lansdown 2002). For example, parents in Tanzania described how they attempted to change the attitudes of the community toward their child and how they draw strength from such campaigns as they learnt to appreciate the positive elements of parenting a child with a disability (Aldersey 2012).

Maintaining Motivation

Naming these four proactive strategies for changing perceptions does not do justice to the vast amount of physical and emotional energy required by parents to sustain these actions in the face of rejection and intransigence. Many families are defeated by the task but fortunately in every country there are parents who have persisted and shown remarkable leadership that has benefited many thousands up to now and will do so for millions more in the future.

Practical Actions

In this final section, we want to identify certain strategies especially suited to developing countries that bring together the proactive influences we have described and that are a counter to the reactive influences that many families still experience.

Parent and friends associations. The value of parent associations in changing perceptions within families and communities is well attested internationally as they can combine a national presence founded on a network of local groups. As already noted, they can be a source of emotional and practical support to new parents, especially as they come to terms with having a child with a disability. They can provide information to counter ignorance and misrepresentations in wider society. They give parents a sense of solidarity from which they can advocate individually or corporately locally, nationally and internationally. The UN Convention on the Rights of Persons with Disabilities was shaped through the involvement of parental advocacy.

In countries such as Lesotho and Zanzibar, the associations are open to professional 'friends', teachers and nurses, for example, as well as family friends, such as siblings and grandparents, to create a broad coalition of mutual support and widen their sphere of influence (McConkey and Mariga 2010). Most associations exist on a self-help basis, but they can be grown in localities with support from sympathetic professionals such as community-based rehabilitation workers or personnel from national parent associations. Training can be provided to members to equip them to be community educators or to assist parents with income generation (McConkey et al. 2000). Many present-day community-based support services for people with disabilities were started by parent groups.

Parent associations are not without their difficulties and shortcomings. In rural areas, villages are further apart and the availability and cost of transport, allied to taking time away from farming activities, can prevent families from attending meetings. Professionals have an important role to play in identifying the support that families need to maintain their resilience and to think of new ways of providing support to the persons with an intellectual disability and their families, making use of available community resources rather than expensive special programs (World Health Organization and World Bank 2011).

Village gatherings. Parent associations and other advocacy groups focus on village or community gatherings as a means of communicating their messages about intellectual disability as the messages can be harmonized with local cultural values and activities. Such gatherings are held with the permission of community elders and draw on the oral traditions that remain strong in rural communities especially. They use culturally appropriate music and dance to draw an audience often made up of all ages. Drama and songs recount the stories, experiences and emotions of parents and people with disabilities, which are tailored to that particular culture. Speeches from an invited dignitary are used to reinforce the messages as are posters and wall paintings that provide ongoing reminders of key slogans such as 'Disability is not Inability'. These gatherings aim to nurture a pride in disability, in families and in local communities.

Radio broadcasts. Engagement with wider audiences is best achieved through radio, which is widely listened to in many developing countries. Program producers and presenters in local radio stations are told of forthcoming events such as village meetings or talks to be given by invited speakers. The advent of mobile phones opens up possibilities of phone-in programs where callers can debate issues, get information and make contact with other like-minded persons. Dramas and story-telling relating to intellectual disability are also well suited to radio. Oral communication in local languages is much cheaper than the production of print materials with their associated translation and distribution costs.

Support from community leaders. The opinion leaders within communities are key allies for families wishing to bring about change. This should include village chiefs and elders, traditional healers and religious leaders, as well as elected politicians and officials. Building personal relationships seems to be an effective means of gaining their support for specific initiatives within local communities, such as those proposed by parent associations. Engaging with those leaders who have a relative with a disability can be especially fruitful as they have personal insights and reactions to share. The support of community leaders can be crucial when it comes to removing discriminatory practices such as school exclusions, access to health services and charges levied by minibus and taxi companies for transporting people in wheelchairs.

The role of traditional healers in combating stigma deserves particular attention. Many families turn to them, yet they too lack understanding about the causes of intellectual disability and fall back on supernatural explanations, such as that disability is a punishment for the breaking of tribal taboos by family members. These traditional healers could contribute positively to reducing stigma if they seek to understand and accept other explanations (Kromberg et al. 2008).

Productive work. In many cultures, one's human status is judged by the extent to which people can participate in valued activities within that society (Aldersey et al. 2014). The active participation of children and young adults with intellectual disabilities in family and community life therefore conveys a strong challenge to negative attitudes, especially when they can be seen to be contributing to family life, such as undertaking household tasks like fetching water and firewood or taking part in community activities such as team sports. In rural agrarian settings, most of the livelihood activities do not require any abstract thinking, so someone with a mild to moderate intellectual disability, who does not have physical limitations, can be involved in subsistence farming, household chores and most activities of daily living. Hence, parents and professionals need to prepare children to become productive members of their community so as to counter beliefs around their helplessness. Ultimately being accepted within communities depends not on labels but on the relationships that people forge with their peers. Hence, participation in schooling, sports and religious activities enable others to relate to the person and the person with them. Indeed, international evidence confirms that personal contact is a potent force for challenging stigma (Macmillan et al. 2014).

Looking to the Future

In this chapter we have chosen to focus on the family as the channel for tackling stigma. But theirs is not the only channel for change and indeed family efforts need to be reinforced by legal rights, national policies that are enforced and changes in discriminatory practices of professionals and services to name but a few. We accept too that reliance on families and local communities to tackle stigma will likely result in greater disparities within countries in their attitudes to intellectual disability as there is unlikely to be uniform implementation of common actions. We are also conscious of placing extra burdens on families and implying that they are to blame for the stigma their relative experiences. So in looking to the future, let's be clear of the key messages on tackling stigma. Our aim is to build relationships between people who are perceived to be different with their families and with their local communities. People's negative reactions to the label 'intellectual disability' can be initially separated from their perceptions of individuals with whom they have built a relationship. This process can be proactively facilitated within families and communities, thereby reducing the stigma associated with the label. In so doing, societal responses to intellectual disability will change over time and across cultures. In a nutshell, that is the journey we have inherited from previous generations and it is one we must continue to advance in coalitions with all interested and involved parties. But we continue to assert that central to these endeavors is the leadership and example that families provide. It is they who have brought us thus far on the journey and they who will see us home.

Key Learning Points

- Families are uniquely placed to challenge negative perceptions in society. In many developing countries they are the main advocates for change.
- Families have had to overcome common reactions such as shame and failure and become more proactive in changing the perceptions of other family members and their immediate community.
- These reactive and proactive influences coexist. Parents need allies to maintain their resilience.
- Practical strategies include the formation of parent associations, the use of village gatherings, radio broadcasts and gaining the support of community leaders.
- Building relationships among families and communities with people who are perceived to be different is the basis for reducing stigma.

Accessible Summary

- People with intellectual disabilities are treated unfairly in every country of the world and especially in poorer countries.
- Families have led the way in changing attitudes, despite the negative reactions they experience from others.
- The support from other parents has helped families to promote more positive attitudes in local communities.
- Village gatherings, radio broadcasts and support from community leaders have been good ways of doing this.
- Families need support from professionals and politicians nationally to match their local efforts.

References

Aldersey, H. M. (2012). Family perceptions of intellectual disability: Understanding of support in Dar es Salaam. *African Journal of Disability, 1,* 1–12. doi:10.4102/ajod.v1i1.32.

Aldersey, H., Turnbull, A., & Turnbull, R. (2014). Factors contributing to construction of personhood of individuals with intellectual and developmental disabilities in Kinshasa, Democratic Republic of Congo. *Canadian Journal of Disability Studies, 3,* 29–61. doi:10.15353/cjds.v3i2.156

Ali, A., Kock, E., Molteno, C., Mfiki, N., King, M., & Strydom, A. (2015). Ethnicity and self-reported experiences of stigma in adults with intellectual disability in Cape Town, South Africa. *Journal of Intellectual Disability Research, 59,* 530–540. doi:10.1111/jir.12158.

Eide, A., & Ingstad, B. (2011). *Disability and poverty: A global challenge.* Bristol, UK: Policy Press.

Einfeld, S. L., Stancliffe, R. J., Gray, K. M., Sofronoff, K., Rice, L., Emerson, E., et al. (2012). Interventions provided by parents for children with intellectual disabilities in low and middle income countries. *Journal of Applied Research in Intellectual Disabilities, 25,* 135–142. doi:10.1111/j.1468-3148.2011.00678.

Essop, F. (2012). Parents' and special care workers' understanding of "acceptance" and "denial" in relation to a child's intellectual disability. In *Unpublished Master's thesis.* Disability Studies Division: University of Cape Town, South Africa.

Haihambo, C., & Lightfoot, E. (2010). Cultural beliefs regarding people with disabilities in Namibia: Implications for inclusion of people with disabilities. *International Journal of Education, 25*, 76–87.

Ingstad, B. (2001). Disability in the developing world. In G. L. Albrecht, K. D. Seelman, & M. Bury (Eds.), *Handbook of disability studies* (pp. 772–792). Thousand Oaks, CA: Sage Publications.

Kahonde, C. (2015). *A grounded theory study of family caregivers' responses to sexuality and relationship support needs of young adults with intellectual disabilities.* PhD thesis in preparation, University of Cape Town, South Africa.

Kelly, A., Ghalaieny, T., & Devitt, C. (2012). A pilot study of early intervention for families with children with or at risk of an intellectual disability in Northern Malawi. *Journal of Policy and Practice in Intellectual Disabilities, 9*, 195–205. doi:10.1111/j.1741-1130.2012.00354.

Kromberg, J., Zwane, E., Manga, P., Venter, A., Rosen, E., & Christianson, A. (2008). Intellectual disability in the context of a South African population. *Journal of Policy and Practice in Intellectual Disabilities, 5*, 89–95. doi:10.1111/j.1741-1130.2008.00153.

Lansdown, G. (2002). *Disabled children in South Africa: Progress in implementing the Convention on the Rights of the Child.* Report retrieved from www.daa.org.uk/uploads/pdf/SA%20Childrens%20report%20.pdf

McConkey, R., Dunne, J., & Blitz, N. (2009). *Shared lives: Building relationships and community with people who have intellectual disabilities.* Amsterdam, Netherlands: Sense Publishers.

McConkey, R., & Mariga, L. (2010). Building social capital for inclusive education: Insights from Zanzibar. *Journal of Research in Special Educational Needs, 11*, 12–19. doi:10.1111/j.1471-3802.2010.01174.

McConkey, R., Mariga, L., Braadland, N., & Mphole, P. (2000). Parents as trainers about disability in low income countries. *International Journal of Disability, Development and Education, 47*, 309–317. doi:10.1080/713671113.

McKenzie, J., & McConkey, R. (2015). Caring for adults with intellectual disability: The perspectives of family carers in South Africa. *Journal of Applied Research in Intellectual Disabilities. Advance online publication.* doi:10.1111/jar.12209.

McKenzie, J. A., McConkey, R., & Adnams, C. (2013). Intellectual disability in Africa: Implications for research and service development. *Disability and Rehabilitation, 35*, 1750–1755. doi:10.3109/09638288.2012.751461.

McKenzie, J., & Muller, B. (2006). Parents and therapists: Dilemmas in partnership. In B. Watermeyer, L. Swartz, T. Lorenzo, M. Schneider, &

M. Priestley (Eds.), *Disability and social change: A South African agenda* (pp. 311–323). Cape Town, South Africa: Human Sciences Research Council Press.

Macmillan, M., Tarrant, M., Abraham, C., & Morris, C. (2014). The association between children's contact with people with disabilities and their attitudes towards disability: A systematic review. *Developmental Medicine and Child Neurology, 56,* 529–546. doi:10.1111/dmcn.12326.

Mirza, I., Tareen, A., Davidson, L. L., & Rahman, A. (2009). Community management of intellectual disabilities in Pakistan: A mixed methods study. *Journal   of   Intellectual   Disability   Research,   53,   559–570.* doi:10.1111/j.1365-2788.2009.01176.

Parmenter, T. R. (2001). Intellectual disabilities—Quo vadis? In G. L. Albrecht, K. D. Seelman, & M. Bury (Eds.), *Handbook of disability studies* (pp. 267–296). Thousand Oaks, CA: Sage Publications.

Siperstein, G. N., Norins, J., Corbin, S., & Shriver, T. (2003). *Multinational study of attitudes towards individuals with intellectual disabilities.* Washington, DC: Special Olympics Inc.

Tarusarira, W. (2015). *Support for Zimbabwean families with a disabled child seeking asylum in South Africa.* MPhil thesis in preparation: University of Cape Town, South Africa.

World Health Organization & World Bank (2011). *World report on disability.* Geneva, Switzerland: WHO.

13

The Law as a Source of Stigma or Empowerment: Legal Capacity and Persons with Intellectual Disabilities

Janos Fiala-Butora and Michael Ashley Stein

When it comes to disability-related stigma, the law is often perceived as playing a positive role. Anti-discrimination and anti-harassment laws can protect persons with disabilities from unfair treatment. Constitutional provisions can serve to reinforce their dignity and equality by explicitly acknowledging their fundamental rights. Human rights treaties, especially the UN Convention on the Rights of Persons with Disabilities (CRPD, UN General Assembly 2007), spell out human rights protections, with the CRPD taking the added step of requiring governments to tackle stigma and discrimination by, among others, raising awareness about persons with disabilities. Further, mainstream human rights bodies, such as the UN Human Rights Committee, have recently started to recognize the interests of persons with disabilities in formulating their jurisprudence and recommendations. Notably, the European Court of Human Rights held in 2010 in *Kiss v. Hungary* (2010) that persons with

J. Fiala-Butora (✉) • M.A. Stein
Harvard Law School, Harvard University, Cambridge, MA, USA
e-mail: janos.fiala@gmail.com

© The Editor(s) (if applicable) and The Author(s) 2016
K. Scior, S. Werner (eds.), *Intellectual Disability and Stigma*,
DOI 10.1057/978-1-137-52499-7_13

intellectual disabilities are a historically marginalized group who will benefit from strict scrutiny in the Court's jurisprudence.

The law is therefore often depicted to be on the side of persons fighting stigma and inequality. This chapter, however, argues that in reality the situation is more complicated. The law seemingly furthers the interests of persons with intellectual disabilities, but at the same time is also frequently the source of their stigmatization and exclusion. For although a plethora of legal instruments superficially help persons with intellectual disabilities, many established legal institutions build on centuries-old stereotypes of these individuals as helpless and incapable objects of care rather than as persons with agency. These assumptions often are unstated and unrecognized. Yet they nonetheless motivate the daily interaction between the law and the disability in a profound way, by reinforcing misperceptions that persons with intellectual disabilities are incapable and provide the means through which those individuals are socially disempowered and excluded.

The Case of Guardianship

To illustrate the general claim made above, this chapter describes how guardianship stigmatizes and violates the human rights of persons with intellectual disabilities globally on a daily basis. And yet to avoid the negative consequences of guardianship, we argue that even overtly recognizing the stigmatizing effects of the law is insufficient to counter their impact. Hidden and embedded assumptions of legal institutions must be uncovered and new institutions created that build on positive imagery and presumptions regarding the agency and abilities of persons with intellectual disabilities. Only then can legal systems amend their daily practices and exert a positive influence on socio-legal perceptions of persons with intellectual disabilities. This chapter demonstrates how the CRPD provides an avenue for such legal reform by replacing guardianship with supported decision-making.

Guardianship is a legal institution that exists in some form or other in all countries of the world, conceivably to protect the interests of persons with disabilities who are unable to manage their own affairs (Nowak 1993).

It involves the limitation of a person's right to make legally valid decisions (the limitation of their *legal capacity*) and the authorization of another person (the guardian) to make decisions on the person's behalf. The newly *legally incapacitated* person loses the right to make decisions about their property and even their own body: about medical decisions, family matters such as care over their children, where they live, who they associate with, and so on. These issues will now be decided by the person's guardian. Because incapacitation is obviously a severe interference with personal autonomy and integrity, guardianship is thought of as a measure of last resort which can be ordered only by a court (or another State-sanctioned administrative agency) and is utilized only for a narrow circle of persons with intellectual and psychosocial disabilities (the latter group is also referred to as individuals with mental disabilities).

Guardianship has changed little in its 2000-year history. On the surface, it is applied through a functional test and affects only those persons who are found by a medical assessment to lack capacity to make their own decisions. However, in practice, the main determinant of incapacitation is the existence of an intellectual (or psychosocial) disability (Dhanda 2007). The person's actual skills or desires matter little (Szegediné and Sebestyén 1982). Studies of guardianship systems have found that guardianship is overused in many countries (Salzman 2011). In addition, most incapacitations result in plenary guardianship, the most severe form of guardianship, which restricts a person's rights to make decisions in all areas of life (Mental Disability Advocacy Center (MDAC) 2013).

The overuse of guardianship has serious effects on persons with intellectual disabilities (Kohn et al. 2013). First, individuals are denied legal capacity in areas where they may well be functionally capable of making decisions, including consent to medical treatment (Plesó v. Hungary 2012), voting (Fiala-Butora et al. 2014), marriage, work, applying to courts (Salontaji-Drobnjak v. Serbia 2009), and participation in adoption proceedings (X. v. Croatia 2008). This is because courts undervalue their skills, and thus consider persons with intellectual disabilities as less capable than they in fact are.

Due to these legal limitations, it becomes much more difficult for a person with an intellectual disability to secure their interests. This is because the guardian has control over their life and is legally entitled to make decisions on the person's behalf. In consequence, it is enormously difficult, if not impossible, for the person to challenge the guardian's decisions. If they and their guardian disagree, it is the guardian's will which nearly always prevails (Salzman 2011). Ironically and tragically, while guardianship is supposed to protect persons with disabilities from abuse, it makes abuse by guardians not only possible but also commonplace (MDAC 2013).

The denial of rights also has an important pedagogic (or anti-therapeutic) effect. When a person cannot exercise certain rights, or make certain decisions because they are made on their behalf by others, they gradually lose their functional ability to exercise rights in the respective areas (Kohn et al. 2013). As an empirical matter, the condition of persons under guardianship deteriorates, and it is rare for any of them to recover their decision-making abilities once stripped of their legal capacity and precluded from exerting their agency (Salzman 2011).

Guardianship is likewise an important social marker of lack of skills. It signals to others that the person is unable to make their own decisions and is associated with the severe inability of an individual. After all, if only the most incapable persons with intellectual disabilities are incapacitated, it follows that those under guardianship are severely disabled and unable to act on their own behalf.

Although the above misplaced correlation between guardianship and inability is widely believed, it is far from the truth. It is not uncommon for persons able to work, live alone or with a partner, and attending to all of their own affairs to nevertheless end up under guardianship. Yet, strikingly, interviews conducted by the Hungarian Civil Liberties Union with persons under guardianship show that at times it is solely the placement under guardianship which reveals to others that the person has a disability. For example, one interviewee explained that her new neighbors did not notice she had a disability until they found out that she was not allowed to vote because she was under guardianship (Hungarian Civil Liberties Union [Társaság a Szabadságjogokért, TASZ] 2012). From that, the neighbors deduced that there must be 'something wrong' with her and her condition must be severe if courts thought it appropriate to appoint a guardian.

These examples are not merely the result of faulty applications of an otherwise well-designed legal system. Guardianship laws automatically produce inflated numbers of incapacitated persons. Of course, the degree of overuse varies across jurisdictions, but it cannot be completely avoided. Even the best assessment tools will produce false incapacitations. Overuse is unavoidable in great part because the system is built on the presumption that persons with intellectual disabilities in general lack capacity to manage their affairs, and, in order to protect them, others need to make decisions on their behalves.

Guardianship laws play an important role in maintaining this long-standing societal prejudice. Guardianship has institutionalized the idea that to help a person with an intellectual disability, their skills and abilities have to be supplanted. It creates persons who are objects of care by prohibiting them from helping themselves—from working, learning, marrying, and making decisions in general. Yet, persons with intellectual disabilities are not a socially marginalized population because of their disability; they are excluded from social participation in part through the operation of guardianship laws.

By treating persons with intellectual disabilities as objects of protection, and at the same time denying their agency, the law strengthens outdated stereotypes that lead to exclusionary practices. Thus, legal institutions aimed at helping persons with intellectual disabilities often harm them. The stigmatization this chapter addresses is not a necessary effect of otherwise beneficial measures, but rather an unintended and avoidable outcome. It is commonplace rather than rare that this system has serious problems and leads to many human rights abuses. The reason guardianship still exists is that there does not seem to be a better solution. Or, at least until recently, there has not been one.

The Alternative—Supported Decision-Making

For millennia, guardianship has been the only solution to help persons with decision-making difficulties. However, in recent years, substituted decision-making has emerged as an alternative. The concept was developed in the domestic laws of Sweden and Canada (Gordon 2000) and received worldwide recognition during the negotiations of the CRPD, adopted in 2006. Article 12 of the CRPD requires that persons with disabilities exercise their legal capacity on an equal basis with persons without disabilities, which many argue means without any restrictions of their legal capacity (Minkowitz 2010).

Supported decision-making rests on the notion that even though some persons with intellectual disabilities might have difficulties making decisions, those difficulties do not justify making decisions on their behalves (Carney 2012). Instead, those individuals should receive assistance from supporters to make their own decisions (Bach and Kerzner 2010), and with such assistance they are able to make their own decisions (Dhanda 2007). Indeed, this process is not all that different from how individuals without disabilities make decisions. With complicated issues such as buying a house or investing money, everybody relies on informal support of family, friends, experts in the area, and other trusted persons (Lord and Stein 2013). Persons with intellectual disabilities might require a higher level of support, even in areas where most people get along on their own or with a minimum of assistance (such as with shopping or cooking), but that is not a qualitatively different situation (Gordon 2000). Guardianship law makes an arbitrary choice by labeling the use of support by persons with disabilities as a proof of incapacitation, but accepts support utilized by persons without disabilities as the natural consequence of fully autonomous and competent decisions.

The goal of legal reform, required by the CRPD, is to create a legal framework which validates the supported decisions of persons with intellectual disabilities. This is not an easy task since difficulties and embedded resistance arise from many quarters. Legislators, academics, and advocates are, for example, debating how to protect supported persons from possible abuse and how to incorporate persons with higher support needs who are arguably unable to make decisions even with support, into a support framework. The purpose of this chapter is not to give an overview of the possible solutions, something that has been done elsewhere (Fiala-Butora 2015), but to underline the connection between stigma and the law's treatment of legal capacity.

In contrast with guardianship, supported decision-making does not underestimate the abilities of persons with intellectual disabilities. It relies on whatever abilities they have and strengthens their capacity by providing support. There are no legal restrictions on what a person with a disability is allowed to do; any emphasis is put on overcoming their lack of knowledge, experience, and skills. This has an opposite pedagogic or therapeutic effect to guardianship: regardless of the starting position, the abilities of a person participating in supported decision-making should develop, rather than diminish as is common under guardianship.

There is a dearth of empirical evidence about whether supported decision-making can deliver on these promises in practice (Kohn et al. 2013). It is, however, clear that its legal design forces others to interact with the person with an intellectual disability. They cannot be hidden in the background, or be made voiceless or invisible while others communicate with their guardian. By talking directly with the person with a disability, contracting parties form a personal and realistic impression about the person's skills—and they will have their supporters to ensure that they perform well in the process.

No doubt some persons with intellectual disabilities will find it difficult to take care of their own interests, especially if they were prevented from doing so in the past. Others will perhaps not receive the support they need. It is sure, however, that the underlying assumptions on which supported decision-making is built are much more favorable to persons with disabilities. It requires all involved to act on the assumption that persons with intellectual disabilities are able to make decisions given the opportunity and means, and thereby pushes legal transactions to reflect the idea of persons with intellectual disabilities as capable and equal actors.

How to Transform Legal Institutions—The Perspective of Stigma

Supported decision-making is already an existing practice in some countries of the world, such as Canada and Sweden, and is proliferating in others through legal reform. It is tempting to suggest that when existing guardianship laws are replaced with laws based on support, the underlying problems will be resolved. However, the challenge is much more difficult to meet as the stigma reflected in and created by the law is not easy to overcome.

Prejudices against persons with disabilities—and specifically, the widely held belief that persons with intellectual (and psychosocial) disabilities are unable to manage their own affairs—are deeply socially entrenched. For millennia these beliefs have manifested themselves in guardianship laws which precluded persons with disabilities to make decisions on their own. In a circular way, these laws also shaped societal conventions regarding the misperceived inability of people with disabilities. Thus, guardianship laws are not solely responsible for the image of a person with an intellectual disability as incompetent; the prejudice is older and much more entrenched.

The law is important, however, in the way prejudice against individuals with intellectual disabilities currently manifests. The guardianship system deprives many otherwise capable people of their legal capacity. They are considered incapable of independent life once they were placed under guardianship, even if they had been able to work and live alone before that legal procedure. Some persons may not even know for years that they are legally incapacitated: they continue to take care of themselves and go about their lives while in the eyes of the law they are considered incapable of having those very same independent lives (Sýkora v. the Czech Republic 2012). Once rights are taken away from them, persons with intellectual disabilities gradually lose these skills, and guardianship becomes a self-fulfilling prophecy: those deprived of their legal capacity often become dependent on various forms of assistance. Guardianship law, often arbitrarily administered, plays a key role in determining who becomes a totally incapable, severely disabled person in need of society's help, and in defining the nature of that dependency.

Nevertheless, and despite the unintended injurious effect, the law can also have a positive influence on societal attitudes. The task of systemic reform in this context is to put in place legal institutions that promote the image of persons with disabilities as equally capable and empowered with agency. However, abolishing all existing guardianship laws and replacing them with support mechanisms, while helpful, is insufficient. This is especially true for countries with an established guardianship system where the instantiated culture does not consider persons with disabilities as autonomous. In those States, social workers, medical professionals, public administration, guardians, and family members acting under current guardianship regimes are all working under the view of persons with disabilities as objects of care rather than individuals with decision-making abilities. Simply abolishing guardianship will not immediately change that attitude. To the contrary, they would likely respond by reinventing the repressive institutional culture in a new legal framework by renaming 'guardianship' as 'supported decision-making'. Thus, even changing the criteria of guardianship so that it does not formally restrict legal capacity is not enough.

Besides establishing a new general framework, legislators must also identify specific obstacles in which this institutional culture manifests itself and directly overrule them. Safeguards must be put in place so that persons with disabilities can indeed make decisions which are currently most often denied to them. Hence, legal reform has to affect the way banks engage with their clients and offer loans, doctors talk to patients, child custody is exercised by parents, public administration handles customers, courts hear witnesses, and many other areas which currently constitute a direct obstacle to persons with disabilities exercising their legal capacity.

The law cannot in itself change embedded societal structures overnight. That is a much more complex task, requiring a longer period of time and other factors to be present. The law can and should, however, establish the structure and create the instruments to allow society to gradually accept and incorporate the notion that persons with disabilities can make their own decisions. By recognizing persons with disabilities as decision-makers under the law, supported decision-making forces all other actors to communicate with them instead of their guardians. Some will no doubt find this burdensome, but the law's normative goal should be to expand those areas where the wishes of persons with disabilities will be honored rather than to exclude persons with disabilities from decision-making on the ground of administrative convenience. In this process it is crucial that we uncover the hidden assumptions that continue to undermine the equal place and legal capacity of persons with intellectual disabilities.

Conclusions

This chapter has argued that the stigmatizing effects of the law are not always evident. Legal institutions can directly contribute to building a positive image of persons with intellectual disabilities by, for example, prohibiting open discrimination against them or expressly securing their fundamental rights. At the same time, legal institutions are built on incorrect assumptions about persons with intellectual disabilities. Through their daily operation they allow these prejudicial assumptions to influence the social environment. This negative effect is harder to observe, but nevertheless very damaging to the public perception of persons with intellectual disabilities.

Guardianship is an example of a widely used legal mechanism that is built on the idea of persons with intellectual disabilities as incapable of managing their own affairs. Due to more than 2000 years of guardianship laws, unfounded stereotypes regarding the inability of persons with intellectual disabilities to make their own decisions has been deeply embedded across cultures. Family members, medical and legal professionals, service providers, and all kinds of caregivers have learned to ignore the wishes of persons with intellectual disabilities, and instead to make decisions on their behalves, to preserve their 'best interests'.

Supported decision-making, a newly emerged alternative to guardianship, shows that protecting the human rights of persons with intellectual disabilities does not have to come at the cost of undermining their capacity and social perception. Stigmatization is not a necessary cost of help, but rather an obstacle to be overcome. Implementing supported decision-making will be a long process, because it requires changing societal norms about how to interact with persons with intellectual disabilities.

While this seems to be a daunting task, one must recall that existing prejudicial attitudes were to a great extent created and are maintained through the operation of guardianship laws. The law can therefore equally play a role in dismantling those social constructs. To achieve this goal, the task of legal reform should be to uncover hidden assumptions behind our legal institutions that covertly contribute to stigmatizing persons with intellectual disabilities. Guardianship serves as one example in this chapter. Similar seemingly disability-neutral mechanisms excluding persons with intellectual disabilities from equal participation can be found in other areas of the law, from labor law through criminal law to family law and other sectors (Fiala-Butora 2013).

The CRPD provides an impetus for reexamining our institutions from a disability human rights perspective. It sets a high standard by requiring the full inclusion and equal participation of persons with intellectual disabilities in all areas of life. In many areas, it directly identifies the existing obstacles which until now went unnoticed by domestic legislators and courts. In others, it will be the task of self-advocates, supporters, legislators, and academics to uncover and root out the outdated prejudices deeply embedded in our legal system.

Key Learning Points

- Legal institutions can be based on prejudiced assumptions and have a stigmatizing effect on persons with intellectual disabilities.
- Guardianship is an example of a seemingly benign institution. It is based on a presumption that persons with intellectual disabilities are incapable of decision-making and reinforces this stereotype through its operation.
- Guardianship still exists because it is wrongly considered irreplaceable. However, supported decision-making has emerged as an alternative that strengthens the capacity of persons with intellectual disabilities instead of limiting their right to make decisions.
- To shift legal systems from guardianship to supported decision-making, current social norms and expectations need to be challenged. The law helped to create prejudiced attitudes and it can help change them as well.
- Legal reform should uncover hidden prejudice in laws and replace outdated institutions with new ones built on realistic and empirically founded understandings of persons with intellectual disabilities.
- The widely adopted CRPD provides good momentum for large-scale legal reform.

Accessible Summary

- The law often treats persons with intellectual disabilities as unable to make decisions for themselves.
- Guardianship stops persons with intellectual disabilities from making their own decisions.
- Supported decision-making helps persons with intellectual disabilities to make their own decisions.
- We need to replace guardianship with supported decision-making. It is not easy, because many people are used to the old laws and think persons with intellectual disabilities cannot make their own decisions.
- Changing laws can also help change people's minds.
- The Convention on the Rights of Persons with Disabilities is pushing countries to change their laws. We should use the Convention to change laws that are bad for persons with intellectual disabilities.

References

Bach, M., & Kerzner, L. (2010). *A new paradigm for protecting autonomy and the right to legal Capacity.* (Paper prepared for the Law Commission of Ontario).

Carney, T. (2012). Guardianship, "social" citizenship, & theorizing substitute decision-making law. *Sydney Law School Research Paper, 12/25.*

Dhanda, A. (2007). Legal capacity in the disability rights convention: Stranglehold of the past or lodestar for the future? *Syracuse Journal of International Law and Commerce, 34,* 429–462.

Fiala-Butora, J. (2013). Disabling torture: The obligation to investigate ill-treatment of persons with disabilities. *Columbia Human Rights Law Review, 45,* 214–280.

Fiala-Butora, J. (2015). Reconstructing personhood: Legal capacity of persons with disabilities. SJD Dissertation, Harvard Law School, MA, forthcoming.

Fiala-Butora, J., Stein, M. A., & Lord, J. E. (2014). The democratic life of the Union: Towards equal voting participation for Europeans with disabilities. *Harvard International Law Journal, 55,* 71–104.

Gordon, R. M. (2000). The emergence of assisted (supported) decision-making in the Canadian law of adult guardianship and substitute decision-making. *International Journal of Law and Psychiatry, 23,* 61–77.

Hungarian Civil Liberties Union [Társaság a Szabadságjogokért, TASZ]. (2012). *Választójog és fogyatékosság* [Suffrage and Disability]. Retrieved from http://www.youtube.com/watch?v=PBgao8ZklGY

Kohn, N. A., Blumenthal, J. A., & Campbell, A. T. (2013). Supported decision-making: A viable alternative to guardianship? *Penn State Law Review, 117*, 1111–1157.

Lord, J. E., & Stein, M. A. (2013). Contingent participation and coercive care: Feminist and communitarian theories of disability and legal capacity. In B. McSherry & I. Freckelton (Eds.), *Coercive care: Rights, law and policy*. Abingdon, UK: Routledge.

Mental Disability Advocacy Center (MDAC). (2013). *Legal Capacity in Europe*. Retrieved from http://mdac.info/sites/mdac.info/files/legal_capacity_in_europe.pdf

Minkowitz, T. (2010). Abolishing mental health laws to comply with the Convention on the Rights of Persons with Disabilities. In B. McSherry & P. Weller (Eds.), *Rethinking rights based mental health laws*. Oxford, UK: Hart Publishing.

Nowak, M. (1993). *U.N. Covenant on Civil and Political Rights: CCPR Commentary*. Kehl am Rhein, Germany: N.P. Engel.

Salzman, L. (2011). Guardianship for persons with mental illness—A legal and appropriate alternative? *Saint Louis University Journal of Health Law and Policy, 4*, 279–329.

Szegediné Dr., & Sebestyén, K. (1982). A gondnokság alá helyezés iránti perekről [About guardianship proceedings]. *Magyar Jog, 7*, 606–615.

UN General Assembly. (2007). *Convention on the Rights of Persons with Disabilities: Resolution*. Adopted by the General Assembly, 24 January 2007.

Legislation

Kiss v. Hungary, No. 38832/06 (Eur. Ct. Hum. Rts., May 20, 2010).

Plesó v. Hungary, No. 41242/08 (Eur. Ct. Hum. Rts., October 2, 2012).

Salontaji-Drobnjak v. Serbia, no. 36500/05 (Eur. Ct. Hum. Rts., October 13, 2009).

Sýkora v. the Czech Republic, No. 23419/07 (Eur. Ct. Hum. Rts., 22 November 2012).

X. v. Croatia, no 11223/04, (Eur. Ct. Hum. Rts., July 17, 2008).

.

14

Intellectual Disability, Group Identification, and Self-Evaluation

Jason Crabtree, William Mandy, and Hannah Mustard

Previous chapters have considered the potential consequences of stigma on the well-being and life chances of people with intellectual disabilities as well as the potential psychological consequences of internalizing negative societal views. This chapter will extend these discussions to consider how identifying with others who share the label of intellectual disability has the potential to mediate the internalization of negative societal views (stigma) and protect positive self-evaluations. Clinical implications of the research findings are discussed, including how positive self-evaluation may be promoted among individuals with intellectual disabilities.

J. Crabtree (✉)
Westminster Learning Disabilities Service, London, UK
e-mail: jcrabtree@westminster.gov.uk

W. Mandy
Division of Psychology & Language Sciences, University College London, London, UK

H. Mustard
Central and North West London NHS Foundation Trust, London, UK

© The Editor(s) (if applicable) and The Author(s) 2016
K. Scior, S. Werner (eds.), *Intellectual Disability and Stigma*,
DOI 10.1057/978-1-137-52499-7_14

Theoretical Background

Early models of self-identity such as Cooley's (1902) 'Looking Glass' self and Mead's (1934) Symbolic Interactionist perspective suggested that the self cannot be separated from the society in which it is located. As a result, individuals' self-evaluations are considered a direct consequence of the views that others hold of them. Similarly, Gergen's (1977) Social Constructionist theory proposes that a person's self-evaluations are formed through social interactions. Accordingly, individuals with intellectual disabilities will simply interpret stigma held by others toward them as a reflection of their 'true' value and internalize, leading to negative self-evaluations.

Research has found that the self-evaluations made by individuals belonging to a number of stigmatized groups are frequently comparable to those of individuals not belonging to stigmatized groups (e.g., ethnic minority groups, Verkuyten 1994; children with mild intellectual disabilities, Crabtree and Rutland 2001; individuals with mental health problems, Hayward and Bright 1997). It therefore seems too crude to suggest that merely belonging to a stigmatized group leads to low self-evaluation (Camp et al. 2002).

Social Identity Theory (Tajfel and Turner 1979) offers a more complex understanding of the development of self-identity and evaluation and accounts for how members of stigmatized groups may maintain positive self-evaluations. It suggests that individuals' self-evaluations depend on the views that society has of their group and how this compares to other social groups. Therefore, positive self-evaluations can be achieved when it is possible to make favorable comparisons between one's in-group and out-groups. Where this is not possible, as in the case of belonging to a stigmatized group, individuals' resultant self-evaluations are likely to be negative. The theory postulates that individuals strive to maintain positive self-evaluations, and therefore may seek to distance themselves from the stigmatized in-group and align themselves with more socially valued groups. In the case of individuals who have no choice in leaving the group (i.e., the group has no 'permeability'), Tajfel (1978) suggested that individuals may promote positive self-evaluation through engaging in group action to bring about social change. However, a high level of group identification would appear to be a necessary prerequisite for such action.

In a comprehensive review of the literature, Crocker and Major (1989) found limited support for the notion that members of stigmatized groups (including individuals with intellectual disabilities) automatically experience low self-evaluations. Instead, members of stigmatized groups attribute the negative evaluations of others to prejudice, make use of in-group social comparisons rather than out-group comparisons to boost positive self-evaluations, and place greater value on the attributes in which their group compares favorably, while devaluing those in which their group compares less favorably.

Branscombe et al. (1999) developed Crocker and Major's (1989) ideas in their Rejection-Identification model of group identification and self-evaluation. They suggested that identifying as a member of a stigmatized group provides social support and resources to resist the discrimination and prejudice experienced by the group. This then mediates the relationship between identifying as a member of a stigmatized group and how individuals evaluate themselves in order to promote more positive self-evaluation.

In summary, contemporary theories of group identity suggest that self-evaluations of stigmatized group members can be protected via a number of mechanisms, made available to them as a result of identifying with the group, despite it being stigmatized. These include the following:

1. The provision of direct social support
2. Providing a group of similar others with which to compare one's attributes
3. Allowing for greater value to be placed on positive attributes belonging to the group or attributes in which the group differs little from others
4. Supporting the rejection of stigmatized societal views as invalid or misrepresented

These mechanisms have been found in research on the self-evaluations made by members of a number of stigmatized groups. It is unclear, however, whether these mediating mechanisms are used in the same way or to the same extent by individuals with intellectual disabilities. Below we consider the limited amount of research in this area and attempt to draw some conclusions regarding the impact on self-evaluations of identifying with a group whose 'membership' is based on significant intellectual impairment.

Group Identity and Self-Esteem Among Individuals with Intellectual Disabilities

There is a dearth of literature that has explicitly explored the link between group identification and self-evaluation among individuals with intellectual disabilities. Much of the literature reported here frequently makes inferences about group identification, rather than explicitly measuring the degree to which individuals with intellectual disabilities actually identify themselves as such. Finlay and Lyons (1998), for example, investigated the significance of the label 'learning difficulties' (the term commonly used by self-advocates in the UK to denote intellectual disability) for the self-evaluations made by individuals with mild intellectual disabilities. Two-thirds of their sample recognized that they had an intellectual disability when asked directly, but the label was not often used spontaneously in their self-descriptions. Participants who devalued others with intellectual disabilities did not report more negative self-evaluations even when they identified with the label, and conversely those who identified with the label did not evaluate the label any more positively than those who rejected it. These findings suggest that firstly, it cannot be assumed that all individuals with intellectual disabilities automatically identify with this label; and secondly, that group-evaluation and self-evaluation processes occur independently in people with intellectual disabilities.

These researchers went on to investigate how sense of self is constructed by people with intellectual disabilities through their social comparisons with others (Finlay and Lyons 2000). They found that the attributes on which individuals compared themselves to others belonging to both their in-group and out-groups were those most likely to result in positive self-evaluations. More specifically, participants made in-group comparisons on attributes such as level of ability and behavioral disturbance. That is, when comparing themselves to in-group members, they chose to compare themselves to individuals who were less able or who displayed higher levels of behavioral disturbance. Attributes selected to make comparisons against members of out-groups included morally questionable or negative behavior, such as people who steal. Thus, in each case individuals with intellectual disabilities were making use of self-protective strategies in evaluating their sense of self.

The above findings would also appear to suggest that participants attempted to distance themselves from the in-group in order to protect their self-identity and could be deemed to offer support for Tajfel and Turner's (1979) model of identity. It could, however, be argued that comparing oneself to the in-group on group-based, stigmatized characteristics such as ability and behavior is in itself an indication of recognizing that one belongs to that group (Hinkle and Brown 1990). If this were assumed to be the case, then the presence of in-group comparisons in Finlay and Lyons' studies suggests that some group identification did exist, but that individuals attempted to position themselves at the more capable end of the group's spectrum of intellectual ability. Such social comparisons would therefore suggest both a sense of identification with the intellectual disability group and a desire to distance oneself from more stigmatized members of the group.

Coping strategies used by individuals with intellectual disabilities to manage social stigma in the context of transitioning from institutional settings and the family home were explored by Jahoda and Markova (2004). They concluded that interviewees were aware both of the stigma associated with intellectual disability and that this affected how they were treated by others. Two key coping strategies to manage stigma that are linked to group identification were identified. Either participants identified with the in-group and regarded themselves as part of a minority group who rejected prejudice, or they attempted to distance themselves from others with intellectual disabilities and associated stigmatizing 'institutionalized' services. More specifically, those moving from institutionalized settings spoke of greater feelings of shame due to being visibly defined as an inpatient (via hospital tags) and a wish to hide the fact that they lived at the hospital. Those living in community settings with a potentially greater opportunity to conceal their difference more positively identified with the intellectual disability group. These findings suggest that self-stigma is linked to being identified as using a stigmatized service and perhaps to whether or not an individual has the choice to conceal a negative group identity.

While not explicitly measuring group identity, Crabtree and Rutland (2001) compared the self-evaluations made by young people aged 11–16 years with mild intellectual disabilities attending 'special schools' (i.e., segregated schools) with their typically developing peers attending mainstream schools. Overall they found no significant difference between the self-evaluations of these two groups, adding to the argument that individuals with intellectual disabilities employ mechanisms to protect self-evaluations. This study attempted to artificially manipulate the social comparison group used by the participants with intellectual disabilities by asking them to compare themselves to predefined groups ('young people like you' and 'young people in other schools'). As anticipated, who the students compared themselves to affected their self-evaluations—comparisons with more similar and/or less able (in-group) peers were associated with more positive self-evaluations. The students also placed greater value on non-academic attributes, such as physical appearance and athletic ability, when comparing themselves to their typically developing peers.

In a follow-on study, Crabtree and Meredith (2003) compared the self-evaluations of adolescents with mild intellectual disabilities attending both mainstream and special schools. Those attending special schools where there was a readily available group of similar others tended to make in-group social comparisons, while those attending mainstream schools most frequently made out-group social comparisons with typically developing peers. Interestingly, while differences between groups were found in terms of their self-evaluations of their maths and general intellectual abilities, no other differences were found in their self-evaluations on a range of other academic and non-academic domains. Thus, while identifying with similar others may affect positive self-evaluations in stigmatized groups somewhat, other processes, such as placing greater value on attributes that are not impaired, are also important in determining overall self-evaluations.

A small number of studies have attempted to explicitly measure group identification and its link to self-evaluations in people with intellectual disabilities. In a study involving individuals attending a day center, Dagnan and Waring (2004) included two items to assess levels of group identification (feeling part of a group or on their own and feeling the same or different as other people). In addition to finding relatively low levels of group identification, negative self-evaluative beliefs were found to be correlated with scores on a measure of stigma perception and were also associated with low self-rated social attractiveness. They concluded, somewhat contrary to much of the previously reported research, that there is a link between perceived stigma and self-evaluation. Furthermore, those living in staffed housing experienced a greater degree of self-stigma than those living independently. This relationship was fully mediated by level of verbal ability: those whose intellectual disability was milder (and who demonstrated higher levels of verbal ability) lived independently and experienced less self-stigma than those who needed extra support due to the severity of their intellectual disability. These differences echo Jahoda and Markova's (2004) findings that people living more independently, and who were therefore able to distance themselves from the intellectual disability group when they chose to, experienced less self-stigma.

It is possible that the lack of association between group identification and self-evaluation found in Dagnan and Waring's (2004) study may be accounted for by the way in which group identification was measured rather than the absence of this relationship. Only two items were used to gauge group identification, and there was a lack of specificity regarding which group of 'other people' participants were comparing themselves to. Therefore, the apparently opposing evidence from Dagnan and Waring's study should be treated with some caution. Further research is required that uses more robust methods to explore levels of group identification in participants with intellectual disabilities.

In Paterson et al.'s (2012) study of the relationship between stigma, social comparison, and self-evaluations, individuals with intellectual disabilities chose to make comparisons with others (both those belonging to the in-group and out-group) on attributes on which they felt themselves to be in a comparatively better position. Participants who identified themselves as someone with an intellectual disability *and* compared themselves to less able members of the group made more positive self-evaluations. Interestingly, when comparing themselves with a broader target social comparison group of 'people living in their city' the selective use of attributes on which to compare themselves to others appeared to come into play, with those who rated themselves as more socially attractive and able reporting higher self-evaluations. This again suggests that downward social comparisons have a protective effect on self-evaluations when an individual identifies with a stigmatized group.

Conclusions

From the research presented in this chapter it appears that the relationship between group identification and self-evaluation in people with intellectual disabilities is complex. Firstly, some individuals do not explicitly appear to acknowledge the label of intellectual disability as applying to themselves (Finlay and Lyons 1998), potentially as a means of distancing themselves from belonging to a stigmatized group.

Secondly, for those individuals identifying with the group the evidence presented suggests that there are a number of mechanisms afforded to them by group membership that appear to buffer the potentially negative consequences of belonging to a stigmatized group. These include (1) comparisons with less able in-group members; (2) mediating the value placed on attributes based on the performance of the in-group compared to other groups; and (3) shared group identification to reject stigma.

In terms of clinical implications and future research directions, it seems important to consider how those with intellectual disabilities compare to other groups for whom initiatives to reduce stigma and protect self-evaluations are more developed. There are certainly similarities between stigma research in the mental health arena and research involving people with intellectual disabilities in terms of both populations' awareness of stigma. However, there appear to be some differences between the two groups in how self-evaluation is protected. There seems to be more of an emphasis in the mental health literature on the impact of social support from other group members, whether from defined support groups or through a sense of belonging to a wider community, in mediating the relationship between stigma and self-evaluation (Crabtree et al. 2010; Watson et al. 2007). This contrasts with the findings from the intellectual disability literature, which suggests that people assigned to this group are more likely to try and distance themselves from other members, whether physically (Jahoda and Markova 2004) or through downward comparison (Finlay and Lyons 2000; Jahoda and Markova 2004; Paterson et al. 2012). It is possible that individuals with intellectual disabilities also receive social support from identifying with this group and that this provides a resource for coping with stigma. Future research should investigate the role of group identification, social support, and stigma resistance among people with intellectual disabilities, as it is not clear to what extent peer support can protect the self-evaluations made by this population. Evidence of downward comparisons may in fact suggest a greater tendency to stigmatize one's own group, compared to groups where peer support and united group strategies against stigma are more readily found. Greater attention is called for to ensure that people with intellectual disabilities can access peer-to-peer support, advocacy, and group-based coping resources to minimize the potential of experiencing both group and self-stigma.

An important issue raised by the literature presented in this chapter is whether group identification occurs when an individual is either not 'out' about their diagnosis or does not use services that bring them into contact with others with a shared diagnosis of intellectual disability. Given the general direction of service provision for those with intellectual disabilities, focused on individualized support and person-centered approaches, opportunities for developing a shared group identity may well be reduced.

The emphasis on the central role of peer support and collectively speaking up within the stigma literature appears to be notably absent from the intellectual disability literature. This perhaps indicates a persistence of perceiving people with intellectual disabilities as receivers of support from those without disabilities, rather than peers with intellectual disabilities. More research is clearly needed to investigate whether peer support offers the same self-protective value as it does for other stigmatized groups.

Key Learning Points

- Viewing oneself as belonging to a group of 'people with intellectual disabilities' does not automatically result in negative self-evaluations.
- Individuals with intellectual disabilities appear to use three key strategies to buffer stigma and maintain positive self-evaluations:

- Selective use of in-group and out-group social comparisons.
- Selective valuing of personal and group attributes.
- Distancing from the group of 'people with intellectual disabilities'.
- Social comparisons, either with less able peers or those belonging to groups presenting with other stigmatizing attributes, are the most frequently identified strategy.

Accessible Summary

- Having intellectual disabilities does not mean people inevitably feel bad about themselves.
- People with intellectual disabilities use different ways to feel good about themselves:
  - Comparing themselves to less able people or people who behave in disruptive ways
  - Placing more importance on the things they do well
  - Sometimes not seeing themselves as having an intellectual disability
- More research is needed to look at the benefits peer support has on how people with intellectual disabilities feel about themselves.

References

Branscombe, N. R., Schmitt, M. T., & Harvey, R. D. (1999). Perceiving pervasive discrimination among African-Americans: Implications for group identification and wellbeing. *Journal of Personality and Social Psychology, 77,* 135–149. doi:10.1037/0022-3514.77.1.135.

Camp, D. L., Finlay, W. M., & Lyons, E. (2002). Is low self-esteem an inevitable consequence of stigma? An example of women with chronic mental health problems. *Social Science and Medicine, 55,* 823–834. doi:10.1016/S0277-9536(01)00205-2.

Cooley, C. H. (1902). *Two major works: Social organization and human nature and the social order.* Glencoe, UK: Free Press.

Crabtree, J. W., Haslam, S. A., Postmes, T., & Haslam, C. (2010). Mental health support groups, stigma and self-esteem: Positive and negative implications of group identification. *Journal of Social Issues, 66*, 553–569. doi:10.1111/j.1540-4560.2010.01662.x.

Crabtree, J. W., & Meredith, C. (2003). Self-concept and social comparisons in learning disabled students attending mainstream and special schools: Does integration have an impact? In R. G. Craven & H. Marsh (Eds.), *Self-concept Theory, Research and Practice: Advances for the New Millennium* (pp. 187–193). University of Western Sydney, Australia: 2000 SELF Research Centre.

Crabtree, J., & Rutland, A. (2001). Self-evaluation and social comparison amongst adolescents with learning disabilities. *Journal of Community and Applied Psychology, 11*, 347–359. doi:10.1002/casp.634.

Crocker, J., & Major, B. (1989). Social stigma and self-esteem: The self-protective properties of stigma. *Psychological Review, 96*, 608–630. doi:10.1037/0033-295X.96.4.608.

Dagnan, D., & Waring, M. (2004). Linking stigma to psychological distress: Testing a social-cognitive model of the experience of people with intellectual disabilities. *Clinical Psychology and Psychotherapy, 11*, 247–254. doi:10.1002/cpp.413.

Finlay, M., & Lyons, E. (1998). Social identity and people with learning difficulties: Implications for self-advocacy groups. *Disability and Society, 13*, 37–51. doi:10.1080/09687599826902.

Finlay, M., & Lyons, E. (2000). Social categorizations, social comparisons and stigma: Presentations of self in people with learning difficulties. *British Journal of Social Psychology, 39*, 129–146. doi:10.1348/014466600164372.

Gergen, K. J. (1977). *The concept of self*. New York, NY: Holt, Reinhart & Winston.

Hayward, P., & Bright, J. (1997). *Stigma and mental illness: A review and critique. Journal of Mental Health, 6*, 345–354. doi:10.1080/09638239718671.

Hinkle, S., & Brown, R. (1990). Intergroup comparisons and social identity: Some links and lacunae. In D. Abrams & M. A. Hogg (Eds.), *Social identity theory: Constructive and critical advances* (pp. 48–70). New York, NY: Harvester Wheatsheaf.

Jahoda, A., & Markova, I. (2004). Coping with social stigma: People with intellectual disabilities moving from institutions and family home. *Journal of Intellectual Disability Research, 48*, 719–729. doi:10.1111/j.1365-2788.2003.00561.x.

Mead, G. H. (1934). *Mind, self and society from the standpoint of a social behaviorist*. Chicago, IL: University of Chicago Press.

Paterson, L., McKenzie, K., & Lindsay, B. (2012). Stigma, social comparison and self-esteem in adults with an intellectual disability. *Journal of Applied Research in Intellectual Disabilities, 25*, 166–176. doi:10.1111/j.1468-3148.2011.00651.x.

Tajfel, H. (1978). Inter-individual behavior and intergroup behavior. In H. Tajfel (Ed.), *Differentiation between social groups: Studies in the social psychology of intergroup relations* (pp. 61–76). London, UK: Academic Press.

Tajfel, H., & Turner, J. C. (1979). An integrative theory of intergroup conflict. In W. G. Austin & S. Worchel (Eds.), *The social psychology of intergroup relations* (pp. 33–47). Monterey, CA: Brooks/Cole.

Verkuyten, M. (1994). Self-esteem among ethnic minority youth in Western countries. *Social Indicators Research, 32,* 21–47. doi:10.1007/BF01078464.

Watson, A. C., Corrigan, P. W., Larson, J. E., & Sells, M. (2007). Self-stigma in people with mental illness. *Schizophrenia Bulletin, 33,* 1312–1318. doi:10.1093/schbul/sbl076.

Epilogue

Katrina Scior and Shirli Werner

Since the days of the almost complete denial of the personhood and rights of people with intellectual disabilities and their large-scale confinement in institutions in many countries, much progress has been made. Many no longer question the human-ness of persons with intellectual disabilities and the days of their physical segregation from society appear numbered in many, but by no means all, parts of the world. In the fight for respect and acceptance, the UN Convention on the Rights of Persons with Disabilities (CRPD) can be seen as a very important step forward, though one that needs to be accompanied by action on many levels. The inclusion of persons with intellectual disabilities under the Convention, at least theoretically, commits signatory states to enact domestic laws and measures to improve their rights and to abolish legislation, customs, and practices that discriminate against them. Nevertheless, the experts from various fields brought together in this book are unanimous in concluding that we are a long way from abolishing stigma and accepting children and adults with intellectual disabilities fully into society. For example, while in many Western countries there appears to be a growing willingness among the general public to include people with intellectual disabilities within their communities, there are many signs that there is a continuing

© The Editor(s) (if applicable) and The Author(s) 2016
K. Scior, S. Werner (eds.), *Intellectual Disability and Stigma*,
DOI 10.1057/978-1-137-52499-7

reluctance to welcome them as equals into inclusive schools and work places. Further, research that taps into more deeply held implicit attitudes suggests that these continue to be grounded in negative constructions of intellectual disability. In many low- and middle-income countries the fight for equal rights for people with intellectual disabilities has barely begun and largely relies on the efforts of parents. At global level then, there is still a huge way to go until the equal human value of such persons is not only being paid lip service to but truly accepted.

Many may question whether we will ever reach a point of true acceptance and full inclusion for individuals with intellectual disabilities. In putting together this first text book on intellectual disability stigma, it is our firm conviction that this is not only a goal very much worth striving for, but also one that is attainable. If we look to the early days of the civil rights movement, for example, many entertained similar doubts about a future in which members of different races would be seen as equals. Going back a little bit further, fierce debates were held as to whether women had sufficient capability for reasoning to justify their right to vote. One factor that makes the fight against intellectual disability stigma unquestionably harder is that many persons with intellectual disabilities require support to make their voice heard and to engage in collective action. Article 12 of the CRPD recognizes that all individuals should hold the right to legal capacity. Individuals with intellectual disabilities have the basic human right to self-determination and autonomy, to being provided with the opportunity to make their own decisions. This indicates growing recognition that the central role of supporters, advocates, and researchers should not be one of doing or speaking *for* but of facilitating people doing and speaking themselves. This recognition may well be at the heart of many services and organizations but is still very alien in many others. In fact, the message of the huge importance and value of self-advocacy emerges again and again throughout this book.

As Pat Corrigan notes in the foreword to this book, in the intellectual disability field our work as experts has mostly focused on developing innovative ways for people to overcome their impairments to meet personal goals. Certainly focusing solely on the individual's impairments does not meet the aim of tearing down barriers which are inherent in communities and within society. Thus, our agenda in moving forward must be to develop effective strategies to tear down community barriers to these goals while not losing sight of underlying impairments and the associated need for support. As we note in Chap. 9, contact between individuals with intellectual disabilities and others in the community seems to be the most promising way to reduce stigma. Further, stigma change efforts should begin early in life and be provided to all age groups; they also must not lose sight of the fact that persons with intellectual disabilities in low- and middle-income countries are as much, and in many cases more, subjected to stigma as those in high-income countries where most anti-stigma efforts take place to date. In this process we suspect those of us in the roles of experts, advocates, or supporters will need to ask ourselves searching questions about our own deeply held beliefs about human-ness and the huge value accorded to intellectual prowess and autonomy, as well as our own emotional responses to disability.

Further, advancing research in this field is a mandatory step. Pat Corrigan in his foreword reminds us that our role as researchers should be to humbly guide how the fight against intellectual disability stigma is most likely to be effective and what strategies carry more risks than likely benefits. On this note, we encourage our colleagues in the world of research to become more active in examining the effects of different strategies. At present, the intellectual disability field is alive with diverse efforts to achieve attitude change but there is currently very little consideration of whether such efforts have the desired effect and where resources are best spent. In an effort to advance this field, it is highly important for different stakeholders to join forces. Collaboration between self-advocates, parents/families, disabled people's organizations, nongovernmental organizations, statutory services, and researchers is highly important. Individuals with intellectual disabilities themselves, and those who support them and are most familiar with them, rather than so-called experts, have most knowledge on how stigma affects their lives and should be empowered to take an active role in delivering stigma change interventions.

While research and innovations have mainly focused on high-income countries, as noted above, we need to recognize that we have left millions of people with intellectual disabilities and those frequently battling for their most basic rights ignored. Thus, more collaboration across world regions is needed as is a greater willingness for those in high-income countries to support efforts in low- and middle-income countries. Furthermore, organizations focused on challenging intellectual disability stigma across the world (such as Inclusion International and Special Olympics) as well as those operating at national and community level should collaborate with researchers to ensure that resources are used in the most effective way and set a united and evidence-driven agenda for stigma change.

Index

© The Editor(s) (if applicable) and The Author(s) 2016
K. Scior, S. Werner (eds.), *Intellectual Disability and Stigma*,
DOI 10.1057/978-1-137-52499-7

Printed by Printforce, the Netherlands